When we are threatened with genocide, totalitarianism, dystopianism, and paranoia, there are different overlapping ways of keeping hope for the future alive: thoughtful reflection, direct political action, and the creative imagination. Barbara Morrill's devotion to studying the life and work of Etty Hillesum resonates with us today because they both offer us the most extraordinary example from the Holocaust of the indomitable spirit of the individual keeping hope for the future of humanity alive.

Thomas Singer, MD and Jungian analyst, editor of Cultural Complexes and the Soul of America and Mind of State: Conversations on the Conflicts Stirring US Politics and Society

Dr. Morrill's recounting of the life and philosophy of Etty Hillesum is exactly the medicine needed for our time. Etty's words and life offer profound guidance about how to stay connected with the soul's wisdom in the midst of the most harrowing of outer circumstance. Morrill draws on Jungian psychology to help us navigate our own experiences of collective trauma. Etty's life and wisdom guide us in how to stay connected with the compassionate truth that lives at the center of our beings.

Shoshana Fershtman, Jungian analyst and clinical psychologist, author of T*he Mystical Exodus in Jungian Perspective: Transforming Trauma and the Wellsprings of Renewal*

In her exploration of Etty Hillesum's writing and life, Morrill deepens our understanding, not only of Hillesum, but also of Europe under the Nazi's and the contemporary rise of authoritarianism and xenophobia. While a psychologist, deeply interested in Etty's inner development during an extraordinary time, Morrill also provides a sociological view, illuminating the intersection between the individual and their culture. Morrill builds upon Hillesum's exquisite writing to challenge us to think deeply about cultivating individual growth amid societal trauma.

Judie Wexler, president emerita, California Institute of Integral Studies, and president, Congregation Sherith Israel

The Jungian Inspired Holocaust Writings of Etty Hillesum

Within this fascinating new book, Barbara Morrill analyses the journal writings of Etty Hillesum, a young Jewish woman in the 1940s, as she began analysis with a Jungian oriented practitioner in 1941.

While Anne Frank is an inspirational figure, little is known about Etty Hillesum, also from Amsterdam, who kept a diary recounting her life and experiences during early World War II. This book is a compelling example of how we can use Etty Hillesum's writings in the present to stand firm against the problems we're currently facing globally. Being a Jungian oriented Integral psychologist and professor, the author examines what Hillesum recorded in her time, as well as employing Etty's ideas to illuminate the chaos in our time. She explores Hillesum's own process of individuation and realization, encouraging others to "develop yourselves!"

This will be a unique volume of interest to Jungian analysts, analysts in training, as well as readers with an interest in the time period and concern about democracy and "our times."

Barbara Morrill, PhD, was program chair, associate professor, and core faculty in the Integral Counseling Program at the California Institute of Integral Studies in San Francisco from 2009–2022. She is now faculty emerita. She received her MA from Boston College in Massachusetts and her PhD from the Institute of Transpersonal Psychology (now known as Sofia University) in Palo Alto, California. She is a clinical psychologist licensed in CA and has been in private practice for over 30 years. Barbara has spent much of her life exploring social, psychological, and spiritual development.

The Jungian Inspired Holocaust Writings of Etty Hillesum

To Write is to Act

Barbara Morrill

NEW YORK AND LONDON

Designed cover image: © The Jewish Museum in Amsterdam

First published 2025
by Routledge
605 Third Avenue, New York, NY 10158

and by Routledge
4 Park Square, Milton Park, Abingdon, Oxon, OX14 4RN

Routledge is an imprint of the Taylor & Francis Group, an informa business

© 2025 Barbara Morrill

The right of Barbara Morrill to be identified as author of this work has been asserted in accordance with sections 77 and 78 of the Copyright, Designs and Patents Act 1988.

All rights reserved. No part of this book may be reprinted or reproduced or utilised in any form or by any electronic, mechanical, or other means, now known or hereafter invented, including photocopying and recording, or in any information storage or retrieval system, without permission in writing from the publishers.

Trademark notice: Product or corporate names may be trademarks or registered trademarks, and are used only for identification and explanation without intent to infringe.

ISBN: 9781032756066 (hbk)
ISBN: 9781032756073 (pbk)
ISBN: 9781003474784 (ebk)

DOI: 10.4324/9781003474784

Typeset in Times New Roman
by Newgen Publishing UK

This book is dedicated to:

Etty Hillesum
whose voice was important in her time,
in our time, and for all time
1914–1943 at Auschwitz

and

Friends

and

Survivors of the Holocaust

Jetteke Frijda, Social Worker, Amsterdam
1925–2017

and, her brother,
Nico Frijda, Psychologist, Amsterdam
1927–2015

HOW COULD IT HAPPEN?

The emotions stemming from those past events are still alive and acute, however long the time that passed since. The emotions include panic, not just fearful memories. They include living grief, not just sad recollections. They include stupefaction, complete lack of grasp of what has happened and how it could have happened...and whenever I come across the[se] lines [of an old Dutch poem related to war] - whenever they enter my thoughts there is this brief urge to sit down, this brief feeling behind the eyes. In fact, it is not the emotions that have not passed but that the issues that precipitated the emotions are not over. They still are in operation, they still are current affairs. What can that mean? Let us begin with stupefaction. Perhaps every survivor of mass destruction—of the persecution of the Jews, of the retaliatory killing of all inhabitants of Putten in Holland, Oradour in France, Lidice in the Czech Republic, the Serbian massacres in Bosnia, and the killing frenzies in Rwanda—has experienced this: the naïve disbelief, the naïve amazement on how it has been or is possible. The stupefied disbelief comes to the surface suddenly, when seeing a picture or reading an allusion. The question returns again and again: how on earth could it have happened. It just does not fit one's conception of life and the world.

Nico H. Frijda, The Laws of Emotion (2007)
Lawrence Erlbaum Associates, Inc.

Contents

Foreword by Klaas A. D. Smelik		*xi*
Preface by Barbara Morrill		*xiii*
Introduction		1
One	Her Times: Historical Context	17
Two	Unfolding Toward Being: Jungian Inspired Developmental Stages of Individuation and Realization	26
Three	Etty Hillesum's Diary in Relationship to The Stages of Realization	34
Four	Camp Westerbork: Her Choice	59
Five	Our Time: 2016–2024	77
Six	The Significance of Etty Hillesum's Writings in our Time and all Time	100
Epilogue	The Evolution of the Public's View of Etty Hillesum's Diary since the 1980s	123
Acknowledgments		*130*

*Appendix A: Etty Hillesum's Letter to Friends That Was
    Sent to the Dutch Resistance Two Weeks before Her Own
    Departure for Auschwitz*   *134*
*Appendix B: Examples of Action Based upon Etty
    Hillesum's Writings Today*   *139*
Bibliography   *142*
Index   *149*

Foreword

Aware that the Nazis were out to destroy the entire Jewish people, Etty Hillesum understood that she had only a short time left to communicate her ideas and experiences to her future readers. Nevertheless, she was convinced that she had a message for the time after the war, even if she would not live it herself. She writes about this:

> I would like to live long enough to be able to explain it all again later, and if I am not allowed to do that, well, then someone else will do it and someone else will continue to live my life where mine has been broken off, and therefore I must live it as well and as completely and as convincingly as possible until my last breath, so that the one who comes after me does not have to start all over again and does not have to struggle so much. Isn't that also doing something for posterity?

Another will do it ... The ideas of Etty Hillesum must be passed on—that was her wish and herein also lies my motivation to distribute her bequeathed writings in original and in translation as much as possible—a task with which I have been working to fulfill for forty years now. Because thanks to her, we do not have to start over. Etty Hillesum has given us a basis to better understand our own lives and our own times and to find an answer to the many challenges we face.

Barbara Morrill's book is a compelling example of how we can use Etty Hillesum's diaries and letters in the present to stand firm in the problems of our time. Being a Jungian oriented Integral psychologist and professor, she not only analyzes what Etty Hillesum recorded in her time, she employs Hillesum's ideas to explain to us readers what is going on in our time. Using Hillesum's writings, she wants to show us a direction on how to get out of the mud—to use Etty Hillesum's metaphor:

> To sum up, I would say this: Nazi barbarism awakens in us the same barbarism which would work with the same methods if we were allowed to do what we want today. This barbarism of ours we must inwardly reject, we must not cultivate this hatred within us, because then the world will not get any further out of the mire.

And anyone who follows the daily news will agree that we still don't seem to have come a step further out of the mud since World War II. On the contrary! Barbara Morrill's book is therefore more necessary now than ever, and we can be grateful to her for devoting so many years to this project. I therefore wish the book many readers.

Prof. Dr. Klaas A. D. Smelik, editor of the diaries and letters of Etty Hillesum, English Edition, 2002: *Etty: The Letters and Diaries of Etty Hillesum, 1941–1943*

November 2022

Preface

Etty Hillesum, a young Dutch Jewish woman of twenty-seven, found an inner path to liberation and "union with the ground of her being" in the face of the horror of her times, the Nazi genocide sweeping across Europe, which ultimately engulfed both Etty and her family in late 1943. Etty Hillesum's life moved from chaotic family dysfunction to the healing of her own inner distress, depression, mood swings, and somatic complaints, toward a vast inner life of spaciousness and presence, even with the awareness of the Nazi evil that awaited European Jewry. Her mode of action and resistance was journal writing and contributing to others, and as Denise de Costa says, "It was with her pen, rather than with her sword that she battled to save humanity" (1998, 141).

Because of her reflections upon her experiences, both inner and outer, Etty Hillesum's writings serve as more than a literal chronicle of the events of her times. In fact, our attention is brought to her introspection as a mode of resistance itself. Rachel Feldhay Brenner, author of *Writing as Resistance: Four Women Confronting the Holocaust*, says of Etty Hillesum, Anne Frank, Edith Stein, and Simon Weil:

> Their legacies demonstrate conclusively that they correctly assessed the "radical otherness" of the catastrophe and consciously defied terror. The foresight, awareness, and comprehension of these four women thinker-writers at the *time* of their resistance is compelling ... The four resisted Hitlerian tyranny through the act of writing. (Brenner 2003, 4)

Etty's reflections are important to her journey of self-realization as well as her coping with and resisting one of most diabolical genocides the world has ever known. Her work and life stand as a model for engaging the seemingly ubiquitous rise of fascism or nationalism throughout much of Europe and the United States in our time and, in a broader sense, the tension that exists between democratic and autocratic principles, or open and closed systems, in all times. In her writing there is an inner voice, a process of "reposing in oneself" that models standing in one's truth in our time, when democracy and truth itself are consistently challenged. Etty's writings are significant and powerful in their imagery and their immediacy on the page; they are both timely and timeless. How does one become whole through trauma and tragedy and, particularly in Etty's case, when the dominant culture is out to exclude and finally exterminate her and all those around her? She lets us know how she becomes whole as she resists the inner destruction of the oppressor, whether, as she says, it is Ivan the Terrible, or Hitler.

In writing this book, I want to cultivate a perspective at the intersection of spirituality, psychology, and cultural context. It is fueled by my activism around oppression of all kinds, as well as the narrow religious upbringing of evangelical Christianity, that tiny and parochial message of "one must be saved by accepting *one* truth or end up in hell without it." What about spaciousness and the mystery of inner and outer vastness juxtaposed with the tender and ordinary everyday movements of the human heart, kindness to oneself and others—immanence and transcendence?

This writing is also informed by the realization of how much I was driven to understand the Holocaust consuming Europe in the 1930s and 1940s and the institution of slavery in the United States and the subsequent civil rights movement of the 1960s—those massive movements of hatred and dehumanization and the fight to overcome them—that I was sandwiched between as a girl born in 1950. My drive toward psychology was an effort to understand human nature, yet it seemed insufficient to address the soul's journey and my deeper quest for meaning and wholeness without inquiring into spirituality, transcendence, and the more formal religious traditions and their own effect on the human experience as well as our psychological and cultural conditioning around love and hate and inclusion and exclusion.

Initially, I turned to Jung for such an integration of the two—psychology and spirituality—and then my aim was to integrate Eastern traditions and practices into my training for this journey to understand both the individual and cultural complexes of a person. More contemporary Jungian scholarship has allowed me to look at the power of cultural complexes, our different forms of attachment wounding, and intergenerational trauma as well as the political and religious dogma that perpetuate such trauma. All of this housed in the human being; it is the human condition.

What is also true is that I related to Etty's psychological and spiritual journey, influenced by the work of Jung, which I dabbled in as early as my mid-thirties. I began a process of leaving my ancestral home of New England, and my roots in Christianity, toward a wider world of inner experience, Eastern spiritual influences and practices, academic communities of integral thought, where psychology was not just aberrant behavior to fix, but, as Maslow introduced, a "fourth force" that explored self-actualized individuals that connected with Jung's vision of wholeness or self-realization, the Self that was larger than mere ego or "ordinary" consciousness, in other words, freedom … freedom from within.

Etty was already modern as she began her journey toward becoming more and more herself, shedding so many layers of deficiency and fear and confusion to become a more fully whole, independent woman who fiercely and resolutely faced into systematic, mechanized annihilation, doing for others what she could as she prayed to be the "thinking heart of the barracks." She became a chronicler of an incomprehensible time in history. Through her writing she gives us a taste of her courage, wholeness, and presence, a guide for us as we face into this moment—the essence of our times of fierce political polarization, authoritarian leanings that Etty would surely recognize, a pandemic impacting the entire world, and climate change wreaking havoc on our planet, given generations of mistreatment in the name of industrial progress. Here, now, may we recognize, as Etty did, the courage to be ... to be present, engaged, and always learning to reach out to the other.

I must also name another important force in writing this particular book at this moment in history. While I was preparing for giving a presentation at the Etty Hillesum Research Foundation conference in 2018, the United States had gone through a huge change of direction in 2016 when Donald Trump became the forty-fifth president of the United States. Trump's authoritarian leanings, his lies and doubling down on the lies, has only increased. Even after losing the 2020 election to Joseph R. Biden, he may very well win another election in 2024. Without knowing what we know now I had geared my 2018 Etty Hillesum paper and subsequent article in this direction: "The Contours of These Times: Etty Hillesum as Chronicler of Love Transcending Hate in Her Times, for Our Time, for All Time." I have expanded on this theme in this book as well as presenting a deeper story of Etty as a person of action though her writings, given her experience at Camp Westerbork.

I concur with many of my Dutch friends, "teachers," and writers about Etty Hillesum, that as an English speaker, not being able to read the scores of Dutch books available, I was limited to her diary alone and a significant journey to Amsterdam, one in which I walked in Etty's footsteps, which I describe in the Introduction. It was on my trip to Ghent University in 2014 when I met the Etty Hillesum research community at a conference where I was presenting for the first time, that I knew there was another entire realm of Etty's life of which I was not fully aware. This book fills in so much of the richness of Etty's unconventional life, the "givenness" of her Jewish background, regardless of being "assimilated" or secular. She lived a modern life for her times, borrowing from and curious about so many other spiritual traditions and people. I feel I know her, and now, much more about the grueling reality of her last journey, which claimed her life along with millions of others.

The richness of my relationships with the Dutch Etty Hillesum research community, as well as my international online Etty group, through their open sharing of research and support for my own experience of Etty's words and essence, has allowed me deeper access to Etty's life. They continue to assist and encourage me as we meet this destabilizing time when democracy is no longer a "given" in the United States and throughout the world.

Barbara Morrill
September 2022

Introduction

Twenty-five years ago, I saw a one-woman show staring Naomi Newman, put on by the Traveling Jewish Theatre. She began with a statement that I have roughly remembered: "stories move in circles—overlapping circles—as there are stories between stories and stories inside stories." My experience has been that in the liminal space where individual stories circle, merge, and overlap, synchronicities can unexpectedly occur. One person's outer story suddenly touches another's inner story, opening a portal for a *mutual* story to reveal itself—a narrative that revisions individual histories into timeless commonalities, offering fresh perspectives, insights, and awareness. This book is exactly that—an overlapping story that emerged from the liminal space that intersects Etty Hillesum's life and times in 1940s Nazi-occupied Holland with my own life and times in contemporary twenty-first-century America.

For those who have not been introduced to Etty Hillesum, let me begin with a short summary of her life. The essence of her story is this: Etty Hillesum, a young Jewish Dutch woman, found an inner path to liberation and union with the "nondual ground of existence" in the face of the annihilation of the Holocaust. Etty was born on September 15, 1914, in Middelburg, the Netherlands. Her family moved several times, finally ending up in Deventer. Her father, a Dutch Jew, taught classical languages and was a quiet, scholarly man with a sense of humor. Etty's mother was a Russian Jew who had escaped to the Netherlands following a pogrom; she has been described as passionate, chaotic, and domineering. This marriage of opposites created a tempestuous relationship and household, and although Etty admired her father, she was critical of her mother. Her two younger brothers were intellectually gifted; one was a musician, the other a physician. Both brothers had severe psychological difficulties and were hospitalized at different times for schizophrenia (Smelik 2002, xi).[1]

Etty went to Amsterdam in 1932 to study law at the University of Amsterdam and then went on to study Slavic languages, psychology, and Russian language and literature. She tutored a number of private pupils for Russian language lessons. During her university years she was involved in left-wing antifascist student circles. In 1937 Etty moved into the household of Han Wegerif, an accountant, as his housekeeper. After some time Etty and Han developed an intimate relationship,

Figure 0.1 Hillesum family portrait, circa 1931. From the collection of The Jewish Historical Museum, the Netherlands.

which seemed to provide her with warmth and stability. There were several members of the household that made up this "family of five," including Maria Tuinzing, a nurse who became one of Etty's best friends (Hillesum [Etty] 1996, xvii).[2]

Etty met Julius Spier in February 1941. He was a psychochirologist, one who read hands for diagnostic purposes, and was a former student of C. G. Jung. She immediately became his patient and, soon after, his secretary. Spier was a psychologically gifted and charismatic figure who gathered around him a group of students, predominantly women, to whom he both lectured and provided individual therapy. His psychological approach would be considered unorthodox today, as it often included wrestling bouts and multirole relationships. Etty became part of this

Figure 0.2 Julius Spier celebrating fifty years old, circa 1937. Photo courtesy of Alexandra Nagel (private collection).

group, called the "Spier Club," and as she wrote about Spier, she tells us that she "fell under the spell of the inner freedom that seemed to emanate from him" (ET 2002, 5).

Etty's psychological and spiritual journey began with Spier. She started a diary, writing not only about her inner life but also the life around her. Her relationship with Spier served as the catalyst for her own growth. She challenged and tested herself against him, and this struggle dominates the early journals. They resisted consummating the relationship for a considerable time, as Spier had a fiancée waiting for him in England and Hillesum had a relationship with "Pa" Han Wegerif. Etty and Julius's relationship evolved from erotic obsession to a deeply transformative love that became their joint project.

In July 1942, she became an employee of the Jewish Council, and soon after applied for a position to help the Jews at the Westerbork transit camp, the main Dutch transit camp where the Nazis held the Jews before sending them to concentration or death camps. (Another Dutch transit camp was in Vught.) She turned down offers to go into hiding and continued, through her Jewish Council privilege, the ability to travel back and forth between Amsterdam and Westerbork for approximately two weeks at a time, for three different times from July 1942 until June 5, 1943, when she was no longer able to leave Westerbork. She was deported to Auschwitz on September 7, 1943, along with her parents and brother. Her parents were killed immediately by gas chamber upon arriving at Auschwitz on September 10th, while Etty's death was recorded as November 30, 1943. Before her final departure, Etty gave her diaries and a bundle of letters to her housemate, Maria Tuinzing, with directions to give the notebooks to Klass Smelik in case she didn't return.

My story first intersected with Etty's history quite directly when I was between eight and ten years old and watching the mid-sized black-and-white TV in our 1950s lower-middle-class cottage home in Hingham, south of Boston, Massachusetts. I was watching the yearly reruns on Holocaust Liberation Day. The TV showed grainy black-and-white footage of General Eisenhower liberating one of the concentration camps, which I later learned was Ohrdruf in Germany. I watched stupefied, frozen, overwhelmed by such unspeakable horror. The images were seared into my young mind. Although I don't recall any discussions with my parents about it, I was left with a strong internal experience of frozen shock: *Why? How could this possibly happen?*

I was born in 1950, sandwiched between World War II and the Holocaust and the beginning of the civil rights movement in the United States in the 1960s. Of primarily British and Dutch ancestry, I came of age in an evangelical Baptist home, with parents who were lower middle or working class with high school educations; in fact, my father only went as far as the tenth grade. My mother's brother, my uncle, was a marine who fought in Guadalcanal in World War II and was injured and survived. I had two considerably older brothers, and the younger one of them, who is eleven years my senior, was the first in our family to go to college. My parents were quite surprised by this son, who on his own had received a scholarship to Brown University and would later go on to Yale Divinity School and finish with a doctorate in Religious Thought from Duke University. In my parents' minds ran this thought which they shared with my brother: "This doesn't happen to people like us; we are the little people." Little people yes, but come to find out, direct descendants of British colonizers. Given our simple and economically spare background, we were surprised to later learn we were early Puritan settlers of Massachusetts on one side and Dutch settlers of "New Amsterdam," landing near today's Wall St. in New York City, on the other. We were also related to the member of Congress in the 1800s, Justin Smith Morrill, who wrote the legislation for the Morrill Land Grant Act, allowing for swaths of land across the US to be used for institutions of higher learning for agriculture and mechanical arts, as well as traditional studies in the arts and sciences. A second Land Grant Act, in the 1890s was initiated for African Americans to attend universities in the south since they had been denied opportunities to attend land grant institutions in the south. It is important to note that Justin Morrill, along with Abraham Lincoln, voted against slavery expanding into the western territories of the United States yet they were still not advocates of equality—slavery could still exist in the places it already existed.

The circumstances were quite different for a girl growing up in the fifties and sixties on "the other side of the tracks" in a town that was more of a middle and upper class one, with public schools from which we greatly benefited. Several of my friends lived on Main Street, which ran through the middle of the town that Eleanor Roosevelt called one of the most charming in New England.

Although my parents were in awe of my brother's success, they certainly didn't feel their children were preordained for academic accomplishment, and particularly their only daughter, given their cultural class conditioning and economic reality. When, as a teen, I asked about college, they were ambivalent and thought I could possibly go to an inexpensive college to become a teacher, as a fallback, should something happen to my "husband." I was quite nonplussed by that comment at the time, as most of my girlfriends' parents said similar things. And it was true that although I was a good student, but not a high achiever, I always saw my potential as "less than" my brother's. I idealized him and believed he was "gifted" and was sure I was not. Much like Etty, I felt a deep sense of inadequacy during my teenage and young adult years.

My brother was my Spier figure in an educational and spiritual manner. He was questioning the dogma of Christianity before I reached that experience myself. He moved away from our rigid evangelical background and toward higher education. He spent his junior year as a student in France and sent me dolls from every country that he visited. His experiences opened me to a life of broadening my horizons through adventure and travel, art and history, and the beauty and wonder of other cultures. We were also emotionally connected in a way that was foreign for my father to engage with his daughter in a personal way. In essence, my brother became a "modern" father figure and mentor, as my father, like many in that generation, did not know what to do with his teenage daughter, particularly one whose life ambitions were quite different from his own.

When I was ten, a year or more from the time I saw those Holocaust archival photos on television, my brother sent me a letter from Yale Divinity School. He was twenty-one, and I was ten and had just written to him from summer camp. In his letter, he wrote, "Dear Itsy Bitsy Sister, I just read your letter and it seems all you spoke about were boys, parties and clothes. Have you ever considered Ultimate Reality?" ... What? This was an important anecdote for my college age self, who was already becoming conscious of her inner and outer world. As it happened, I have considered "Ultimate Reality" extensively over all these years. Given my brother's modeling, I wanted what he was having, including freedom, adventure, and education.

Much like Etty, who was born the same year as my mother, I had a fear of ending up as a "traditional housewife," trapped in a domestic life of mediocrity and potential meaninglessness without a career of my own. My mother was a proud homemaker, and I rebelled against the domestic skills that she was most proud of, from "spring" cleaning—the annual tradition of washing and ironing and thoroughly cleaning everything in sight, including all of the machine-washed laundry hanging on the clothesline to be freshly "air-dried"—to her quite beautiful and professional artisan craftwork of knitting sweaters, hooking rugs, and crocheting bedspreads. Today my home is filled with these actual works of art. Her disappointment that

I did not follow suit in homemaking or religion was palpable and omnipresent. My accomplishments were a curiosity to her at best.

When I was nine years old, I attended an evening church service with my mother at the Baptist church. A traveling evangelist drew chalk pictures as he spoke about the Jesus story, followed by the inevitable *altar call*, defined by the Oxford dictionary as a "summons to the altar at a Christian worship service to those wishing to show (or renew) their commitment." At that age I had no commitment to renew, only the pressure of my mother elbowing me in the ribs to go forward to "accept the Lord Jesus Christ into my heart as my personal savior." I dutifully did, and the upshot was a prayer with the evangelist and a true baptism a year later at ten years old to become a member of our evangelical Baptist church. Ten turned out to be a big year.

In 1968, as a beginning college student, I became involved with the battle for civil rights for Black people on my college campus in North Carolina where in my dorm the radio was on and a "grand dragon" of the Ku Klux Klan was rejoicing about the assassination of Martin Luther King. I was flabbergasted and frightened as now I felt was in a foreign land as, growing up south of Boston, my high school was integrated through busing and we were proud of Lloyd Garrison, a prominent Boston abolitionist in the mid-1800s. Overt Jim Crow laws were not that long ago, but more than subtle ones were alive and well at that time in a small village in the US south. Cultural complexes were at play and becoming conscious. It was the beginning of my awareness of white institutional racism as well as the view of many Christians of that time—and this time—that Christianity was the "premiere," or possibly the only true American religion.

Around my second year of college, I finally challenged my mother about this exclusive "club of salvation" reserved for Christians. It was clear that, although my mother looked favorably upon Jewish people, she felt they hadn't been "saved"— that was their only problem—so they could not get into "heaven." *Saved from what, I wondered?* Needless to say, I was exasperated by such a claim, and now, armed with education, I told her how ridiculous that seemed: how could millions of people from other belief traditions be cast into hell by a loving God?

A decade before moving to California for graduate school, I visited the Jung Institute in Switzerland and listened to a talk by Joseph Wheelwright, an analyst from San Francisco. After that talk and a boat ride on Lake Zurich, the dye was cast, and I knew what I had to do. I wanted to understand human nature as well as the archetypal patterns and forces that impact our conditioning.

My early experiences were determinative in my becoming a depth psychologist and a seeker, drawn toward transpersonal or integral psychology, Jungian archetypal psychology and the practices of Eastern traditions as well as an activist and researcher around human rights, racism, antisemitism, and the limitations of organized religion, particularly the one I grew up in.

Ten years later at thirty years old, I took a position as Associate Dean of Student Life at Wheaton College, a women's college at the time, in Norton, Massachusetts. A school that was on the cutting edge of feminist thinking with a faculty-led process and publication called "Toward a Balanced Curriculum." A school that gave me opportunity in areas of women's leadership development and diversity trainings for new students, and a leader myself as secretary of a Society Organized Against Racism—SOAR, that had a membership of twelve to fifteen colleges. It was at Wheaton that I realized liberal zeal can also be blind to the reality of the conditioning of white majority people who are not indigenous to this American land, but have settled here in the early period of British and Western European colonizing. The spiritual and theological notion of "essentialism" leaves out difference and awareness of needs, rituals, and the particularities and suffering of exclusion of the "other." This was 1980, and the academic community was waking up all over the East Coast to the true needs of students of color. I learned this most painfully and gratefully as the second year of my tenure at Wheaton, Black students wanted to leave the Student Union and start the Black Student Union. At first, I resisted it, as I was focused on how can we work with the whole to recognize your needs? And after hiring Black consultants and days of dialogue I saw through this spiritual notion of "we are all the same as human beings" is akin to "color blindness" without recognizing the differences, the political reality, and stain of racism and exclusion that the whole Student Union had not experienced, only part of it. As Patricia Collins (a prominent African American scholar) taught me through her books—the real need of these students "was the freedom both to be different and yet part of the 'solidarity' of humanity" (Collins 1991, 54) Hence, 1981 became the first year of the Black Student Union at Wheaton College.

I left Wheaton in 1985 to become president of a new startup in Connecticut called "Connecticut Works" that placed women on welfare into private sector jobs that provided a stipend for childcare. It provided career training, skill-building in the lab we had developed in the space, and its unique feature was a coordinator who helped women work out the childcare needs and work with them around transportation and even a clothing swap and share for first interviews.

The hard work of those years gave me a sense of my outer strengths and capacities, but I realized I needed to begin an inner journey. Activism was rewarding, but it was only one dimension of a deeper connection to my own true nature and not relying on only outer action to make lasting change. I left family and friends and moved to California in 1988 to attend the Institute of Transpersonal Psychology in Menlo Park. In 1994, I completed my dissertation "Quest for Wholeness: The Individuation Process of Seven African American Women, A Case Study." The purpose of this study was to look at the triple jeopardy of Black women; of how racism, sexism, and classism impacted their lives in a multitude of areas such as self-worth, health, violence, as well as financial equality, and spirituality, and/or what they drew from in the forms of inner and outer support and guidance.

Although I did not become a Jungian analyst, I have always been centered around the psychological, including Jungian archetypal psychology and the spiritual, cultural, and political implications of intergenerational trauma patterns from racism and antisemitism.

I became a student of the Holocaust, reading all I could of the history and impact of the twelve years of the National Socialist Party rule in Europe and its impact in the US, a period that changed our very foundation. I was consumed by survivors' stories, reading all the accounts and diaries that were being published, including those most famous accounts by Elie Wiesel, Anne Frank, Primo Levi, and Viktor Frankl.

In the late 1990s, I discovered *An Interrupted Life*, an abridged copy of Etty Hillesum's diary. It changed my life. From the beginning, I saw Etty as an independent, unconventional woman who wanted to write, to express herself, and who wanted to liberate herself from the "tightly coiled ball of twine" (Etty 1996, 3) existing within, and who then, through her work with Spier and her own inner work, discovered her own way of holding onto the beauty of life amidst the signs of her own probable demise along with millions of others.

In 2005, after reading Etty's unabridged diary, first published in English in 2002, I discovered a more integral perspective toward Etty Hillesum through the lens of both Jungian psychology and Eastern and Western spiritual practices, including my thirteen-year involvement in the Diamond Approach. I drew upon the work of A. H. Almaas and Karen Johnson, the developers of the Diamond Approach, to set the stage for this new experiential path, which combines Eastern teachings and practices with the concepts of Western depth psychology. In the Diamond Approach, development is seen as occurring in spiraling and overlapping stages. I examined Etty Hillesum's spiritual and psychological journey in the context of these stages, which are much like the alchemical stages of individuation in the Jungian world that I have utilized in this book. I am also informed by the Diamond Approach's method of inquiry. Whereas Jung's process was an intellectual one, unless one entered Jungian oriented therapy, the Diamond Approach was a much more here and now method of becoming aware of one's actual experience in the moment, from body to sensation to insight to presence.

I chose to walk in Etty's footsteps in Amsterdam, Holland, in 2006, using her book to guide me in walking over "5 streets and a canal" to visit Julius Spier's flat at 27 Courbetstraat in South Amsterdam, from where she lived with Han Wegerif (and community) on Gabriel Metsustraat 6.

As I approached Julius Spier's flat, I looked across the street and saw an African or African American young woman getting on her bicycle. I said hello and asked if she had heard of Etty Hillesum. She was from Ghana, West Africa, but grew up in Los Angeles. She did not know of Etty, but we spoke about the Anne Frank House, and then she had an idea: "I just moved in two weeks ago, but there is an old woman in the flat below me who has lived here for a long time, and she might know of her. Let me go in and see if she will speak with you."

Suzette came out about ten minutes later, looking a bit stunned, and told me that not only did the woman know about Etty and Spier as Spier once lived directly across the street, but also she was Jewish and was hidden by Christians in the Dutch countryside during the war—and *she was best friends with Margot Frank, Anne's sister, and was at Anne Frank's birthday party when she got her plaid diary.*

As I stepped into Jetteke Frijda's flat, I felt as if I had entered an archetypal frame of mind, as if I were stepping back into another time in history. Jetteke was eighty-two years old, and I was fifty-six. Present time and timelessness were interwoven, thanks to Jetteke's perfect English. She told me her story and her strong connection to Margot Frank, as they were the only two Jewish girls in their school. We also discussed our well-known brothers who had each published books that very year! Jetteke's brother was Nico Frijda, a psychologist in Amsterdam who had just published *The Laws of Emotion*. My brother's (Richard Morrill) book *was Strategic Leadership*: *Integrating Strategy and Leadership in Colleges and Universities*. Both Jetteke and I were both quite proud of our brothers yet felt eclipsed by them in our growing up as girls in the 1940s, 1950s, and 1960s

After several visits with Jetteke that week, including meeting her cousin for dinner one night, she gave me a paper copy, in Dutch, of her story during the war. I took it home to California, had it translated, and returned to Amsterdam the next summer, stayed in an upstairs flat with Suzette, the woman from Ghana, and walked downstairs every day to tape Jetteke as she told her story. I wrote an unpublished paper, comparing and contrasting Jetteke Frijda's and Etty Hillesum's experiences during the Holocaust and presented it at a transpersonal psychology conference in India in 2008. This exploration of Etty Hillesum and the life around her has become both my personal and academic pursuit for the past eighteen years. Because of this direct intersection with Jetteke, Anne, Margot, and Etty's time in history, it feels important to add that Jetteke began therapy in earnest many years after the war, which was in the unpublished biography I have mentioned. While she was an established and well-known social work professional in Holland, she began to lose her grip on reality as she had never processed the rage she had toward her mother during the war. She would only work with a cognitive behavioralist, and one who was Jewish. As it turned out this professional was a very distant cousin who she ultimately trusted. This took many years and was full of explosions of rage at her therapist, many periods where she would walk out, go on strike, and come back, again and again. The breakthrough came as her therapist asked her to make a scrapbook of everything that was positive about her mother, because as a child they were close. It was a devastating reality Jetteke had to confront—that her mother fell in love with another man and left her husband and three children as the war began, and flew to Switzerland with her new paramour. Years after the war, her mother returned to Holland without this man and Jetteke finally responded to her positively when she found out her mother had Alzheimer's disease and took care of her to the end of her life. This is ultimately what Jetteke herself died of in late 2017.

This was my first public opportunity to tell Etty Hillesum's and Jetteke Frijda's stories and what mattered most to me was that Jetteke, whose personality was quite different from Etty's, was satisfied with the paper I presented at that conference. In fact, she felt seen. Jetteke was a pragmatist and was very direct about the fact that she could not get past Etty's "all-consuming" love story with Spier. She felt "Anne Frank was a 'chatterbox,'" and that "Margot was the real intellect, so wondered why was Anne the one who became famous?" She even asked Otto Frank, Anne and Margot's father, the only one of the family to return alive from the camps, the same question once Anne's diary was published. Otto was clear with Jetteke and told her Margot's diary was never found, if she even had one.

In 2009, I accepted a position as a faculty member in the Integral Psychology Counseling master's program at the California Institute of Integral Studies in San Francisco. A year later, I became chair of the department, serving in that role for the next six years, and taught as part of the core faculty for the following eight years. Today, I have recently retired as a core faculty member in the same department after fourteen years and have recently become Faculty Emerita at this unique institution. Students have both been my guides to understanding as well as teaching about the intersection of psychology, spirituality, and cultural context.

I continue to be deeply moved and fascinated by this fragile yet powerful woman, Etty Hillesum, and shared her story, her powerful and tender words with my students as a culmination of a semester's learning about therapeutic communication, compassion, presence, and practice with a final class about this woman who exemplified transformation at the nexus of her spiritual and psychological quest at a time of radical cultural genocide.

Jetteke and I would go on to have a twelve-year correspondence, and we visited in person perhaps four times, the last time in 2014 (with both Jetteke and her brother Nico who was visiting for the day). Nico told me about his own trip to Auschwitz with his son just the year before to honor their father who was killed there. It was at that time that Jetteke let me know that she had Alzheimer's disease. In 2017, I went to her flat as she was no longer replying to my messages online. As I approached that familiar place across the street from Spier's former flat, I saw a for-sale sign above her building, although her name was still beside her doorbell. I pressed it, and a neighbor came out and told me that Jetteke had died six months before. I also found out that her brother Nico, eighteen months her junior, had died in 2015, about eighteen months before her. I walked away with not only my own grief, but also the realization that we were nearing the end of this first generation of Holocaust survivors and the fear of more Holocaust denying, increased antisemitism, and the rewriting of history by authoritarian-leaning governments all over the world, including now, in the United States.

Anne Frank and Etty Hillesum—Amsterdam

As Jetteke eventually realized, the world came to know of this Dutch Jewish girl she called a "chatterbox." Anne Frank was a diarist wanting to be a writer. She is known to have written: "Despite everything, I believe that people are really good at heart" (Frank 1952). A short time later she and her sister Margot perished in the Holocaust at the same concentration camp, Bergen Belsen in 1945. Anne's diary was saved by Miep Gies, who worked for Otto Frank, and it was Otto who began to work to get portions of the diary published. The first edition of Anne's diary was published in 1952, seven years after WWII.

Only three miles away in Amsterdam, Etty Hillesum, twice Anne's age, commenced her journal writing in 1941, as she began analysis with a Jungian oriented practitioner, Julius Spier. Etty wanted to become a writer, and similarly to Anne her voice is also one of love and not hate. Etty was killed at an extermination camp, Auschwitz-Birkenau, near the end of 1943. Anne and Etty never met, and most likely never met, nor crossed paths, as Anne was also at Westerbork transit camp, yet it was in 1944, months after Etty had been deported.

In my journey to Amsterdam, it was Jetteke Frijda who had the experience of being best friends with Margot Frank and professed to be at Anne's 13th birthday party, on June 12, 1942, where Anne received her plaid notebook—actually, it was a smaller scrap book she used as a notebook and Jetteke was most likely there the day after, when the friends celebrated Anne, as she received her special plaid gift the day before with her parents and sister. She was quite excited about this gift, which came just one month before the Frank family went into hiding.

Etty began her diary in March of 1941 and by September 15th of 1942, Spier had died of cancer They had eighteen months together. Etty left for the last time to Westerbork in June of 1943 and was deported to Auschwitz three months later on September 7th.

One Jewish teenager and one Jewish young woman from the same city passed, crossed, and circled each other in their writing journey at the time of the war's escalation to complete Hitler's primary mission—to rid Europe and the world if possible, of Jewish blood. As Denise de Costa says:

> While the Nazis were doing their best to destroy the Jews, Frank and Hillesum were working on their personal development. Though their freedom to do so grew more restricted, language was a channel of expression no one could take away from them. Both devoted themselves to writing: in language they found a new home, a safe haven to which they could retreat. (de Costa 1998, 4)

Both Anne and Etty fought their chaotic moods and depression in their lives and in their journals in order to be to be optimistic. In Etty's case, she was on the journey of analysis toward self-realization and wanted to become a chronicler of this maelstrom for the Jewish people who would survive. Whereas, Anne, as a teen "clung to her dreams of that extraordinary future that awaited her." Both women, struggled with their mothers—Etty, because her mother was "hysterical" and somewhat gross to her in her food habits and lack of rationality, while Anne wanted to live a life "different from other girls and later on, different from ordinary housewives" (de Costa 1998, 5).

Both women became aware of being the "other" as being Jewish and being female at that time in history meant radical exclusion. Both distanced themselves from traditional roles of being housewives and mothers yet Anne did so without denying her womanhood:

> I know that I am a woman, a woman with inner strength, Plenty of courage! If God lets me live, I shall achieve more than Mother ever has. I shall not remain insignificant, I shall work in the world for mankind! (de Costa 1998, 5 from Frank 1952, 601)

Etty Hillesum also had many thoughts about women and wondered why women were not at the top of various professions, and realized hers was a patriarchal world. Etty was also a very sensual and sexual young woman with many boy friends, and still came to understand that "femininity was not exclusively bound to the body." She could also draw on an ancient bond between the feminine and the soul (ET 2002, 301). A woman's task, which she had taken on, lost its negative connotation (to renounce the body) and was transformed into a positive act (to use one's spiritual strength): "It is really true, I think: Men can only reach their own feelings through ours, women's feelings" (de Costa 1998, 9; ET 2002, 300).

Both women needed God. Anne, went back and forth from God causing this suffering upon the Jews, while at other times she placed the blame on people having the capacity for rage and murder and destruction. She would often come back to believing God would lift the suffering again. Denise de Costa says she needed God in order to become a good person while "upholding her own sense of honor and obeying her own conscience" (de Costa 1998, 5 from Frank 1952, 605). In short, even though life was extraordinarily difficult for her as a Jew, she kept the faith. Etty, also needed God, although she used the notion of God in different ways at different times. At times, she called God "reposing in herself," to protecting God and not blaming him for this genocide—but taking responsibility for protecting the God within herself and wanted that for others as well. She also quoted Jung several times when Jung calls God an experience of the ineffable. She was a modern mystic and existential thinker. Time was running out for the Jews and prayers to God were more constant and of longer duration. She is reminiscent of a devoted rebbe with an intimate relationship with God as the Beloved.

The differences between them have most to do with Etty growing up in a more assimilated, secular fashion. She was an old soul, growing up quicky with two younger brothers both diagnosed with schizophrenia which she was terrified of having. She may have kept some of the traditions of her Jewish religion as a child and teenager, yet it was not an observant home, even though Etty's father was intellectually extremely knowledgeable about Judaism.

As we can see, Anne and family were observant and Anne was thirteen when going into hiding. And while Anne's most quoted phrase has more to do with what people want to remember about her, Denise de Costa feels it was taken out of context, as when she wrote those words she was in a serious mood, realizing how hard it was for young people to grow up in wartime:

> "For in its innermost depths, childhood is lonelier than old age." I read this saying in some book , and I've always remembered it, and found it to be true. Is it true then that grown-ups have a more difficult time here than we do? No, I know it isn't. Older people have formed their opinions about everything and don't waver before they act. It's twice as hard for us young ones to hold our ground, and maintain our opinions, in a time when all ideals are being shattered and destroyed, when people are showing their worst side, and do not know whether to believe in truth and right and God. ... It's really a wonder that I haven't

dropped all my ideals, because they seem so absurd and impossible to carry out. Yet I keep them, because in spite of everything I still believe that people are really good at heart.

I simply can't build up my hopes on a foundation consisting of confusion, misery, and death. I see the world gradually being turned into a wilderness, I hear the ever-approaching thunder, which will destroy us too. I can feel the sufferings of millions and yet if I look up into the heavens, I think that everything will turn out all right, and that this cruelty too, will end, and that peace and tranquility will return again. In the meantime, I must uphold my ideals, for perhaps the time will come when I shall be able to carry them out! (Frank 1952, 693–694)

As we will see, Etty has some of the idealism, self-involvement, and growing despair of Anne's. Yet given Etty's age, maturity, intellect, and support of an analyst, her deepening "experience" will lead the way. After Spier died, she grew stronger in her resolve and in inhabiting the ground of her being, bringing Presence to those around her.

Both of these young women were rare and special beings—Anne Frank and Etty Hillesum. We know they are joined by hundreds of thousands of young people whose writings either did not exist or were not found. And to know two of them from Amsterdam a few miles apart…is a gift to all of us.

Why? How Could This Happen?

This question, first asked at the age of nine or ten by a naive American girl in 1950s Boston, has followed me for the rest of my life. As I became a student of Jungian psychology, and ultimately a practicing Integral therapist and professor, I have come to see the deep underlying roots that continue to nurture cultural hate.

Thomas Singer, a contemporary Jungian analyst and scholar, has done a significant amount of work to build upon the Jungian theory of the individual complex (and Etty spends a great deal of time working through her own individual complexes). *Individual complexes* can be understood as internalized messages that drive externalized behavior, related to personal thriving or suffering. Singer's notion of *cultural complexes* expands this same dynamic to include a group's *collective* conditioning and underlying messages in these same arenas of thriving and suffering. Often described as "the water we swim in," cultural complexes are invisible but extremely potent ways of seeing the world and others around us (Singer 2020, xxii).

We are shaped by many forces: our time in history and country of origin; our parents and their conditioning, their attributes as well their flaws; our culture, our governments, and politics, our race and ethnicity, our class, and gender, our religious origins, or lack of them; the color of our skin; our societal privilege or class to name just a few. As Singer says, cultural complexes are autonomous, repetitive, validate their own point of view and are resistant to facts, tend to be simplistic, have strong emotions, and can form the core of a healthy identity (2020, xxii–xxiii). Singer says that cultural complexes can be seen

> as being part of the filtering system ... that dwells in each of us and the groups with which we most strongly identify. Distilled over generations, cultural complexes filter and dictate through their own narratives, the meaning, emotion, thought, memory, image, and behavior of inner and outer events. (Singer 2020, xxii)

In telling Etty Hillesum's story, I feel it important to share what informs my perspective, arising from both the individual and cultural complexes of my time in American history. It is also true that Etty's time, place, religion, and ethnic identity laid the groundwork for her journey to becoming a chronicler of Jewish experience during one of the worst travesties of human destruction the world has known.

Psyche, says Singer, is not only real in individuals, but also exists in groups, often referred to as the group psyche or collective psyche. "Psyche is inside us—forming an inner sociology—and all around us, taking many shapes and forms that can shift predictably like the tides or overwhelm unpredictably like a tsunami" (Singer 2020, xxi). Here is how Jung stated it:

> Therefore it seems to me far more reasonable to accord the psyche the same validity as the empirical world, and to admit that the former has as much "reality" as the latter. As I see it, the psyche is a world in which the ego is contained. Maybe there are fishes who believe that they contain the sea. (Jung 1929/1968, CW 13, para. 75; quoted in Singer 2020, xxi)

There are many individual and cultural complexes existing in Etty Hillesum's time, as there are in the people who influenced her the most—her family, friends, teachers, and Julius Spier—their religious and ethnic identities as well as the political and social zeitgeist of their time in history. C. G. Jung influenced Julius Spier, and both Jung and Spier influenced Etty Hillesum and therefore Jungian ideas will provide a framework of my exploration of how these ideas interface with their story as well as my own.

Chapter One, "Her Times: Historical Context," I discuss the context of Hitler's coming to power up to the Dutch capitulation and the particular experience of the Jews of Amsterdam.

Chapter Two, "Unfolding Toward Being: Developmental Stages of Etty's Realization," will address, first, Jung's stages of Individuation as well as Feminist Jungian scholars' views through the years, including Carol Christ's (pronounced "Crist") stages toward wholeness that I have adapted.

Chapter Three, "Etty Hillesum's Diary in Relationship to Stages of Realization," will be Etty's psychological and spiritual journey, through various quotes from her two-and-a-half years of diaries and letters. This chapter will use a feminist and whole person neo-Jungian lens to look at her stages of evolution, which sets the inner foundation for her presence and actions at Camp Westerbork.

Chapter Four, "Camp Westerbork: Her Choice," will explain her purpose in going to Westerbork, and not going into hiding. Her experiences at the camp and her contributions to her tribe as well as to history—as a chronicler—will be covered.

Chapter Five, "Our Time: 2016–2024," will present the growing impulse toward authoritarian regimes across the globe, particularly in the United States.

Chapter Six will look at "The Significance of Etty Hillesum's Writings in Our Time and All Time," in terms of the lasting significance of Etty's writings and what they point to in terms "of *living fully, outwardly and inwardly, not to ignore external reality for the sake of the inner life, or the reverse—that's quite a task*" (ET 2002, 53; italics mine).

The **Epilogue** will speak about the evolution of the public's view of Etty Hillesum's diary since the 1980s.

When I found Etty Hillesum's diary around twenty-five years ago, I experienced an immediate familiarity with her as she seemed a modern woman; in fact, she seemed like "everywoman" as well as a companion, a psychological and spiritual seeker who became a guide for me in living this human life of suffering and soaring. Where our stories radically differed was that she was a Jewish woman in the 1930s and 1940s. What Etty had to live through for the last several years of her life and what she was murdered for during the Holocaust are incomprehensible for so many of us—unless one has grown up Jewish in Europe or Black in the United States and while these histories have multiple distinctive differences, they share the experience of being hated—and have been shaped by experiences of exile and exclusion, terror, torture, and extreme suffering that have become deeply embedded in one's own fabric through the generations. While Black people were not exterminated as part of a mechanized plan, they were dehumanized and used as chattel and as utilities to produce economic success for white people, and were tortured and lynched by everyday citizens as well as the infamous Ku Klux Klan. Both groups were assessed as less than desirable humans that should not procreate by the science of eugenics and conspiracy theories about both groups continue to predominate. Historically, since the first century CE, Jewish individuals and their cultural and religious traditions have caused scorn and hatred and antisemitic sentiment that can and has erupted into full-scale genocide. White supremacists in our times are determined, still, to keep the white race pure—free from people of color and are determined that, as we know of late, from the chant in Charlottesville by white supremacists that "Jews will not replace us."

Our times demand our reflection and action. In her times, Etty's writing was her action. Journaling about self-growth at such times is action. Writing was her act of healing, an act of Beauty, an act of political activism, an act of advocacy, an act of witnessing, an act of remembering, of documenting, and in her words, an act of chronicling—which became an act of warning and an act of truth-telling, of soul survival and hope. In our times, drawing upon Etty Hillesum's example, we may also find that *to write is to act.*

Notes

1 Hereafter references to Klaas A. D. Smelik, ed., *Etty: The Letters and Diaries of Etty Hillesum 1941–1943*, trans. Arnold J. Pomerans (Grand Rapids, MI: William B. Eerdman's Publishing Company, 2002) will be cited as ET 2002, followed by the relevant page number.
2 Hereafter references to Etty Hillesum, *An Interrupted Life: The Diaries of Etty Hillesum, 1941–1943*, notes and introduction by Jan G. Gaarlandt (New York: Henry Holt and Company, 1996) will be cited as Etty 1996, followed by the relevant page number.

Chapter One

Her Times
Historical Context

> And then, it suddenly happened: I was able to feel the contours of these times with my fingertips. How is it that this stretch of heathland surrounded by barbed wire, through which so much human misery has flooded nevertheless remains inscribed in my memory as something almost lovely? How is it that my spirit, far from being oppressed seems lighter and brighter there? It is because I read the signs of the times and they did not seem meaningless to me ...
>
> Etty Hillesum (ET 2002, 526)

For nearly two thousand years Jewish individuals had been the quintessential "other" in European Christian culture. It began with the theological negation of Jews, Judaism, and Jewish scripture in the first century CE because of their refusal to accept Jesus as the long-anticipated Messiah. With the developing Christianity of late antiquity, a process began of marginalizing, scapegoating, and dehumanizing Jews, describing them in the vilest of terms. Jews were known as the murderers of God; they were in league with the devil and responsible for all the world's evil (Reuther 1997, 117–128).

Given this very particular and ongoing kind of scapegoating, hatred for Jews was well established in the very cells of Europe, as Germany met up with Adolf Hitler, the totalitarian dictator and psychopathic murderer of the Third Reich. Hitler was the absolute shadow figure of Paul von Hindenburg, the democratic-leaning aristocrat of the Weimar Republic. In his book *The Death of Democracy: Hitler's Rise to Power and the Downfall of the Weimar Republic* (2018), Benjamin Carter Hett describes Hitler's rise as an element of the collapse of a republic confronting the difficulties of globalization, not unlike our own times. The Germans would become self-sufficient by conquering territory and developing their own economy in isolation. "As Goebbels put it" says Hett, "We want to build a wall, a protective wall" (Snyder 2018). Hitler maintained that the dilemmas of globalization were not the result of economic forces but an international Jewish conspiracy. The Germans, then, became the victims and the totalitarian regime fueled a coalescing fear response among the population.

The antisemitic and ubiquitous propaganda, lying, and political maneuvering were not limited to the Nazis of that day. In a prescient nod to American politics,

Hett describes Hindenburg and his advisers as those who regarded the Nazi movement as a considerable opportunity for creating a majority for the Right. According to Hett, Hindenburg had the legal authority to dissolve the Reichstag and rule by decree, but instead he changed the government to a group of feuding parties, so that in the election of 1932, the Nazis would win, and Hitler would become chancellor in 1933. It did not occur to the Hindenburg camp that the Nazis would do as well as they did, or that their leader Hitler would escape their control. As Hett concludes, "And so the feckless schemes of the conservatives realized the violent dreams of the Nazis" (Snyder 2018, 4). Hindenburg died in 1934 believing he had saved Germany and his own reputation, when, in fact, he had created the conditions for the greatest horror of the twentieth century (Snyder 2018).

While Hitler was telling the biggest of lies in his conspiracies about the Jews, "he said clearly what he was doing and what he planned to do, this is the essential paradox of Adolf Hitler" (Hett 2018, 38). It is both chilling and enlightening that former US President Donald Trump was and still is using the same playbook and would be open about so many of the things that he would be impeached for as a way to justify his crimes and lies as normalcy.

Hitler and Russia's Putin are of a similar kind of ruthless and murderous totalitarian tyrant. Hitler, in the 1930s and 1940s, well known for his SS treacherous secret police headed by Himmler, while Putin, still in lifetime power, currently comes from the Stalinist Russian tradition as well as from KGB training, both an intelligence agency as well as secret police. He is known for the disappearance of anyone who opposes him.

Copious numbers of authoritarian politicians worldwide double down on their lies consistently. While today's strongmen are considered "personalist" dictators: Victor Orbán, in Hungary, formerly Trump in the US, formerly Bolsonaro in Brazil, and Netanyahu in Israel who has recently won again with a far right platform. The central goal of this kind of personalist authoritarian is to gain more and more power, instead of terrorizing people physically. This kind of ruler reshapes its citizens through charisma, and enthusiasm of getting more recognition banning the press, as well as marginalizing people who are considered "other" … and injecting fear through conspiracy theories of losing what one has accumulated.

Even more shameful is that Hitler admired America's early genocidal history with Native Americans and its enslavement and lynching of African Americans, which provided both a model and methodology for his genocidal aspirations toward the Jews. Isabel Wilkerson in her current book *Caste* (2020) names it directly:

> He had studied America from afar both envying and admiring it. He praised the country's near genocide of Native Americans and the exiling to reservations for those who had survived. He was pleased that the United States "had shot down the millions of redskins to a few hundred thousand." The Nazis were impressed by the American custom of lynching its subordinate caste of African Americans, having become aware of the ritual torture and mutilations

Her Times: Historical Context 19

that typically accompanied them. *Hitler especially marveled at the American knack for maintaining an air of robust innocence in the wake of mass death.* (Wilkerson 2020, 81; italics added)

Hitler's Final Solution was clicked into high gear in January 1942 in the Wannsee suburbs of Berlin, later known as the Wannsee Conference. Etty Hillesum was wearing the Jewish Star three months later and murdered at Auschwitz Birkenau eighteen months later, as a result of the Final Solution to save Aryan Europe from the stain of "evil" Jewish blood. Because Etty's historical time had much to do with her Dutch and Jewish heritage, it serves the purpose of Etty's larger story to look at the particular and peculiar story of the Dutch Jews.

In 1940, the main principle of Dutch foreign policy was neutrality, as it had been for a century, yet the Netherlands capitulated to the Nazis on May 15, 1940, five days after the Nazi blitzkrieg of the Netherlands, Belgium, and Luxembourg. Etty was in Amsterdam at the time, and she would begin her diary less than a year later.

In it, near the beginning, after another death of a Slavonic's professor, she reflects back to her law school days and her last encounter with one of her professors who she ran into a few hours before the Dutch capitulation to Hitler's Germany:

Figure 1.1 Etty Hillesum Reading the Newspaper circa 1938-1939 Photo taken by Han Wegerif.

Because I am still so young and utterly resolved not to go under, and also because I feel that I am strong enough to pull myself together, I tend to forget how deprived we young people have become and how lonely. Or have I simply been anesthetized? Bonger is dead, Ter Braak, Du Perron, Marsman, all are dead. Pos, and Van den Bergh, and many others are in concentration camps.

I shall never forget Bonger. (Odd, how Van Wijk's death has suddenly brought it all back to me.) It was a few hours before the Dutch capitulation. And suddenly there was the heavy, cumbersome, unmistakable figure of Bonger shuffling along through the Skating Club, blue-tinted glasses, singular, heavy head tilted to one side and looking toward the clouds of smoke that came floating across the town from the faraway oil terminals. This image—the clumsy figure with neck craned and head tilted at the distant clouds of smoke—is something I shall never forget. On an impulse I ran, coatless, out through the doors behind him, caught up with him and said, "Hello, Professor Bonger, I have thought a lot about you these last few days, may I walk a little way with you?" And he gave me a sidelong look through those blue glasses and obviously had no idea who I was, despite two exams and a year at his lectures. Still, those days people felt so close to one another that I just continued walking by his side. I can't remember the precise words we exchanged. It was that afternoon when people thought of nothing but getting away to England, and I asked, "Do you think it makes sense to escape?" And he said, "The young have to stay put." And I, "Do you think democracy can win?" And he, "It's bound to win, but it's going to cost us several generations." And he, fearless Bonger, was suddenly as defenseless as a child, almost gentle, and I felt an irresistible need to put my arms round him and to lead him like a child, and so, with my arm round him, we walked on across the Skating Club. He seemed a broken man and good through and through. All the passion and fire in him had been doused. My heart overflows when I think of how he was that afternoon—he, the college tyrant. And at Jan Willem Brouwers Square I took my leave of him. I stood in front of him, took one of his hands between mine, and he gently lowered his heavy head a little and looked at me through his blue glasses, which hid his eyes, and sounded almost like a stage comic as he said, "My pleasure." And next evening at Becker's, the first thing I heard was, "Bonger is dead!" I said, "That's impossible, I spoke to him last night at seven o'clock." And Becker said, "Then you must have been one of the last people to speak to him. He put a bullet through his brain at eight o'clock." And two of his last words had been addressed to an unknown student, one whom he had looked at kindly through a pair of blue glasses, "My pleasure!"

And Bonger is not the only one. A world is in the process of collapse. But the world will go on, and so for the present shall I, full of good heart and goodwill. Nevertheless, we who are left behind are just a little bit destitute, though inwardly I still feel so rich that the destitution is not fully brought home to me. However, one must keep in touch with the real world and know one's place in it; it is wrong to live only with the eternal truths, for then one is apt to end up behaving like an ostrich. To live fully, outwardly and inwardly, not to ignore external reality for the sake of the inner life, or the reverse—that's quite a task. (ET 2002, 52–53; italics added)

Professor Bonger was not alone; hundreds of Dutch Jews killed themselves on that day and during the several weeks after the capitulation. Although the Dutch army still scored small victories, it could not hold its positions against the Nazis. The cabinet felt that Queen Wilhelmina should flee. Her safety was at stake. Initially, she did not want to go, but she was forced to leave when the situation worsened. A warship took her to England, where the British King received her. The fact that their Queen had fled came as a blow to the Dutch population. Until then, the newspapers had mainly reported on Dutch successes. The situation turned out to be more serious than expected. Some people criticized the Queen for fleeing and called her a coward. However, during the occupation, the Queen would prove to be an important symbol of the fight against Nazi Germany.

The Netherlands, and particularly Amsterdam, was historically known as a place of liberal ideas, tolerance of difference, and concern for the empowerment of the individual. Russell Shorto, in his book *Amsterdam: A History of the World's Most Liberal City* (2013), explains how, given the history of tolerance, that it was all the more "curious" that the Nazis had a special plan for the city. He goes on to say that the Germans "did the Dutch the honor of believing 'pure' Dutch descent was on a par with 'pure' German descent—both, a part of the same Aryan stock. The Germans went about quietly occupying the country and gradually 'neatening up' its racial situation" (Shorto 2013, 265–266). It seems the Dutch, over the preceding decades, had chosen to deal with their increasing racial complexity by beginning a system they called the *pillar system*, or *pillarization*. It was a movement to keep peace and give different groups their own community space: their own newspapers, banks, schools, and even radio stations. The main pillars were Catholic, Protestant, socialist, and liberal. Jews fell under the socialist pillar, and like the other groups, were also cataloged, making the Nazis' job easier (Shorto 2013, 266)

What seems surprising is how much the Dutch aided the Germans in their persecution policy. Two examples stand out: first, Jacob Lentz, a Dutch bureaucrat, "took it upon himself" to create a personal identity card. Lentz wrote a small book about it and brought it to Berlin to display it, as a way to earn credit! The Germans approved and ordered every Dutch citizen to have one. The cards for the Jews were stamped with a large *J*, predating the use of the ubiquitous Jewish Star. Nothing like it had been developed before (Shorto 2013, 266). Louis de Jong, a well-known historian of World War II in the Netherlands, called this device "an indispensable aid to the persecution policy of the German occupation" (de Jong 1990; quoted in Shorto 2013, 266).

As we know, the first visible step in making the Nazi's job more explicit was the administering of the yellow Jewish Star for all Jews in Holland to wear in public attached to their clothing. Etty was at the height of her relationship with Spier in 1942 when the directive of wearing the star came down on April 29, 1942. The first impact on her had to do with Spier. "For something inside me has suddenly changed and I know now that I shall follow S. wherever he goes and share his sorrows" (ET 2002, 355). And, for the first time, she feels a sense of further connection with Spier in being Jewish: "I am so glad that he is a Jew and I a Jewess" (355). It is clear that Etty is aware, radically aware, at this point, while she continues to live her life to the fullest, reminding herself that life is not meaningless. She starts reporting the antisemitic laws that follow in June 1942, "Jews may no longer visit greengrocers' shops, they will soon have to hand in their bicycles, they may no longer travel by tram and they must be off the streets by eight o'clock at night" (ET 2002, 409). Etty learned that all Jews would be transported out of the Netherlands through Drenthe Province and then on to Poland. And the English radio reported that 700,000 Jews perished last year alone, in Germany and the occupied territories (Frenk n.d.). On July 2, 1942, she records this horrific foresight:

> I am in Poland every day, on the battlefields, if that's what one can call them. I often see visions of poisonous green smoke; I am with the hungry, with the ill-treated and the dying, every day, but I am also with the jasmine and with that piece of sky beyond my window; there is room for everything in a single life. (ET 2002, 460)

And on July 11, 1942: "The Jews here are telling each other lovely stories: they say that the Germans are burying us alive or exterminating us with gas. But what is the point of repeating such things even if they should be true?" (ET 2002, 484). She was determined to live in the moment, regardless of the swirling stories, that she seems to realize will become closer and more extensive, while always hopeful that miracles can happen at anytime.

Etty already did some typing work for the Jewish Council. Eventually she would become more involved. The role of the Dutch Jewish Council in Holland, located in Amsterdam, was extremely confidential. According to Hans Knoop, the actions of Abraham Asscher and David Cohen, leaders of the *Joodse Raad* (Jewish Council), were as follows:

> They issued deportation notices and urged the Jews in Het Joodsche Weekblad to obey these summons to the letter ... Cohen declared after the war, "Thanks to our efforts, no Jews suffered from hunger in occupied Holland." That is the case. But thanks to Asscher and Cohen, the deportation of the Jews in the Netherlands achieved a greater measure of perfection and efficiency than anywhere else in occupied Europe. (Knoop 1983, 219)

Whereas de Jong notes "that the path to collaboration is a most slippery one" (de Jong 1990, 11), Jacob Presser, in his groundbreaking history of the Holocaust in the Netherlands, *Ashes in the Wind: The Destruction of Dutch Jewry* (2010), tried to balance his criticism of Asscher and Cohen, noting their intentions to lessen the effects of the stringent rules imposed by the Nazis on the Jewish population. Presser's historical account was quite thorough yet also unusual for a historian as it was fairly subjective as he lived through many of the events he described. He did go into hiding and survived the war; however, his wife was deported. He had an extremely negative view of Asscher and Cohen, feeling them to be willing vehicles of the Nazis. The accusations toward the Jewish Council after the war were about the degree to which they as victims had—naively or mistakenly—conceded too much to Nazi pressure to collect Dutch Jews and help transport them to unknown destinations in "the east." According to Shorto, while all the other members of the Jewish Councils from different countries died in concentration camps, Asscher and Cohen survived. In 1947, they were found guilty by the "Jewish Council of Honor" of abetting the Nazis (Shorto 2013, 267).

Other authors such as Leni Yahil write sympathetically of Asscher and Cohen: "Asscher, and especially Cohen, invoked the humanitarian principle, and believed it was necessary to negotiate with the Germans in order to mitigate the suffering of the Jews through intercession on their behalf" (1987, 224). Piet Schrijvers, who has written a book about David Cohen, feels that the changing views of Asscher and Cohen have circled around to another Dutch Jewish chronicler of the Holocaust who studied law, much like Etty Hillesum, and who survived Bergen-Belsen and the war: Abel Herzburg. His view of the Jewish Council in 1950 was positive because of the "social and material" support it offered to the suffering Dutch Jews. Over the years the most severe allegations have been softened as the reality was mixed and the Jewish Council "played for time," as they sought to preserve as many people in the Dutch Jewish community as possible by haggling deportation numbers down as much as they could. As Schrijvers sees it, "Asscher and Cohen served as perfect scapegoats in order to ease the guilty consciences of numerous Dutch people" (Schrijvers 2018, 327).

Etty Hillesum has also been criticized for her involvement in the Jewish Council. She both predicted and understood the controversy: "Nothing can ever atone for the fact, of course, that one section of the Jewish population is helping to transport the majority out of the country. History will pass judgment in due course" (ET 2002, 541). She was able to hold the tension of both aspects of the Jewish Council and the larger reality of her times, carrying them within herself like a "battlefield." On July 10, 1942, when Etty was also threatened by deportation, she notes in her diary:

> That she should tell about destiny and about a piece of history the likes of which didn't used to be here before. Not in this totalitarian and wholly organized and encompassing form for the whole of Europe. Some people must survive to become chroniclers of these times. I'd like to be a little chronicler in the future. (ET 2002, 484)

On August 24, 1943, she writes one of her last long letters about Camp Westerbork, and after a sleepless Tuesday night before her deportation, she observes:

> That no words and images are adequate to describe nights like these. But still, I must try to convey something of it to you. One always has the feeling here of being the ears and eyes of a piece of Jewish history. (ET 2002, 687)

Dutch Jews had their unique and "peculiar" experience of responding to the occupation, while Dutch resistance took time to evolve. Initially the resistance was more passive, yet they excelled at hiding Dutch Jews. Tragically, however, Jews in the Netherlands had the lowest survival rate of Jews in Europe. For example, whereas 75 percent of the Jews in France survived the Nazi period, only 27 percent of Dutch Jews survived. Of approximately 80,000 Dutch Jews in Amsterdam as the start of the war, an estimated 58,000 were dead by the time it was over, most in concentration camps (Shorto 2013, 267).

It would take many years and several German Chancellors doing pieces of work to aid Germany in dealing with the horrific damage done by the Third Reich, in order to move toward healing. The first Chancellor after the war, Willy Brandt, was reviled for visiting the Warsaw Ghetto in 1970 and falling to his knees. It took until the mid-1980s to integrate deep change in the education of the Holocaust, including reparations to Jewish individuals and families which has been happening since then. Former Chancellor Angela Merkel, recently resigned, is considered one of the most committed to this endeavor to face into that dark side of what brought Germany to the Holocaust and to the modern, insidious problem of growing anti-semitism in Germany. Around 2018, Merkel created a new, high-ranking office to combat antisemitism (Nieman 2019, 13).

Susan Nieman, an American Jewish philosopher, who has lived in Berlin for forty years, wrote an important book, *Learning from the Germans; Race and the Memory of Evil*, in 2019. The book is about the long and slow process of Germany coming to terms with the dark side of its past and focused on how changes could happen in the United States, and her focus was the deep south and American racism, and how to begin a process of change in these times. It seems Etty Hillesum would concur with Susan Nieman when she says:

> Facing the past doesn't work like a vaccine: there's no one off shot for racism. For years, Germans have been discovering that undoing racist damage is a complex and multi-layered process. In arguing for learning from the Germans, I have also argued from learning from their mistakes. Most initial German attempts to work off the past were slow, reluctant, and incomplete. But they combined to create a historically new insight: you cannot have a healthy present if you bury the shame of your past. They also created a precedent: it is possible to change a nation's self-image, to switch perspective from self-pitying victim to accountable perpetrator. (Nieman 2019, 389–390)

She ends with an inscription from the National Peace and Justice Memorial in Alabama, US (2018) that is apt for Etty Hillesum's experience as well as her life perspective:

> For the hanged and beaten.
> For the shot, drowned, and burned.
> For the tortured, tormented, and terrorized.

For those abandoned by the Rule of Law.

We will remember.

With hope because hopelessness is the enemy of justice.
With courage because peace requires bravery.
With persistence because justice is a constant struggle.
With faith because we shall overcome.

Chapter Two

Unfolding Toward Being

Jungian Inspired Developmental Stages of Individuation and Realization

> "Being at rest in oneself" indeed! It's so hard "being at rest" on thistles
>
> (ET 2002, 153)

There are many developmental theories or spiritual stages that I could utilize to describe Etty's process of individuation, but I will describe her unfolding using a Jungian and more modern neo-Jungian context than that of Jung's historical time and culture. Julius Spier, Etty's therapist, teacher, and significant life relationship, was greatly influenced by Jung and the mores of that time, which were quite loose between analyst and patient, especially in Berlin and Zurich.

Jung, impressed by Spier's talent at palm-reading as a diagnostic vehicle, provided him professional connections and support by writing the preface to Spier's first and only book, *The Hands of Children: An Introduction to Psycho-Chirology* (1944/2014), which was published posthumously during the war. Spier coupled his intuitive diagnostic skill with Jung's psychodynamic principles.

Jung's Stages of Individuation

Twentieth-century psychology has contributed a great deal to a developmental view of human life. Life is now commonly seen as a series of stages, or developmental phases. Jung was one of the earliest theorists to go beyond childhood to midlife stages and death. According to Jung, the search for self-realization or wholeness is known as the way of individuation and is the main goal of the therapeutic process. In fact, the quest for wholeness is often seen as the religious goal or "ultimate concern" of Jung's psychotherapeutic system:

> There is a destination, a possible goal ... That is the way of individuation. Individuation means becoming an "in-dividual" and, in so far as "individuality" embraces our innermost, last, and incomparable uniqueness, it also implies becoming one's own self. We could therefore translate individuation as "coming to selfhood" or "self-realization." (Jung 1928/1969, CW 7, para. 266)

Jolande Jacobi, a prominent author (*The Way of Individuation*) and theorist in Jung's inner circle, felt that the archetype of most spiritual systems is the birth-life-death-rebirth pattern. She clarified that rebirth in this context means "psychic rebirth within the lifetime of the individual, renewal of the personality in the sense of its growing completion, its tendency toward wholeness" (1967, 61).

Jacobi reminds us that the rebirth of the personality consists of many little "'rebirth moments' because every rebirth is an essential change, a transformation, and the possibility is inherent in all living organisms" (1967, 61). As understood by Jung, the primary concern in the individuation process "is the individual experience of 'death and rebirth' through struggle and suffering, through a conscious, lifelong, unremitting endeavor to broaden the scope of one's consciousness and so attain a greater inner freedom" (Jacobi 1967, 62).

Jung's clinical practice contributed to the formulation of his concept of individuation. He discovered that his patients were often plagued with the problem of meaninglessness at midlife (or earlier based on life circumstances). He believed they had to turn to the spiritual dimension of life (Jung 1930–31/1969, CW 8), which resided within their own psyche. "For ultimately only the 'complete realization of our whole being' can bestow life with meaning" (Smith 1990, 89). For Jung "the psyche demands to be developed and made whole ... the ultimate concern of life" (89).

Jung's Alchemical Stages of Individuation

According to Jung's use of the term, "individuation designates both a process and a goal. As a goal it refers to the realization of the self, while as a process it refers to the stages or 'way' leading to the goal" (cited in Smith 1990, 220). The stages of individuation described by Jung changed throughout the years as he used different metaphors at different times. Curtis Smith (1990) synthesized and condensed Jung's alchemical metaphors, which he used to explain the process of individuation:

- **Nigredo ("blackening")** This stage corresponds to the ego's confrontation with the shadow as it descends into the unconscious and precipitates the beginnings of an intense experience of suffering and uncertainty.
- **Albedo ("whitening")** This stage symbolizes a washing away of the darkness. Its replacement by the light represents the "birth of a new perspective on one's own psychic condition, arising, in part, from the critical examination of the unconscious contents" (Smith 1990, 108). One may even assume this is the end goal of the process, however, intellectual understanding alone is insufficient to bring about the full realization of wholeness. "What is still lacking, said Jung is heart or feeling, which imparts an abiding value to anything we have understood" (279).
- **Rubedo ("reddening")** In this state the reanimated being is "returned to a 'state of 'oneness.' ... In which all opposites are reconciled" (Smith 1990, 104). It

symbolizes "the new birth" in which the emergent Self becomes the symbol of wholeness. At this stage, says Smith, one attains a "unified state of being in which all projections are withdrawn and most psychic conflicts are resolved" (109). Of course, as the psyche is infinite in scope, the journey to wholeness becomes an ongoing process.

Feminist Perspectives on Individuation

Jungian psychology has appealed to women since the early days when Jung's protégés were predominantly female. Demaris Wehr, author of *Jung and Feminism*, believes the primary appeal of Jung's psychology to women is:

> that it is a "meaning-making" psychology ... that it can open up new worlds not only of dreams, fairy tales, and myth but also of poetry, music, dance, arts, and crafts. For Jung, the unconscious was the source of creativity, and Jungian psychology often releases creativity previously unreleased. Analytical psychology offers a balance to an overtly rational, materialistic world and can shed light on the darkness of a soul lacking meaning. It can be a path to a person's spiritual awakening. (Wehr 1987, 6)

More current Jungian feminist authors include Claire Douglas, Sylvia Brinton Perera, Linda Leonard, Marion Woodman, Jean Shinoda Bolen, and Peggy Young-Eisendrath. More recently, Fanny Brewster, a Jungian analyst in New York City, wrote a sorely needed book called *African Americans and Jungian Psychology: Leaving the Shadows* (2017), in which she examines both the weaknesses and strengths of a Jungian perspective to both understand and to take action around the universal human problem of racism as well as the United States' ongoing intergenerational struggle of trauma related to the endemic institution of slavery.

In addition, Carol Christ and Naomi Goldenberg, two feminist theologians who have pointed out the shortcomings of Jungian psychology from a feminist perspective, have retained the parts of depth psychology essential to creativity and spiritual awakening. Christ (1980) made the point that Jungian psychology addresses the situation of the male psyche quite well but offers an inadequate portrait of the female psyche. Naomi Goldenberg has recommended that feminists retain Jung's vision of the importance of myth, ritual, and symbol, yet in her articles and book (1979) she describes what she believes is the greatest flaw in Jung's work:

> Jung often claimed archetypal status for the categories he formulated. Once a description of a national group, of a psychic situation or of either of the two sexes was considered an archetype, it became immune to sociological analysis. It was treated as a universal fact of life, which one simply had to accept. Jung's views on women exhibit the weakness of this archetypal approach. (Goldenberg 1979, 56)

She continues:

> Deciding that our stereotypes are archetypes can only impede our progress. The roots of sexism and racism run deep in human culture. We need to call on the methods of every academic and scientific discipline to discover the reasons for such prejudices and to formulate an effective means of combating them ... If feminists do not redefine the archetype, we are left with only two options: The first is to accept the patriarchal ideas of feminine as ultimate and unchanging and work within those; the second is to indulge in a rival search to find our own archetypes—this time the *true* ones to support our conclusions. (Goldenberg 1979, 61)

Androcentrism, when society is centered around men and their needs, distorts Jung's discussions of women, the anima, and the feminine. As a result, Jung's individuation process may be skewed for women.

Damaris Wehr (1987), Carol Christ (1980), and feminist psychologist Jean Baker Miller (1986) point to a difference between Jung's view of individuation and their own. This difference is based on Jung's view of the ego. One of the important aspects of Jung's individuation process is the subjugation of the ego to the Self, or the defeat of the ego. This death-like experience prepares the way for the birth of the Self and the rebirth of the individual. Wehr questions this vision of self-development of people "who are not strongly based in the ego in the first place ... such is the condition of most women in patriarchy whose egos are not validated by their context" (1987, 101). Jean Baker Miller concurs:

> They [women] do not have the right or the requirement to be full-fledged representatives of the culture. Nor have they been granted the right to act and to judge themselves in terms of the direct benefit to themselves. Both of these rights seem essential to the development of ego and super ego. This does not mean that women do not have organizing principles or relate to a "reality" in a particular way. But women's reality is rooted in the encouragement to "form" themselves into the person who will be of benefit to others. This experience begins at birth and continues through life. Out of it, women develop a psychic structuring for which the term ego, as ordinarily used may not apply. (Miller 1986, 72; quoted in Wehr 1987, 101)

If the ego, for women, does not apply, what is it that women need to "die to" if anything? "Perhaps women," says Wehr, "need to die to the false self system that patriarchy has imposed on them, whatever form it has taken. This is not the same as the annihilation of the ego but dying to the false self would necessarily precede the birth of the true self" (Wehr 1987, 103).

Feminist Jungian analyst and author Jean Shinoda Bolen (1993) would say that it depends on a woman's archetypal structure as to whether she is "dying" to an ego or "waking up." The woman who is more directly influenced by the patriarchy is more apt to have a "focused consciousness" and, in Jungian terms, a "driven animus," making her experience of individuation more like a man's. Whereas the woman with "diffuse awareness" may experience "waking up" to her own self, having been so psychically connected with everyone around her that she had been undifferentiated (Claremont de Castillejo 1973).

Carol Christ (1980) has written extensively about the condition of women's egolessness in patriarchy. This egolessness is in the form of "nothingness," which Christ posits as the first stage of four that women go through in their spiritual quest or quest for wholeness. It is to Christ's developmental stages that I will now turn as a model of individuation for women. This model seems not only appropriate for an essentialist view of women but also particularly relevant for Etty's Hillesum's condensed lifespan as a Jewish woman in her immediate chaotic familial life but also hated by the majority of European culture, for being Jewish—which came to a head in the 1920s, 1930s, and 1940s.

Christ (1980) responds to the aforementioned split between the individual woman and the societal forces that influence her by uniting what she calls a *social* quest and a *spiritual* one. She believes that "women's spiritual and social quests are two dimensions of a single struggle" (8). She goes on to say:

> Women's social quest concerns women's struggle to gain respect, equality, and freedom in society—in work, politics and in relationships with women, men, and children. In the social quest a woman begins in alienation from the human community and seeks new modes of relationship and action in society. (Christ 1980, 8)

She says that women's spiritual quest, on the other hand, undergirds the social quest and is concerned with a "woman's awakening to the depths of her own soul" (Christ 1980, 8). Whereas Jung would refer to these depths as the Self, Christ refers to them as the powers of being—"forces larger than herself that ground her in a new understanding of herself" (9).

It is possible and even common for some women to engage in a social quest without the quest for wholeness, however, these women do not often experience the freedom of consciousness or transformation that can occur when they are grounded in a psychospiritual quest or the process of individuation.

Carol Christ: Stages of Spiritual Quest

Carol Christ's stages of spiritual quest, which I believe are analogous to Jung's alchemical stages of individuation, will be the basis of the developmental model that I will use to depict Etty's stages of growth during the period of time when she began her diary up until her death two-and-a-half years later. I have chosen Christ's model as the cornerstone because she integrates the social and spiritual quest and underscores the importance of the social spiritual quest. Her language is more modern, nonracist (Jung's "blackening" as death, destruction, and suffering, "whitening" as pure), nonsexist, and it has been developed for women by a woman in a position to observe and listen to other women. Most importantly, Christ has written her schema based on women's experiences and what she sees are the differences in men's individuation and spiritual unfolding. And although Christ is a majority woman, her commitment is to the diversity of women's experience: "The full reality of 'women's experience,' is not contained in any one voice but in the rising chorus that speaks from many standpoints, pressing toward the creation of a society in which all can be heard" (1980, 4).

As in all stage theories, these stages may proceed linearly, but often they spiral and overlap. The stages are as follows:

1. **Nothingness** The mystic's notion of the "dark night of the soul" is analogous to the stage of Nothingness. Christ says that " 'the dark night' is a metaphor for the sense of emptiness felt by those who have broken their ties with conventional sources of value but have not yet discovered their grounding in new sources" (1980, 14). Although the dark night is a human experience, Christ argues that is often different from men's because of the internalized oppression that women experience (15). Polly Young-Eisendrath (1986), Christ (1980), and Wehr (1987) all describe the depth of feelings that arise when women internalize the voices of their oppressors, those voices of inferiority, inadequacy, and self-hatred. Jungian analyst Sylvia Brinton Perera (1981) offers her perspective on an ancient Sumerian myth, the "Descent of Inanna," and compares it to a contemporary woman's quest for wholeness. The first stage of the quest resembles Christ's Nothingness stage as Inanna descends to the underworld, is stripped of her queenly regalia—her power—and hangs on a meat hook for several days, "dying" to a scattered self she once knew. Perera goes on to say, "Though shaken even destroyed as we knew ourselves, we are re-coalesced in a new pattern, spewed back into ordinary life" (1981, 142). In short, Estella Lauter and Carol Rupprecht see that Perera's rendition of Inanna's descent into Ereshkigal's underworld or death realm offers a model for "disidentification with patriarchal values" encoded into a woman's psyche (1985, 20). "All descents imply suffering and all of them can serve as initiations" (Perera 1981, 50). Christ (1980) posits that Nothingness can manifest as a variety of feelings or experiences for women, from anxiety to emptiness to a despair so all-encompassing that they doubt the worth of their own lives and even contemplate suicide.

2. **Awakening** Awakening is a metaphor that, again, mystics often use to describe the experience of enlightenment, which involves a "transition in consciousness and a new perception of reality" (Christ 1980, 18). Awakening suggests that one wakes up to what is already there. Women often describe their awakening, according to Christ, as "a coming to self, rather than a giving up of self, as a grounding of selfhood in the powers of being, rather than a surrender of self to the powers of being" (20). Roberto Assagioli, an Italian psychiatrist who is

considered one of the pioneers of transpersonal psychology and of psychosynthesis, in particular, says this of awakening:

> The awakening of the soul is usually followed by a period of joyful inner expansion assuming different forms from one person to another. Sometimes it is the mystical aspect and enlightenment which are dominant; in other cases new energies are released in the form of selfless, heroic action, benevolent service or artistic creativity. (Assagioli 1991, 13)

Christ (1980) has studied and observed that women's Awakenings can often come through a mystical experience. That mystical experience can often happen in nature. Simone de Beauvoir (1970), a feminist theorist, has noted that women often experience a transcendence in nature that is closed to them in society. In addition, the cycles of nature and the nature of women's cycles seem to lead to a natural affinity between them. Another awakening for women, says Christ, can be experienced through social groups or movements—as the quests for freedom, truth, and justice can unleash the powers of being.

3. **Insight** Although Christ names stage three Insight, she only refers to it in passing. It is my understanding that she sees it as a stage that builds upon the Awakening stage. It extends the mystical Insight, such as a time to create symbols to express the deepening experience. In short, the Insight from awakening is reflected upon.

4. **New Naming** New Naming speaks to the integration of the prior stages and becomes the rebirth. As Christ says, it is "a new reconstituted orientation to self and world achieved through experiencing the powers of being" (1980, 23). And much like Jung's "union of opposites" in his final stage of individuation, Christ speaks of a women's quest for wholeness that "overcomes the dualisms" (8), a revaluing of the so-called negative sides of the dualisms, and a uniting of spirit and body, rational and irrational, life and death. She feels this is also a time to experience the uniting of the spiritual and social quest.

Jung's alchemical model of individuation and Christ's model of spiritual quest seem quite similar at first glance; however, context is entirely left out of Jung's model. Christ's descriptions of the stages are geared to women's lives, and her emphasis on the social quest reminds us, for women, and particularly for wholeness, that means equality in society as well as an expansion of consciousness. The major difference, other than the more inclusive language in Christ's model, is found in *how* women go through these stages, as that has not been studied.

In reviewing these stages it becomes clear that they describe the overall process of individuation throughout a lifetime, or even the process of transformation during a day, month, or year. The death-rebirth movement occurs over and over again during different stages or cycles of life, making, of course, the quest for wholeness an ongoing and ever-expanding journey.

Given the importance of the social quest, and the cultural complexes of Etty Hillesum's time in history, it seems important to modify Christ's stages by adding a fourth stage that amplifies Etty Hillesum's spiritual journey during the Shoah.

Carol Christ speaks about the integration of one's social and spiritual quest in her New Naming stage when she describes it as an "overcoming of the dualisms of self and world" (1980, 13). As I see it, this stage has to do with this synthesis *within* the person—that the quest for equality within society and one's spiritual awakening have been resolved, transformed, or integrated *internally*.

In line with the feminist and spiritual new powers of being or new Self of the New Naming stage, there is also a *return* to share those with the community. As a result of this journey of self-realization, I would add an additional stage.

5. **Integration/Boundless Dimension** This stage is where women can often bring back an *elixir* (of education, love, inner wisdom, knowledge of resources, protest, empowerment), hard-won from their own struggle, to provide opportunities to their larger community, race, tribe, gender, or family, and in so doing restore balance and equality in the world. It is the place where the transformed being comes back to themselves and then, wherever they find themselves to give back, to act.

In looking at Christ's stages from the point of view of Jewish women during the Holocaust, I would do two things before applying this model to Etty. First, I have combined stages two and three as one second stage called Awakening/Insight because there seems to be little differentiation between them in Christ's model. As mentioned, I have then added the stage Integration/Boundless Dimension. The model I am creating has its origins in the work of Jung, has been reconstituted with a more feminist orientation by Carol Christ, and I have added to it based on my research about Etty Hillesum. The stages, or phases, of my hybrid model are as follows:

1. Nothingness
2. Awakening/Insight
3. New Naming
4. Integration/Boundless Dimension

I will turn to these stages as Etty Hillesum meets Julius Spier and begins her diary, a very thorough description of her daily to weekly, sometimes monthly, moods and reflections, with the immediacy and often her experience and transmission of presence on each and every page.

Chapter Three

Etty Hillesum's Diary in Relationship to The Stages of Realization

> It is a slow and painful process, this striving after true inner freedom.
> Etty Hillesum (ET 2002, 134)

Etty Hillesum and Julius Spier—the Beginning of the Diary

We are able to follow Etty Hillesum's process of inner development because she began a diary at the moment of starting therapy with Julius Spier. He suggested that she write. In the first stages of spiritual and therapeutic work the use of a journal is common, as is the seeking of a teacher. It seems Etty was ripe for both as she met Julius Spier for the first time as a subject in having her hands read by Spier on February 3, 1941. That session startled her because of its accuracy. She then went to a lecture Spier gave in his sister's house on February 8, 1941, and began her diary on Saturday, March 8, 1941, the day after she had her, presumably *first*, private session with Spier. She was impressed by him again, regardless of some early criticisms of him. It is clear from her first diary entry, that Etty Hillesum had found both her psychological analyst or therapist as well as her spiritual teacher, which was a relationship that would evolve into something much larger over the next year and a half.

In reading the diary I realized very quickly that Etty is not only a natural seeker, but also a talented writer, which renders her diary unique and all the more compelling. Because of this chaotic moment in her life, she had begun a path toward her own transformation as a human and spiritual being but also as a writer, and as ultimately an important chronicler in the history of the Holocaust as it was happening.

Spier, known as *S.* in Etty's journal, as mentioned, was a psychochirologist (a reader of hands) and a psychological practitioner associated with C. G. Jung. He had, in fact, studied with Jung in Kussnacht, Switzerland, from 1926 to 1929. Jung was supportive of Spier's work as a chirologist for diagnostic purposes and suggested that he open a practice in Berlin, which he did. There, he met Herta Levi, a student who later became his fiancée in 1939 before he moved to Amsterdam, seeking more safety from the Nazis. He suggested that Herta become his assistant as he hoped marriage would give them a legal reason to be together for his work. After September of '39 traveling had become more problematic. Until 1940, the Netherlands was considered neutral.

Carl Jung had been supporting Spier's work since 1928 by introducing him to other professionals outside of Germany who gave him exposure and opportunities. His psychological approach would be considered unorthodox today, as it often included wrestling bouts and multirole relationships. Etty Hillesum became his patient, student, and secretary very quickly and part of his group, the "Spier Club." She shared, "I fell under the spell of the inner freedom that seemed to emanate from him" (ET 2002, 5).

What she saw in Spier went beyond his obvious personality conflicts and limitations. Spier became intimately close to certain of his female patients, in much the

Figure 3.1 At Julius Spier's home, circa 1941–1942. From the collection of The Jewish Historical Museum, the Netherlands.

same way that Jung did, although Spier went a step further in using a strange diagnostic tool in which he would physically wrestle with his patients to see if they could "flip" him. None had until Etty. Given his intensity and charisma, Etty Hillesum was at risk for becoming overwhelmed by him or, at the very least, making him the center of her being. In modern times, the unequal power dynamics between therapist and patient and the concern around exploitation have become central to ethical principles in the psychological profession. The "Me Too" movement has further underscored the experience of women being expected to pay a sexual price for mentoring or professional opportunities in many other sectors such as the entertainment industry and US gymnastics. Spier could be intimate in his personal style particularly with women patients and students, often with sensual and intimate touching. He poured affection on them because he believed that there wasn't enough authentic love in analysis. Although that may be true, these early passages describing times with Spier's "harem" cause alarm for most. As Carol Lee Flinders, in her book *Enduring Lives: Portraits of Women and Faith in Action*, says so beautifully and to the point:

Figure 3.2 Julius Spier, circa 1930. From the collection of The Jewish Historical Museum, the Netherlands.

Mediator he may have been, but in effect, Spier threw almost as many obstacles in Etty's path as he removed. We could resent him more for this if those obstacles hadn't become the making of her ... If Etty had in many ways met her match in Spier, so had Spier met his in Etty. (Flinders 2006, 44)

Gratefully, Spier was well intentioned at core, and their relationship became "a joint venture" of learning to love each other as well as "all of humanity." In time, Etty could meet him directly with her growing inner power, and because of each of them, their partnership became its own transforming love story. She wanted what he had: his spiritual presence, his deep wisdom, and love of the truth and of humankind, and his ability to see through things as they really were. He also introduced his group to a larger perspective in reading the Bible, the Psalms, the New Testament, Rilke, St. Augustine, and Dostoyevsky. But most importantly for Etty, he helped her to face reality by inquiring into whatever came up in her, so she could allow it and, ultimately, accept it.

Etty Hillesum began her diary nine months after Hitler's takeover of the Netherlands. She focused upon her inner journey, and importantly, she was writing it at the time of the Holocaust not afterward. This renders her diary unique in Holocaust literature and all the more gripping. Her experience at Camp Westerbork makes this known because of her letters to friends—that were sent by them to a larger audience which will become clear in Chapter Four entitled "Camp Westerbork: Her Choice."

Phase One—Nothingness

Since there are only two-and-a-half years of Etty's words and experiences to describe these four phases of the journey toward the realization of her true nature, the stages are compressed and overlap greatly and are often not as distinct and differentiated as I point them out to be. Most readers and authors writing about Hillesum, however, recognize the gradual yet dramatic change in the tonality of Etty's personality and life as she moves toward the unfolding of her being, toward realization. Etty's shift is both measured and sudden, given the circumstances of her moment in history and the choices she makes. In this early stage, women often repeat the same patterns of perception and behavior that they have developed through their conditioning. Even though they are stuck in the repetition, the potential exists in this phase to break through conventional experience and reveal its limitations, opening from emptiness, chaos, and nothingness to the beginning of awareness.

This is a phase where the dynamics of family relationships come into full awareness. Although little is known of Etty's early childhood years, it is clear in her teenage and early adult years that she struggled intensely in relationship to her mother while idealizing her father. She deemed her mother to be chaotic and hysterical, and her father to be accomplished, stoic, and erudite. These early familial impressions and experiences have much to do with setting the stage for the negating of her own worth as well as her great fear that she had the mental illness that her brothers shared and the tendency to merge with older men for security, love, and learning. She shares the Russian sense of drama, emotionality, and somatic complaints of her mother, yet identifies with the intellectual curiosity and capacity of her father. Her budding transparency suggests an inner strength with striking immediacy and vulnerability. What is illuminated at this first stage of Nothingness is the chaos within her family and her own scattered and immature personality. She seems lost, anxious, tearful, and "stripped of strength," for example:

> Here in this strange family, there is such a remarkable mixture of barbarism and culture that you are stripped of all your strength … In the past, my picturesque family would cost me a bucket of tears every night. I can't explain those tears as of yet; they came from somewhere in the dark collective unconscious. Nowadays I am not so wasteful of this precious fluid, but it is not easy to live here. (ET 2002, 83)

And here we see very early that Etty sees her mother as hysterical, demanding and like a complaining, self-absorbed "cry-baby"—elements, she would discover, that were part of her own personality, which is quite common to discover with a same-sex parent and why the intensity and anguish become exacerbated:

> Had a respectable conversation in Russian with Mother, who suddenly seems a spirited, decent person again. Then I am all at once dreadfully sorry for having had such ugly feelings and am sure that I have misjudged her, but a few hours later an exasperated little devil inside me suddenly riles against her again: "You horrible cry-baby, stop all that rubbish, you're honestly quite mad, what a mad person you are." I think these thoughts very soberly and with a wry sort of humor, and love is far removed from me then. Etty, Etty, don't let yourself down like that! And isn't it high time you were asleep? (ET 2002, 81–83)

As the entries indicate, amid the chaos, there is just the beginning of her own witnessing of her critic, which is reminiscent of a "reparenting" of herself, an opening to self-compassion: "Etty, Etty, don't let yourself down like that!" Along with her overwhelm, anger, guilt, and regret, Etty Hillesum also had a fear of identifying with her mother and becoming a conventional housewife. This fear was linked to her own body ailments and compulsions around food and missing out on things, a fear of not feeling "filled up" in a number of ways that she saw in her mother:

> Her gluttony gave her the air of being terrified of missing out on anything. There was something terribly pathetic about her as well as something bestially repulsive. That's how it seemed to me. In fact, she was just an ordinary housewife in a blue lace dress eating her soup. If I could only fathom what I really felt deep down, why I observed her so closely, then I would understand a great deal about

my mother. That fear of missing out on things makes you miss out on everything. Keeps you from reality. (ET 2002, 147)

She worries about her own self-control around food and fears ruining her own digestion by eating too much. She would compare herself to her mother talking about food as if nothing else mattered and her own greed around food, knowing she would pay dearly for that extra morsel, and yet "I can't stop myself" (ET 2002, 146). Etty's disgust at her mother and her own lack of control suggests she is beginning to name these primal forces of greed and desire and longing that can take over though she has not yet touched the inner experience behind the obsession.

When Etty began therapy with Spier, in fact after the very first session, she indicated the very thing that the phase of Nothingness can lead to without some kind of psychological or medical intervention: suicidal ideation. Early on in the diary it is related to her internalized chaos and shame and fear of having the same mental illness as her family and relatives and particularly, her brothers:

> You know, yesterday, when I could do nothing but look stupidly at you, I experienced such a clash of conflicting thoughts and feelings that I was quite shattered and would have yelled out loud had I had even less self-control. I experienced strong erotic feelings for you, which I thought I would have got over by now, and at the same time a strong aversion to you, and there was also a sudden feeling of utter loneliness, a suspicion that life is terribly difficult, that one has to face it all on one's own, that help from outside is out of the question, and uncertainty, fear, all of that, too. A small slice of chaos was suddenly staring at me from deep down inside my soul. And when I had left you and was going back home, *I wanted a car to run me over, and thought, ah, well, I must be out of my mind, like the rest of my family, something I always think when I feel the slightest bit desperate. But I know again now that I am not mad, I simply need to do a lot of work on myself before I develop into an adult and a complete human being.* And you will be helping me, won't you? Well, I have written you a few lines now; they have cost me a lot of trouble. I write with the greatest reluctance, and always feel inhibited and uncertain when I do. Yet, I want to become a writer one day, would you believe it? (ET 2002, 3; italics added)

It is also during this phase in her early relationship with Spier that Etty grapples with the feelings that Spier brings up for her. She unabashedly shares her erotic attraction and aversion to Spier, leading to two of the most powerful energies for transformation: desire and repulsion. Initially, Etty prides herself on her skill and passion as a lover. As she says, "I am accomplished in bed, just about seasoned enough I should think, to be counted among the better lovers," yet her deepest commitment is revealed in the continuance of the same sentence: "and love does indeed suit me to perfection, and yet it remains a mere trifle, set apart from what is truly essential, and deep inside me something is still locked away" (ET 2002,

4). This tension will become a dynamic part of the second phase of her journey, but for this first phase of her exploring, her "gender questions," much like the younger Anne Frank, are very much on her mind and heart are on womanhood—both her questions and original thinking about it. The same questions are born of her experience of patriarchy that the birth of feminism will make conscious in general European culture with Simone de Beauvoir's groundbreaking book a decade later, *The Second Sex* (1949). Etty reflects on the comment that Spier makes about the "love of mankind" being greater than the love of one man:

> I too am filled with love for all mankind, but for all I know I shall always continue to be in search of my one man. And I wonder to what extent that is a handicap, a woman's handicap. Whether it is an ancient tradition from which she must liberate herself, or whether it is so much part of her very essence that she would be doing violence to herself if she bestowed her love on all mankind instead of on a single man. (I can't yet see how the two can be combined.) Perhaps that's why there are so few famous women scientists and artists: a woman always looks for the one man on whom she can bestow all her wisdom, warmth, love and creative powers. She longs for a man, not for mankind. (ET 2002, 6)

Other women at times would touch off her inferiority around her fierce critic of comparison. This was a time on contemplation about womanhood and it seems she was quite prescient of what was to come:

> Sometimes, when I pass a woman in the street, a beautiful, well-groomed woman, I completely lose my poise. Then, I feel that my intellect, my struggle, my suffering, are oppressive, ugly, unwomanly ...
> ... Perhaps the true, the essential emancipation of women still has to come. We are not yet full human beings; we are the "weaker sex." We are still tied down and enmeshed in centuries-old traditions. We still have to be born as human beings; that is the great task that lies before us. (ET 2002, 6)

One can observe in Etty Hillesum's writing her modern awareness of the classical history of the simmering gender conflict of women in relationship to men for millennia: of women struggling with the patriarchal objectification by men, often not appreciating women for their full selves from intellect to ambition or their strength, short of child rearing, homemaking, and sexual fulfillment. Etty is recognizing, at the same time, her own wanting to be seen as beautiful and also desired by men as well as "an ultimate confirmation of our worth and womanhood," is in fact only a primitive "instinct." Yes, she appreciated friendship, respect, and love, but still, her primal fantasy included being a "desirable plaything." She recognizes how "infinitely complex" this gender reality is at this stage of her life and was able to see and foretell a phenomenon, first-wave feminism, that would explode into conscious awareness ten years later in Europe and twenty years later in the United States.

Denise de Costa has been a scholar in the Etty community for many years. Her dissertation was published and translated into English in 1998 entitled: *Anne Frank and Etty Hillesum; Inscribing Spirituality and Sexuality*. While she very much equates Anne Frank with the insights of the Belgium-born feminists, Luce Irigaray and Julia Kristiva, she equates the French theorist Helene Cixous with Etty Hillesum. Cixous analyzes Etty Hillesum's diaries and letters in her seminars between 1985 and 1988. De Costa feels that Cixous relates most explicitly to the position of the "other" and not only in terms of sexual difference. As a Jew and an Algerian, Cixous grew up amidst differences, she says:

> I had the "luck" to take my first steps in the blazing hotbed between two holocausts, in the midst, in the very bosom of racism, to be three years old in 1940, one part of me in the concentration camps, one part of me in the colonies. (Cixous 1976; quoted in de Costa 1998, 21)

Ultimately, it is this part of Etty's experience of otherness, concretized by the majority of European society as bad, as dangerous, that destroyed her.

Another area Etty speaks about in the early phase of her journey is loneliness, indicative of depression and anxiety. Etty cycled between existential despair and strength and joy:

> I know two sorts of loneliness. One makes me feel dreadfully unhappy, lost and forlorn, the other makes me feel strong and happy. The first always appears when I feel out of touch with my fellow men, with everything, when I am completely cut off from others and from myself and can see no purpose in life or any connection between things, nor have the slightest idea where I fit in. With the other kind of loneliness, by contrast, I feel very strong and certain and connected with everyone and everything and God. (ET 2002, 82)

In these states of disconnection, the theme of Etty's soul struggle at this point is one of feeling lost. So, when she says, "I need to expose myself unreservedly to someone. And perhaps and above all I also want that someone to appreciate my full worth," we can see why Spier and his eventual psychological and spiritual mastery become so important to her, even if his carnal struggle was in "full cry." Etty is becoming aware of herself and what she needs and wants in relationship. She is committed to record everything that is going on with her and realizes she can't capture all of it in words at this stage. Her agitation gets translated into the somatic complaints of headaches, stomachaches, or digestion problems. She uses metaphors of a "tightly bound ball of twine," the "cork that bottles her up again," to explain this inability to write or "to say things, to express them in such a way that the words become transparent and the spirit behind them can be seen." It is quite telling that when Etty is in one of these cut off and alienated places and she hears from S., she returns to center: "I regained contact with myself, with the deepest and best in me which I call God, and so also with you. A moment came in which I grew one stage further, in which many new perspectives about myself and my bond with you and my fellow beings appeared" (ET 2002, 830).

Many readers may see these early phases, as often my graduate students did, as disjointed and "all over the place" which is exactly the importance of Etty Hillesum's inner journey: this is what therapy facilitates—inquiry into these states and experiences to touch their origin, decipher their felt sense in the body, to make connections with those moments of insight that gather into inner clarity and moments of realization, of "being" itself. It is no easy path, it has many moments and extended periods of lostness, aloneness, anxiety, and continual questioning of "who am I anyway?"—the painful deconstruction of how we had once considered ourselves to be. Add to that a severe trauma, a cultural debacle targeting the annihilation of not only oneself, but one's entire tribe, far outside of the usual developmental struggle to become a person, you will see that Etty Hillesum's development before Auschwitz, at multiple levels, is nothing short of remarkable and allowed her to live fully, as she would not let "them" destroy her essence, her soul, *before* the Nazi's murderous Final Solution of full extermination.

Phase Two—Awakening/Insight

Awakening, as Carol Christ suggests, means waking up to who one already is. Much of the second stage of Etty's journey, described in this diary, is about discovering herself, made possible by being seen and engaged by Spier and her own inquiry into her many states, fantasies, and inner experiences—becoming present to what arises. This stage of individuation gives the soul a sense of fullness — "in-dividuality"—as Jung says, and ability to function as a person in a fluid and dynamic fashion responsive to the environment. The qualities of this stage are budding autonomy, beingness, and personal independence. She used a German word *hineinhorchen* to describe this process of hearkening to herself. She describes it:

> Hearkening to myself, to others, to the world. I listen very intently, with my whole being, and try to fathom the meaning of things. I am always very tense and attentive. I keep looking for something but I don't know what. What I am looking for, of course, is my own truth, but I still have no idea of what it will look like. (ET 2002, 90–91)

There are many points in this second phase where Etty's growing maturation becomes palpable, when on this journey, most of us can feel when something begins to "consolidate" within. I have had the opportunity to witness this, particularly among graduate students, in Etty's age range, wanting to become therapists, and move from insecurity and fear "not knowing how" and feel terribly exposed … until they become more in touch with their inner ground, as they seem to, like a plant, take root. These are not only the stages in this age range, but any age range as I know from my patients and/or clients over so many years as well as my own experience. She gets that this is a "fragile start of a more mature phase." She says:

> A strong straight pillar is growing in my heart, I can almost feel it growing, and around it all the rest resolves; I myself, the world, everything. And the pillar is an earnest (symbol) of my inner security. How terribly important this is for me, being in touch with my inner self! I don't go on losing my balance or tumbling from one world into the next ... Something is being consolidated within me, I seem to be taking root instead of continuously drifting, but it is still no more than the fragile start of a new and more mature phase. You must keep watching your step, little one, but I am well pleased with you all the same, you're pulling through, truly, you are pulling through ... (ET 2002, 85)

Etty often mentions she wants to be a chronicler; one who sees, writes, records, helping others to see, to understand, to expand. This is her mission. She elaborates and underscores her curiosity:

> I want to live to see the future, to become the chronicler of the things that are happening now; oh yes, a chronicler. I notice that over and above all my subjective suffering, *I have an irrepressible objective curiosity, a passionate interest in everything that touches this world and its people and my own motives.* Sometimes I believe that I have a task. Everything that opens around me is to be clarified in my mind and later in my writing. Anyhow, I sprang from this chaos, and it is my business to pull myself out of it. S. calls it "building with noble material; he's a real treasure." (ET 2002, 86; italics added)

This phase is about waking up to reality, and Etty's awareness about work and its importance—its role of engaging her "on the ground" being consistent with studies and working "properly" given her propensity for dreaming and romantic and erotic fantasy becomes a part of her new insight:

> You've just got to work, and that's that. No fantasies, no grandiose ideas, and earth-shattering insights. Making a translation exercise and finding the right words are much more important. And that is something I have to learn and for which I must fight to the death: all fantasies and dreams shall be ejected by force from my brain, and I shall sweep myself clean from within, to make space for real studies, large and small. To tell the truth, I have never worked properly. It's the same with sex. If someone makes an impression on me, I can revel in erotic fantasies for days and nights on end. I don't think I ever realized how much energy that consumes, and how much it is bound to detract from any real contact. Reality does not chime with my imagination, because my imagination tends to run riot. I don't think I ever realized how much energy that consumes, and how much it is bound to detract from any real contact. (ET 2002, 7),

Etty Hillesum's relationship with Spier spans this second stage of individuation or unfolding. For Etty, it seems like her first conscious drive to awaken, not masked by mood swings or illness. She sees and claims her own grappling with her "demon" of jealousy and possessiveness. It is the work of facing into the deconstruction of the ego's hold on self-representation: the crumbling of the edifice and touching of the "abyss." Another way to put it is the cracking of the egoic shell and revealing not only the terror of annihilation, but the deepest human vulnerability without the multiple layers of defense. She observes the conditioning of women and her actual experience:

> We women want to perpetuate ourselves in a man. Yes, I want him to say, "Darling, you are the only one, and I shall love you for evermore." I know, of course, that there is no such thing as eternal love, but unless he declares it for me, nothing has any meaning. And the stupid thing is that I don't really want him, don't want him forever or as the only one in my life, and yet I demand it of him. Do I demand absolute love from others because I'm unable to give it myself? And then I always expect the same level of intensity, when I know from my own experience that it cannot last. And I take flight just as soon as I notice the other becoming lukewarm. That's an inferiority complex of course, something like: if I can't inspire him enough to be on fire for me at all times, then I'd rather have nothing at all. And it's so damned illogical, I must rid myself of it. After all, I wouldn't know what to do if somebody really was on fire for me all day long. It would annoy me and bore me and make me feel tied down. Oh, Etty, Etty! (ET 2002, 105)

These are the kind of struggles that suggest identification at the object-relations level of development, where everything gets viewed from the original and primal need for love, security, and the animal body's physical and sexual urges as central. This stage is also rife with the deficiencies that surface based on personality fixations as well as parental conditioning and modeling. The prevailing historical and cultural beliefs about gender add and reinforce such conditioning.

Etty reveals her wisdom when she reflects on these things and says that her need for Spier to desire "me alone" and for "eternal love" "are some kind of compulsion." She begins to recognize this when she is feeling "extremely" sensual. She obsesses about Spier, "his mouth and hands while everything else pales into insignificance …" As this quote illustrates, she is quite aware this is a compulsive fantasy. She works with her ideals about eternal or undying romantic love, and it seems she moves to the next layer of what she feels is another obstacle to Spier's love, his fiancée, Herta Levi. Etty's fear is that Herta would come to Amsterdam to join Spier on an ongoing basis. She laments:

> I suddenly had the feeling that Hertha was coming back. My heart broke … several times over. I waged a heroic struggle and then took off for faraway Russia. After first having written him a heartrending letter to tell him I was but a frail human being who could not cope with him and Hertha combined. Nor did I want to have anything more to do with his work, and I suddenly puzzled hard

whether I had not chosen the work for the man's sake rather than to the man for his work's sake. And though I knew I would never want to marry him; I could not put up with him having another woman. (ET 2002, 117)

Each of these obsessive fantasies, and the subsequent inner struggles that would ensue, would bring Etty back to her purpose, which was that of learning to love another person unconditionally, wholly, as a way of preparing her (and them) to love all human beings in a similar fashion. The love for one would lead to the love of all. Spier had the same goal and also had his own way of backsliding. But this mission that they shared had the power to transform both of them over time. Clearly, Etty is maturing and becoming more convinced that she is "no longer cut off from that deep undercurrent" within her. It is indeed painstaking work, and Etty rises to this challenge based on her own drive for the truth. It is not evolved or so radiant to begin with, which is important for most seekers to know. It is a grind, like the grains of sand rubbing over the pearl, again and again, to face the reality of her relationship with Spier, as if grinding the toughest grains into a soft and luminous pulp. As she says:

He was probably tired as well, absorbed in something or other. In the past that would have been a shock, I should not have been able to take that neutral conversation. This time, too, I felt for a moment how tired and over-excited I was, because the horribly sober tone he used made me want to let myself go completely for a split second, to burst into tears or something like that. But in another split second I had scolded myself for being so hysterical. In the past I would have been quite unable to reconcile his sober tone with my feelings toward him, and there would have been a head-on-collision. I would have blown the whole thing up out of all proportion. But this morning it suddenly hit me: its ebb tide again. And now I know that the flood tide will be coming back ... And now just this bit more: when it suddenly struck me, again in the bathroom, that it can't always be flood tide in a friendship, and that the ebb tide has to be accepted as something positive and fruitful as well, then, life, too suddenly surged through me again with a calmer beat. (ET 2002, 200–201)

Etty Hillesum struggled with these emotions not unlike hundreds of clients and students throughout my years of psychological practice. If one hasn't been "seen" as separate from the projections and desires of one's parents or caretakers, emptiness can get concealed and continual longing can replace inner acceptance. Longing, if not identified as the flame for discovery that it is, but only as fulfilment through an object, then can become an obsessive even destructive drive rather than a means to "see through" the drive as a vehicle for evolving toward wholeness.

It is during this stage of deepening awareness about herself and reality that she becomes conscious of another form of awareness—of the raging political world around her—the Third Reich. This is one of the first times that Etty addresses her direct experience with the Nazi machine in the form of a young man:

> Very early on Wednesday morning a large group of us were crowded into the Gestapo hall, and at that moment the circumstances of all our lives were the same. All of us occupied the same space, the men behind the desk no less than those about to be questioned. What distinguished each one of us was only our inner attitudes. … When it was my turn to stand in front of his desk, he bawled at me. "What the hell's so funny?" I wanted to say nothing's funny here except you," but refrained. "Your still smirking," he bawled again. And I, in all innocence, "I didn't mean to its my usual expression." And he, "don't give me that, get the hell out of here," his face saying, "I'll deal with you later." And that was presumably meant to scare me to death, but the device was too transparent. (ET 2002, 259)

It is here that we see the living example of Etty's composure, her growing inner esteem, her psychological awareness, her compassion, her presence:

> I am not easily frightened. Not because I am brave, but because I know that I am dealing with human beings and I must try as hard as I can to understand everything that anyone ever does. And that was the real import of this morning; not that a disgruntled young Gestapo Officer yelled at me, but that I felt no indignation, rather a real compassion, and would have liked to ask, "Did you have a very unhappy childhood, has your girlfriend let you down?" Yes, he looked harassed and driven, sullen and weak. I should have liked to start treating him there and then, for I know that pitiful young men like that are dangerous as soon as they are let loose on mankind. (ET 2002, 259)

This marks the very beginning of Etty's attention to the impending threat. At the moment it is held at bay, and within this second stage of her growth she will come to realize, directly, how dangerous "pitiful men like this" are "as soon as they are let loose on mankind."

Yet her personal essence grows as manifested through her grappling with relationships. She also struggles with Pa Han, as she realizes, "It's nasty, and childish and unfair to attempt to work your longing for one man out on another" (ET 2002, 256–257). During the first half of this stage, Etty's mission is actually to grapple with her stuckness, her impasses, her blocks, as well as her fear, in order to become internally free. She has reached a turning point with Spier, a bit more than a year into their relationship. She reveals:

> I suddenly knew for sure that I would be visiting a great many countries, see a great many people, write books, and leave him, … and how I felt freer of him at that moment than ever before, yet also closer to him. And then I said "No matter what happens between us, that feeling of freedom, of being a world unto myself,

of having no claims on you, will always be with me, and that is why I have the courage to tell you everything all the time, the courage even to express my desire, since that doesn't call for any ties. It is sheer desire, nothing more, and it longs for one part of you, and yet I am free of you ..." and I am walking this path right now—that became clear to me yesterday. *I have turned my desire into our joint venture, and we shall no doubt cope with it together.* (ET 2002, 268–269; italics added)

Working it out together clearly signals Etty's evolution in regard to the relationship. It is also clear that she is drawing closer to her Jewish roots. Etty's diary was written in a series of spiral notebooks. At this point, in April 1942, she was nearing the end of the current one. Before she finishes this notebook, the "yellow star" is issued for every Jewish person to wear outside of their homes. A few months earlier she had said, "I wondered again as if I was so 'unworldly' simply because the German measures affect me so little personally." She then goes on to say:

But I don't fool myself for one single moment about the gravity of it all. Yet sometimes I can take the broad historical view of the measures; each new regulation takes its little place in our century, and I try to look at it from the viewpoint of a later age. And the suffering, the ocean of human suffering, and the hatred and all the fighting? (ET 2002, 239)

Although she surmises that these regulations do not affect her strongly, and views history through Jung's archetypal lens, she continues to wake up to the reality of their future. Given this realization, Etty has come to a place at the end of April where she wants to marry Spier so they can go through the times ahead together. She declares:

And I shall tell him this evening: I am not really frightened of anything, I feel so strong; it matters little whether you have to sleep on a hard floor, or whether you are allowed to walk only through certain specified streets, and so on—these are all minor vexations, so insignificant compared with the infinite riches and possibilities we carry within us. We must guard these and remain true to them and keep faith with them. And I shall help you and stay with you, and yet leave you entirely free. And one day I shall surrender you to the girl you mean to marry. I shall support your every step, outwardly and inwardly. I think I have grown mature enough now to bear a great many hard things in life and yet not to grow too hard inside. (ET 2002, 355)

She has indeed grown "mature enough" to even suggest that she "would surrender you [Spier] to the girl you mean to marry" at this moment ... she goes back and forth with her fear of losing Spier to Herta, or any other woman, and of course, to the Nazis. This is what growth actually means—to become aware of the cycles and complexes that pop us back into terror, and over and over again come back to the ground of one's being. Freud's notion of "repetition compulsion," repeating our dysfunctional patterns, is a challenging part of cracking through our conditioning as well as the way our nervous system can be altered through therapy as well as a somatic practice such as meditation, practices that Etty employed.

By the end of May 1942, she is quite reflective as the ever-present squeeze of the Nazis is becoming tighter and tighter. The persecution accelerates with continual restrictions, and it becomes clear to Etty that the Nazi machine is intent upon their destruction. Even so, it seems Etty is touching some kind of deep spiritual feminine receptivity that sustains her. She feels safe, comforted by the "naked breast" of life as well as her own tender heartbeat, even with what she realizes what is happening around her. This becomes a first glimpse of the Boundless Dimension of a further stage, to "recognize that life with its mysteries" was close to her. She speaks tenderly:

> The bare trunks that climb past my window now shelter under a cover of young green leaves. A springy fleece along their naked, tough, ascetic limbs. ... Well, how was it last night in my small bedroom? I went to bed early last night, and from my bed I stared out through the large open window. And it was once more as if life with all its mysteries was close to me, as if I could touch it. I had the feeling that I was resting against the naked breast of life and could feel her gentle and regular heartbeat. I felt safe and protected. And I thought, How strange. It is wartime. There are concentration camps. Small barbarity mounts upon small barbarity ... And these streets and houses are all so close to my own. I know how very nervous people are, I know about the mounting human suffering. I know the persecution and oppression and despotism and the impotent fury and the terrible sadism. I know it all and continue to confront every shred of reality that thrusts itself upon me ... And yet ... at unguarded moments ... my own heartbeat is difficult to describe: so slow and so regular and so soft, almost muffled, but so constant, as if it would never stop, and so good and merciful as well. (ET 2002, 386)

In addition to safety, amid the "strangeness of wartime" and integrating the stories of the barbarities she has heard, she comes back to her experience with Spier and another "awakening" as an awareness arises after a meeting with Spier when Etty is tired, sleepy, and distracted. It speaks to how far she has come in differentiating from him and reveals her depth, and hard-won objectivity, and a certain sobriety on one hand and deepening love for others and herself on the other:

> I used to be genuinely hysterical and desperate then. In the past I would refuse to acknowledge that sort of emptiness in myself, then make forced attempts on all fronts, from the intellectual to the erotic and sexual, to restore contact at any price, and if that failed I would later have orgies of loneliness all on my own. And now I was sitting there so calm and composed, and vaguely sad as well, of

course, thinking, well, this is something that kind soul can do nothing about. In the past I would have expected him, and other friends as well, to work miracles of solace. And now I was bearing my own emptiness and tiredness and malaise, realizing that that too was part and parcel of life, and that there was no need to feel so forlorn. (ET 2002, 405)

Etty's personality is changing into her true nature, she has worked on it herself and with Spier on an ongoing basis, as can be seen from her diary entries in this second phase of her journey toward self-realization. In the following quote, which becomes one of the last ones with Spier, not only has this larger love become embodied, integrated, but also Etty demonstrates that love for her beloved by becoming *his* guide in one of Spier's most vulnerable moments. Time is running out because of the Nazis' acceleration, and Etty, even at a subconscious level at this juncture, is beginning to recognize that S. is ill:

He leaned against the wall in Dicky's room, and I leaned gently and lightly against him, as I had done on countless similar occasions in the past, but this time, it suddenly felt as if the sky had fallen as in a Greek tragedy. For a moment my senses were totally confused, and I felt as though I was standing in the center of infinite space—pervaded by space but also filled with eternity. In that moment a great change took place within us, forever. He remained leaning against the wall for a little and said in an almost plaintive voice, "I must write to my girlfriend tonight, it will be her birthday soon. But what am I to say to her? I haven't the heart for it or the inspiration." (ET 2002, 475)

This is such a riveting moment, as it is an example of how mutual this love is that Etty and S. share. In this moment she is giving back to him what he has contributed to her development and speaks to the deeply sad reality that their time left is short:

And I said to him, "You must start even now and try to reconcile her to the fact that she will never see you again; you must give her something to hold onto for the future. Tell her how the two of you, though physically apart for all these years, have nevertheless been as one, and that she has a duty to carry on if only to keep something of your spirit alive." Yes, that's how people speak to one another these days, and it doesn't even sound unreal anymore. We have embraced a new reality, and everything has taken on new colors and new emphases. And between our eyes and hands and mouths there now flows a constant stream of tenderness, a stream in which all petty desires seem to have been extinguished. All that matters now is to be kind to each other with all the goodness that is in us. And every encounter is also a farewell. (ET 2002, 475)

This is a clear moment of Etty Hillesum's becoming ... and not only becoming herself, but the transcendent voice of the ages seems to be speaking through her—a shining moment in their "joint venture." Yes, "a constant stream of tenderness"

"And every encounter is a farewell." She is leaning in, to both loving and bearing it all, the infinite space and the ending with Spier.

Phase Three—New Naming

New Naming speaks to the integration of the prior stages, and as Carol Christ says, it is a "reconstituted orientation to self and world achieved through experiencing 'the powers of being'" (1980, 23). Much like Jung's "union of opposites" it encompasses this journey toward wholeness that overcomes the dualisms.

Although Etty's relationship and dialogue with God could be discussed at any of the stages of her growth, her notion of God has evolved as she arrives at this phase of New Naming, or rebirth She was no stranger to this idea or construct of God. Early in her life, her father, according to Meins Coetsier in his book *The Existential Philosophy of Etty Hillesum* (2014), studied the Jewish and Christian scriptures, had an interest in Jewish identity, and even contemplated becoming a rabbi, but ultimately Etty's father's spirituality played out as "the detached interest of a bookish scholar" (Coetsier 2014, 23). As Etty moves closer to the experience and purpose of her own existence and wrestles with ultimate questions, she comes to an evolving awareness of what God means to her. And this meaning changes throughout her diary, becoming an ongoing inquiry:

> I am only at the beginning, but the beginning is there, that much I know for certain. It means gathering together all the strength one can, living one's life with God and in God and having God dwell within. (I find the word "God" so primitive at times, it is only a metaphor after all, an approach to our greatest and most continuous inner adventure; I'm sure that I don't even need the word "God," which sometimes strikes me as a primitive, primordial sound. A makeshift construction.) And, at night, when I sometimes have the inclination to speak to God and say very childishly, "God, things just cannot go on like this with me"—and sometimes my prayers can be very desperate and imploring—it is nevertheless as if I were addressing something in myself, trying to plead with a part of myself. (ET 2002, 438–439)

Both Klaas A. D. Smelik, and Meins Coetsier point out Rainer Maria Rilke's significant influence upon Etty as a writer, poet, and kindred spirit. He seems to influence her notion of "God" as well. It was in *The Book of Hours,* written in 1905, that Rilke spoke to God as if he were speaking to himself.. For Etty, "God" is included in some passages as "an imaginary figure" that allows her to express her thoughts more easily. As she says in this passage: "When I pray, I never pray for myself; always for others, or else I hold a silly, naive, or deadly serious dialogue with what is deepest in me, which for the sake of convenience, I call God" (ET 2002, 493).

It is also important to mention Jung's quote about "God," which was significant enough to Etty that she copied it into her notebooks at three different times:

I know people for whom the encounter with the strange power within themselves was such an overwhelming experience that they called it "God." So experienced, "God" too is a *theory* in the most literal sense, a way of looking at the world, an image which the limited human mind creates in order to express an unfathomable and ineffable experience. The experience alone is real, not to be disputed; but the image can be soiled or broken to pieces. (Jung 1964, CW 10, para. 330; quoted in ET 2002, 226)

"God" transforms again and again in Etty's usage throughout the remainder of her time in Amsterdam and Camp Westerbork, even on the way to Auschwitz. Etty is relational and, hence, personal; God becomes her companion in the darkest of times, both personally as a friend and guide and impersonally as the essence and presence of all things.

Etty's relationship with God is one of mutual commitment. It is reminiscent of the Book of Job in the Hebrew Bible, which Rabbi Harold Kushner describes in *When Bad Things Happen to Good People* as "the greatest, fullest, most profound discussion of the subject of good people suffering ever written" (1981, 42). The story of Job is one of deep suffering; Job, a good and successful man, is made to suffer because of a bet between God and Satan that Job will not give up his steadfast faith, even if the worst things befall him. Job doesn't give up on God even through the worst tragedies—his children dying, terrible health conditions, and loss of everything—but then his friends begin to urge him to give up his piety. They begin to blame Job; maybe he is not that pious after all and threw religion overboard: "No wonder God does this to you." Job then blames God for not being a caring God and "spying" on him even when he has lived a good and decent life. Finally, after three cycles of this dialogue of blaming, the book, says Kushner, comes to its "thunderous climax": Job swears to his innocence and challenges God to appear with evidence or to admit that Job is right and has suffered wrongly. What happens next is quite dramatic:

> And God appears. There comes a terrible windstorm, out of the desert, and God answers Job out of the whirlwind. Job's case is so compelling, his challenge so forceful, that God Himself comes down to earth to answer him. But God's answer is hard to understand. He doesn't talk about Job's case at all, neither to detail Job's sins nor to explain his suffering. Instead he says to Job, in effect, What do you know about how to run a world? (Kushner 1981, 40–41)

In relationship to the questions about Job and Etty, I had a delightful visit with Rabbi George Gittelman in Santa Rosa in 2021.[1] We spoke about Etty Hillesum, The Holocaust, Judaism, and the Book of Job in the Hebrew Bible. Rabbi George "got" Etty deeply in a way that spoke much to me about his own spiritual depth. The year before, in 2020, a colleague and part of the Shomrei Torah community, invited me to present a program on Etty online. I also met with Rabbi Dorothy Richman,[2,3] a member of our online Etty Hillesum group, wanting to further understand this notion of Etty's God not being all-powerful or all-caring enough to change the situation for the Jews and that Etty wanted to help Him to help them preserve Himself within them.

One interpretation of Job, from these encounters with both rabbis, is that it was not about God being all-powerful or all-caring but that the author of Job was, in a sense, setting a boundary with humans, so they could experience life fully, whatever it brought forth, not by having God change it based upon who was bad or good. God's presence was the point; he came down to earth to be present to and be in relationship with Job and his challenge and made it clear that His mission was larger:

> Where were you when I planned the earth?
> Tell me, if you are wise
> Do you know who took its dimensions,
> Measuring its length with a cord? ...
> Where were you when I stopped the sea ...
> And set its boundaries, saying "Here you may come,
> But no further"?
> Have you seen where the snow is stored,
> Or visited the storehouse of the hail? ...
> Do you tell the antelope when to calve?
> Do you give the horse his strength?
> Do you show the hawk how to fly?
> (Job 38, 39, translated by author,
> Rabbi Kushner, 1981, 40–41)

As July 1942 approaches, Etty's strength is solidifying further as she faces into the reality of the suffering that is already engulfing both herself and her tribe with the Nazis' promise of full destruction, yet much like the story of Job, Etty seems to know those boundaries and what she feels is her responsibility. She, as is her nature, develops a relationship with God and draws on the divine presence within herself to meet the myriad of larger-than-life challenges she will encounter. She speaks to God in partnership:

> Dear God, these are anxious times. Tonight, for the first time I lay in the dark with burning eyes as scene after scene of human suffering passed before me. I shall promise You one thing, God, just one very small thing: I shall never burden my today with cares about my tomorrow, although that takes some practice. Each day is sufficient unto itself. I shall try to help You, God, to stop my strength ebbing away, though I cannot vouch for it in advance. But one thing is becoming increasingly clear to me: that You cannot help us, that we must help You to help ourselves. And that is all we can manage these days and also all that really matters: that we safeguard that little piece of You, God, in ourselves. And perhaps in others as well. Alas, there doesn't seem to be much You Yourself can do about our circumstances, about our lives. Neither do I hold You responsible.

> You cannot help us, but we must help You and defend Your dwelling place inside us to the last ... (ET 2002, 488)

Right after this declaration of commitment, Etty continues to reinforce this New Naming as she reconciles the opposites, the dualisms of beauty and misery, contraction and expansion and the joint venture now, of Etty Hillesum and God.

> The jasmine behind my house has been completely ruined by the rains and storms of the last few days; its white blossoms are floating about in muddy black pools on the low garage roof. But somewhere inside me the jasmine continues to blossom undisturbed, just as profusely and delicately as ever it did. And it spreads the house in which you dwell, oh God. You can see I look after You. I bring You not only my tears and my forebodings on this stormy grey Sunday morning, I even bring You scented jasmine. (ET 2002, 489)

This jasmine seems to be Etty's offering to the sacred within herself as God dwells in her being, and she "will look after You." And she does bring her tears and forebodings to this house on that Sunday morning as she continues to look after "You" to the last moment that we hear her "voice" from the train.

Etty's journey from the beginning of her diary moves from panic and chaos, lack of self-confidence, anguish, and jealousy, to a clear-eyed response to the "havoc ridden world" she knows is out to destroy her. She says on July 3, 1942:

> that what they are after is our total destruction, I accept it. I know it now and I shall not burden others with my fears. I shall not be bitter if others fail to grasp what is happening to us Jews. I work and continue to live with the same conviction, and I find life meaningful—yes, meaningful—although I hardly dare say so in company these days. Living and dying, sorrow and joy, the blisters on my feet and the jasmine behind the house, the persecution, the unspeakable horrors—it is all as one in me, and I accept it all as one mighty whole and begin to grasp it better if only for myself; without being able to explain to anyone else how it all hangs together. I wish I could live for a long time so that one day I may know how to explain it, and if I am not granted that wish, well, then somebody else will perhaps do it, carry on from where my life has been cut short. And that is why I must try to live a good and faithful life to my last breath: so that those who come after me do not have to start all over again, need not face the same difficulties. Isn't that doing something for future generations? And that is why I must try to live a good and faithful life to my last breath: so that those who come after me do not have to start all over again, need not face the same difficulties. Isn't that doing something for future generations? (ET 2002, 461–462)

In this quote, Etty Hillesum acknowledges to herself that she will not be bitter if "others," which means the Allied powers, were 'failing to grasp what is happening to us Jews.' Etty never mentions the United States in this context. A new Holocaust documentary from Ken Burns and his colleagues (2022) give a different window into the Holocaust with a focus on the US and raises troubling questions about this country's history and actions. The quotas are so pernicious with regard to European refugees, particularly Jewish refugees, trying to get out that it creates a bottleneck that results in the unnecessary deaths of tens of thousands of more people. "That's on Roosevelt. It's on the State Department. It's on the Congress but it's also on the American people" (promotion for the docuseries *The U.S. and the Holocaust*, 2022). This is America's shadow around immigration at the time of the Holocaust, that rages on until this very day.

There are thousands of stories of Jewish families sitting around radios hoping and praying that the Allied powers would intervene, bomb the Nazis' train tracks, or assassinate Hitler (which was attempted and failed) or any number of rumors and/or tufts of hope for the European and East European Jews to hold onto. And it was true for Etty in an environment of hatred for the Germans, and incredible hopelessness and despair, that she found life meaningful which she realized sounded absurd to many—it was her own resistance to hate of any kind. Again, she wants to explain it for future generations—her contribution that only could work for her if she knew what enslaved Jewish people were going through, only then could she be a chronicler. It became her practice to stay conscious and live with meaning and contribute to the chronicling of "these times" so "we do not have to start all over again." She was determined to reinforce the beauty of life which often took the shape of flowers:

> How really beautiful life really is. An inexplicable feeling. It has no anchor in the reality in which we now live. But surely there are also realities other than those one reads about in the paper and hears in the thoughtless and inflamed talk of frightened people? There is also the reality of that small rose-red cyclamen and of the wide horizon one can keep on rediscovering behind all the noise and confusion of the times. (ET 2002, 450)

While Carol Christ says that Etty is coming into the powers of being, Paul Tillich a protestant theologian from the 1960s might say that one is touching the "ground of one's being," at this stage, describing this state in his 1952 book *The Courage to Be*. Etty Hillesum speaks with courage and determination when she speaks on July 10, 1942:

> A hard day, a very hard day. We must learn to shoulder our "common fate"; everyone who seeks to save himself must surely realize that if he does not go another must take his place. As if it really mattered which of us goes. Ours is now a common destiny, and that is something we must not forget. A very hard day. But I keep finding myself in prayer. And that is something I shall always be able to do, even in the smallest space: pray. And that part of our common destiny that I must shoulder myself; I strap it tightly and firmly to my back, it becomes part of me as I walk through the streets even now.

> *And I shall wield this slender fountain pen as if it were a hammer, and my words will have to be so many hammer strokes with which to beat out the story of our fate and of a piece of history as it is and never was before. Not in this totalitarian, massively organized form, spanning the whole of Europe. Still, a few people must survive if only to be the chroniclers of this age. I would very much like to become one of their number.* (ET 2002, 484; italics added)

Within this tumult, Etty seems to be experiencing the deep capacity to hold the whole of her experience. She seems to find meaning in this moment, given her rational ability to see the historical long view, as there is always a Hitler or an Inquisition. As readers we are bearing witness to something else, an energy, a calling, to "beat out the story of our fate." It becomes clear, during this time, that Etty is making decisions about how she wants to move forward. She realizes that by "coming to terms with her life," it means "that the reality of death has become a definite part of my life" (ET 2002, 464). She faces her fear about Spier:

> Though I am tired, and though I am sad or afraid, the whole world is in me all the time, it is always there and keeps growing. ... And I have taken in something this past year that will never leave me again. But he must remain in good health. And safe. They must not take him away, they mustn't. Because I should then have to summon all my strength. But please let nothing happen to him. I wouldn't know how to carry on ... Yes, I would have to live on and pray for him, day and night. I feel so strange. Everything that up until now has seemed so unreal is increasingly becoming a reality, an inner one so far. (ET 2002, 471)

At this point, she is beginning to realize that Spier is ill; his energy is low; he is prone to coughing fits; and "he is breathing as if he is running a race" (ET 2002, 496). She feels she can't put into words what is consolidating in these last July days, afraid of how ill and tired Spier seems and afraid the Nazis will take him away. She has continued her affiliation with the Jewish Council and applied to be transferred to be in the first group of Jews to go to work at a camp, one that turned out to be "Social Welfare for People in Transit," at Camp Westerbork, in the Drenthe Province in the Netherlands. She waits for the orders ... and thinks about packing a rucksack with Jung and Rilke. She recognizes she will go through many more transformations and that she has been "transformed again. Once again there is gladness and lightheadedness and resolve and complete surrender" (ET 2002, 507). She moves from despair to assurance and strength and back again.

And yet she continues to affirm her acceptance, her equanimity. Although Spier and Etty have spoken about going together if he is not called up first, she is doubtful. "I really would rather he stayed behind than come along with me. I should hate to see him suffering by my side. I shall lock him inside me and carry him safely with me and so be with him when I like" (ET 2002, 507).

Etty's diary pauses on July 29th with the words "what if my call-up papers come tomorrow?" Come they did, and Etty becomes clear that she will not marry

Spier; their age differences are too great, and she has watched him become old, just as she has Han, and knows she will always be united with S. by an "inner bond." Before Etty leaves for Camp Westerbork, she has one last time with Spier on July 29th:

> What I really wanted to say is: it suddenly felt as if life in its thousand details, twists, and turns had become perfectly clear and transparent. Just as if I were standing before an Ocean and could look straight through the crystal-clear water to the bottom. I doubt very much if I shall ever be able to write—or shall I yet? It may take a long time before I can describe this moment, a high point in my life. You huddle in the corner on the floor in the room of the man you love and darn his socks, and at the same time you are sitting by the shore of a mighty Ocean so transparent that you can see to the bottom. And that is an unforgettable experience. (ET 2002, 512)

Again, the ordinary and the transcendent—darning the socks of the man you love and sitting by the shore of a mighty Ocean so transparent that you can see to the bottom. This is what makes Etty Hillesum so compelling. She is able to channel the most transpersonal part of our humanity along with the personal—the ordinary. Something that is available for all of us the more practice we have of not splitting these two apart, making spiritual life inherent in the beauty of any ordinary moment if we just stop to recognize it, that we can actually feel the present moment instead of residing in the fear of the idea of it.

This is the last time that Etty Hillesum is with Spier before she goes to Westerbork for the first time for two weeks, as she is now part of the Jewish Council and is given the "privilege" to travel back and forth to Amsterdam until June of 1943. The next time Etty writes in her diary is on September 15, 1942. She has come back from Westerbork as she got word that S. was extremely ill. He died suddenly from cancer two days after she arrived.

> There you lie now in your two small rooms, you dear, great, good man. I once wrote to you, "My heart will always fly to you like a bird, from any place on earth, and it will surely find you."
>
> I had a thousand things to ask you and to learn from you; now I will have to do everything by myself. But I feel so strong that I'm sure I'll manage. What energies I possess have been set free inside me. You taught me to speak the name of God without embarrassment. You were the mediator between God and me, and now you, the mediator, have gone, and my path leads straight to God. It is right that it should be so. And I shall be the mediator for any other soul I can reach. (ET 2002, 516)

This is a profound moment for Etty Hillesum to lose her soul's mate, yet, as always, she is grateful ... "To think that one small human heart can experience so much, Oh God, so much suffering and so much love." She goes on to say that

Figure 3.3 Etty, circa 1939, in the upper room in Hendrik (Hans) Wegerif's house where she wrote her diary and lived before her definitive departure to Westerbork in 1943. From the collection of The Jewish Historical Museum, the Netherlands.

there is such perfect and complete happiness in me, oh God. What he called "reposing in oneself." And that probably best expresses my own love of life: I repose in myself. And that part of myself; that deepest and richest part in which I repose, is what I call "God." (ET 2002, 519)

It is at this point, after Spier's death, that Etty's body has called a "halt," and she stays in Amsterdam to rest until November. She is back in Westerbork for two weeks in November, though struggling and on painkillers. Returning to Amsterdam in December, she learns she has gallstones and is debating with her medical doctor whether to have surgery for this condition, which ultimately is decided against. It then takes more time to recuperate, and she does not return to Westerbork until early June 1943—for good now, until her own deportation to Auschwitz. There will be no more privileges, and she will be considered a prisoner by the end of June 1943 when the Jewish Council is dissolved.

Phase 4—Integration/Boundless Dimension

In this stage of self-realization, all that has gone before in this journey is integrated, and there is a realization of the Boundless Dimension and a convergence of immanence and transcendence.

Now that the soul has journeyed into the mystery and transcended limitations, it flows back into the phenomenal world. One maintains the connection to the boundlessness that has been discovered but integrates "being" into ordinary consciousness.

In the hero's journey mythology, there is often the return; the hero or heroine must enter the world with some elixir or gift to help restore society. In Etty's case, she has not only come back into the "world" as an awakened being, but she has also come back into an even more accelerated, distorted, mechanized "world" of transit and concentration camp destruction, to offer what is her most cherished elixir—her realized self, her realized true nature to love and not hate, and her profound art of writing as creation and resistance. For Etty Hillesum, in addition to loving and providing equanimity in the shattered community of Camp Westerbork in 1942 and 1943, we will also see that for her that writing that has been a vehicle for transformation, at Westerbork, *to write is to act.* The next chapter describes Etty's lived experience of integration, the boundless dimension that makes its way into deep *communitas* as well as the tremendous fear and sorrow of Camp Westerbork, and her warning to others in 1943 before her final deportation to Auschwitz.

Notes

1 Rabbi George Gittleman joined Shomrei Torah in Sonoma County in1996. A native of Kentucky, Rabbi George earned a bachelor of arts degree in American History from the University of Vermont in 1984. In 1991, he embarked on his rabbinical journey after eight years in computer sales, obtaining a master's in Hebrew Letters and ordination from the Reform Seminary, Hebrew Union College, Jewish Institute of Religion in 1996. Rabbi George is also a Senior Rabbinic Fellow at the prestigious Shalom Hartman Institute in Jerusalem and a graduate of the Rabbinic Leadership Program of the Institute for Jewish Spirituality. The Shomrei Torah *mishpacha* (family) has been blessed and strengthened by Rabbi George's leadership in teaching, community-building, and worship.
2 Rabbi Dorothy Richman serves as the rabbi of Makor Or Jewish Meditation Center and is Rabbi Emerita of Congregation Beth Sholom in San Francisco. She teaches Torah widely in the Bay Area and has served as rabbi for Berkeley Hillel and Congregations Sha'ar Zahav and Beth Sholom. Her rabbinate has been deeply influenced by years of service with American Jewish World Service (AJWS) and Bend the Arc: A Jewish Partnership for Justice. She is a soulful leader of traditional and creative ritual and has released *Something of Mine*, an album of original songs largely based on texts from the Jewish tradition, available on Bandcamp.
3 Betty Rogers—unpublished interview in English with Liesl Levie after the war

Chapter Four

Camp Westerbork
Her Choice

I want to share the destiny of my people...

(ET 2002, 761)

Etty Hillesum's decision to volunteer to go to Westerbork via the Jewish Council and not go into hiding has been considered controversial by her close friends as well as by authors and reporters throughout the postwar generation. It was this decision, however, that became the cornerstone of both her self-realization and her resistance. She had ample opportunities and invitations from non-Jewish friends to go into hiding, yet she chose to go to Camp Westerbork transit camp.

Camp Westerbork was first established on October 9, 1939, in Drenthe Province in the Netherlands as the Central Refugee Camp Westerbork to provide a safe haven for Jews who had fled Germany and Austria. On July 1, 1942, the Germans took control of the camp and installed a German commandant, Albert Konrad Gemmker; an SS unit; and Jewish camp police called the *OD* or *Ordedienst*. The Germans added barbed wire and watchtowers, transforming the camp into a transit port for Jews being sent to their deaths.

In July 1942, Etty volunteered through the Jewish Council to go to Camp Westerbork. She wanted to be a social worker and help others, initially young women and girls, as well as her parents and brother who eventually arrived at the camp. It is here that Etty both struggled and flourished, ultimately finding the purpose of her life in the most difficult of times, amid the ubiquitous dust, mud, and winding barbed wire of the camp, working with the sick and persecuted, living in fear of the continual transports east to "work" in Poland.

Etty Hillesum was part of the first group of the Jewish Council in July to prepare for the initial transport of Dutch Jews later in July. Conditions in Westerbork, compared to other camps, were relatively favorable, even with poor hygiene conditions given the dust and mud of the region, lack of privacy, and the continual terror of deportations to "the east" and the unknown. According to Lotte Bergen, "Camp Westerbork did not give the impression that it was the last stop before destruction in the East." She goes on to say that an illusion was created that life behind barbed wire was only temporary. Gemmeker, the German commandant during Etty's time at the camp, with his air of both "correctness" and charisma, contributed to the facade (Bergen 2019, 64).

Etty's Friends and the Postwar Generation

The best person to tell the story of Etty Hillesum's choice not to go into hiding is Klaas A. D. Smelik, the son of Klaas Smelik Sr., Etty's friend and former lover who was also a publisher. He was the keeper of the diaries for many years, with his son Klaas Jr. growing up with his father's mysterious writing desk that contained Etty Hillesum's spiral notebooks that constituted her diary. Etty gave them to her friend and housemate Maria Tuinzing with directions to pass them on to Klaas before she left 6 Gabriel Metsustraat for the last time in early June 1943. We would not have these diaries today without the combined efforts of the Smeliks. Klaas A. D. Smelik, after many failed attempts by his father to have them published, was finally able to get an abridged copy of the manuscript published as *An Interrupted Life,* edited by Dutch publisher Jan Geurt Gaarlandt in 1981. Then, in 1996, Klaas A. D. Smelik was able to publish the much larger, unabridged manuscript with supporting notes as *Etty: The Letters and Diaries of Etty Hillesum,* which was translated and published in English in 2002.

The elder Smelik, who had some communication from the German front in World War II, had an inkling of the type of genocide that the Nazis were preparing for the Jews. He tried to talk Etty into going into hiding, and when that did not work, he and his daughter Johanna tried to kidnap her. As his son Klaas tells it, Klaas Sr. and his daughter Johanna were at a music salon at Han Wegerif's house where Etty lived. At a certain moment, father and daughter made their move:

> Etty was lifted by Klaas from behind, while Johanna held her legs as they descended the steep stairs to the front door of the house. Outside, a taxi was waiting for them. The descent did not go smoothly. Etty resisted and said in her soft voice to Johanna: "You should not do this." The kidnappers abandoned their plan ... (Smelik 2018, 84)

Klaas Smelik Sr. tried again to force Etty to go into hiding:

> I held Etty and tried to convince her once again of the mortal danger she was in ... but she wormed herself free and stood at a distance of about five feet from me. She looked at me very strangely and said, "You don't understand me." "No, I don't understand what on earth you are up to. Why don't you stay here you fool!" Then she said: "*I want to share the destiny of my people.*" When she said that, I knew there was no hope. She would never come to us. (ET 2002, 761; italics added)

In addition to Klaas Sr., Etty's other close friends who were part of the Spier Club were concerned and in disagreement about Etty's choice to stay at Camp Westerbork as part of the Jewish Council. One of those friends was Leonie Snatager (1918–2013), who as a Jewish woman facing the same risks, said in an unpublished interview after

Figure 4.1 Etty and Leonie Snatager (date unknown). From the collection of The Jewish Historical Museum, the Netherlands.

the war that in the summer of 1942, she consciously decided to distance herself from Etty, after her friend had almost convinced her that she should not go into hiding, but should voluntarily go to Camp Westerbork (Smelik 2018, 84, 85).

Her close friends Liesl and Werner Levie, a married couple with two daughters and part of the Spier community, also had a hard time understanding Etty's motivations about hiding and "sharing the destiny of the Jewish people" by joining the Jewish Council and going to Camp Westerbork. In an English interview with Betty Rogers after the war Liesl said the following:

> We regarded it—but we never told her—a bit strange [that she joined the Jewish Council], in relation to her very pro-human attitude, that she was dealing with these horrible people from the Jewish Council. Those were horrible people. My husband knew that very well. Asscher and Cohen and other leaders are not buried in the Jewish Cemetery [today]. My husband did not feel at home there [Jewish Council] at all. Etty also writes about that, but still she stayed. We didn't talk about that with her, imagine that could be the reason she would be taken away, but I often discussed it with my husband. It didn't fit at all with Etty that she was there where one person was sending away the other.

If we hadn't gotten them [the government papers to go to Palestine] we would have gone directly to Auschwitz like Etty and her family. Etty didn't imagine so she never worried about papers. She lived for the moment and she thought she would stay at the Jewish Council. And other people said to her you have to stay in the Jewish Council because the Jewish Council will be spared.

The Jewish Council work changed Etty's view, it seems to me. Yes, it gave her more of a sense to be united with the Jews, not to exclude herself from them. This is what every person has to live. It is his destiny. The Destiny of the Jews.

We always felt, Werner and I, we have the destiny of the Jewish people now and we have to be with them. Perhaps Etty felt the Jewishness later. Because of the work.

It was Werner's great passion to be part of a Zionist, Jewish state in Palestine. Etty heard him, heard us, discuss this many times.

Figure 4.2 Levie family portrait. Photo courtesy of Alexandra Nagel (private collection).

Four close Jewish friends ended up with different attitudes about their Jewishness, the Jewish Council, and hiding. Liesl seems to indicate that Etty's view changed over time from an assimilated Jewish attitude as her diary opens to wanting to be the "thinking heart of the barracks" by the time she has spent the first several periods at Camp Westerbork, much closer to her Jewishness and to her own heart of compassion, living her destiny differently from Leonie, Liesl, and Werner. A quote from Barbara Sullivan, a modern Jungian analyst and author, points to the anguish in any such decision:

> To begin our acquaintance with the other in the realm of being means we begin in the light of the moon. We do not know how this person will work out the terrible dilemmas of human experience until they show us their path. (Sullivan 1989, 81)

Leonie Snatager went into hiding and survived the Holocaust and eventually married and emigrated to the United States in 1948. In 1953, she married Walter Penney, had three children, and became an economist. Bernard Penney, one of her sons, has become a part of the Etty Hillesum community because of the close friendship that Etty had with his mother, and provided Judith Koelemeijer with Leonie's journals for Judith's new biography of Etty Hillesum, published in September 2022.

Werner and Liesl Levie had many stops on the way to Palestine/Israel, including Westerbork where they connected with Etty Hillesum one last time. They were there for a year, during the time that Etty was deported to "Poland" as they, Werner and Liesl, had papers for Palestine. And then on to Bergen-Belson, which they surprisingly survived. This was the camp where Anne Frank and her sister Margot perished—from the horrifying conditions and then from a Typus outbreak in February 1945. In the beginning of April 1945, prisoners from concentration camp Bergen-Belsen were transferred to Theresienstadt. One of the three trains that were used for this transport, was liberated by the Red Army near the village Tröbitz. Many passengers died in the train. Many people still died after the liberation because of the prevailing typhus in Tröbitz. Werner Levie was one of them. Liesl made it to Israel with her daughters. These daughters, Hagar Yudnik and Mikey Yaron, who are still alive and living in Israel, attended the big launch event for Etty Hillesum's biography by Judith Koelemeijer in Amsterdam in September of 2022.

Massenschicksal

Etty said to Klaas Smelik Sr. that she wanted to share the common fate—the *Massenschicksal*—of the Jewish people. What was her thinking, her truth? For Etty, freedom was found through her engagement with the suffering of others, not in her individual survival:

> Many accuse me of indifference and passivity when I refuse to go into hiding; they say that I have given up. They say everyone who can, must try to stay out

of their clutches, it's our bounden duty to try. But that argument is specious. For while everyone tries to save himself, vast numbers are nevertheless disappearing. And the funny thing is, I don't feel I'm in their clutches anyway, whether I stay or am sent away. I find all that talk so cliché-ridden and naive, and can't go along with it anymore. I don't feel in anybody's clutches ... They may well succeed in breaking me physically, but no more than that. I may face cruelty and deprivation the likes of which I cannot imagine in even my wildest fantasies. Yet all this is as nothing to the immeasurable expanse of my faith in God and my inner receptiveness. I shall always be able to stand on my own two feet even when they are planted on the hardest soil of the harshest reality. And my acceptance is not indifference or helplessness. I feel deep moral indignation at a regime that treats human beings in such a way. But events have become too overwhelming and too demonic to be stemmed with personal resentment and bitterness. These responses strike me as being utterly childish and unequal to the "fateful" course of events. (ET 2002, 487)

Her moral indignation in this situation shows itself in the strength of her resistance to the overwhelming forces of hatred and destruction that can take one over and kill a soul before a body gives out. The Nazis' purpose was the dehumanization of the Jewish people, and Etty's moral outrage, as Rachel Brenner suggests, was to prove her "unrelenting defiance to the terror of hopelessness and despair" (2010, 590). Etty continues:

People often get worked up when I say it doesn't really matter whether I go or somebody else does, the main thing is that so many thousands *have* to go. It is not as if I want to fall into the arms of destruction with a resigned smile—far from it. I am only bowing to the inevitable, and even as I do so I am sustained by the certain knowledge that ultimately they cannot rob us of anything that matters. I certainly do not want to go out of some sort of masochism, to be torn away from what has been the basis of my existence these last few years. But I don't think I would feel happy if I were exempted from what so many others have to suffer. They keep telling me that someone like me has a duty to go into hiding because I have so many things to do in life, so much to give. But I know that whatever I may have to give to others, I can give it no matter where I am, here in the circle of my friends or over there, in a concentration camp. And it is sheer arrogance to think oneself too good to share the fate of the masses. And if God Himself should feel that I still have a great deal to do, well then, I shall do it after I have suffered what all the others have to suffer. And whether or not I am a valuable human being will become clear only from my behavior in more arduous circumstances. And if I should not survive, how I die will show me who I really am. It's no longer a question of not getting oneself into a certain situation, come what may, but of how, in whatever situation, one conducts oneself and goes on living. (ET 2002, 487)

Etty says it quite simply, when she says she would not feel happy or, possibly, whole if she were exempted from what others had to suffer. As we move into her daily experience at Westerbork, Etty, in the first phases of her evolution of consciousness, moves from her experience of Nothingness to growing up, to Awakening/Insight and waking up to who one actually is after the conditioning of youth and for most, becoming conscious of the rigid patterns and defenses that develop as well as becoming present to one's experience in the moment. Then to the transformation to the new powers of being, of New Naming and then to Integration and the Boundless Dimension, as Rachel Brenner characterizes it, a shift from "they" to "we" of a shared fate. "Her growing solidarity with the deportees" becomes her community. She reflects: "It has been brought home to me *here*, ... how every atom of hatred added to the world makes it an even more inhospitable place" (Brenner 2010, 590).

In Joanne Braxton's book *Black Women Writing Biography* (1989), she delineated stages of African American women's development beginning with slavery. The Holocaust represented something similar for Jewish women and for a shorter period in current history, however, Braxton uses the phrase "making a way out of no way" where the pressures and hatred against them are so great, that there is no movement, no choice, and they are "defeated... by the external circumstances of their lives" (Washington 1982, 212).

"Making her way out of no way" at this stage of Etty's development was a time of Integration (phase four) for Etty, of growing into the Boundless Dimension that enabled action and empathy and love versus hate within herself, Camp Westerbork, and of the larger community of Dutch Jews as well as all human beings. Again, Etty's wish and prayer was to be the "thinking heart," as Jung would call the opposites from which a new orientation is born: "My head is the workshop, in which all worldly things must be thought through until they become clear, And my heart is the fiery furnace in which everything must be felt and suffered intensely" (ET 2002, 87). Etty's "thinking heart" will continue to appear in her final three months at Westerbork and will allow her to give back to her community at ever deeper levels.

Dailyness in Westerbork

When Etty was called back to Westerbork during the first week of June 1943, for the final time, she was struck by the desperate chaos of the place that she initially experienced in 1942 as one of community and bonding with the staff and its 1,000 "citizens." It now held 10,000 people living in gravely subpar conditions. Overall, Etty's continual concerns and struggles for herself, her family, and the inhabitants had to do with exceedingly poor hygiene. Exacerbating these poor conditions for Etty was the sandy terrain and wind, with sand getting into people's eyes, food, and bodies, causing ever-present illness; the constant anxiety and terror of who would be chosen for the next transport to "Poland" or "the east"; and the role of working in the hospital as a person who both comforted and assisted people in touching something within themselves that would not/could not be crushed by this destructive force. She was also quite concerned about her parents' and brother's health and wellbeing and managed the process of writing to friends, asking them to send rations and occasionally small delicacies such as butter, cakes, or chocolate.

For Etty, Westerbork was the "new focus of Jewish suffering," with its "great waves of human beings from all the nooks and crannies" of Holland, waiting anxiously "to meet their unknown destiny" (ET 2002, 583). One of the more harrowing examples of this was the transport from Vught on June 7, 1943, her first day back since November 1942. Vught was another Dutch transit/concentration camp that was poorly run, with prisoners treated badly. Etty was immediately assigned to help. She writes:

> First of all, we underwent a Lysol treatment, because so many lice always arrive from Vught. From four to nine I dragged screaming children around and carried luggage for exhausted women. It was hard going, and heart-rending. Women with small children, 1,600 (tonight another 1,600 will arrive); the men had been deliberately kept back in Vught. The morning transport is ready; Jopie and I have just been walking along it. Large, empty cattle cars. In Vught two or three children die every day. An old woman asked me helplessly, "Could you tell me, please could you tell me, why we Jews have to suffer so much?" I couldn't answer. There was a woman who had had to feed her four-month-old child on cabbage soup for days. She said, "I keep calling, 'Oh God, oh God'—but does He really still exist?" (ET 2002, 600)

The above is how Etty transcribed this experience into her letter to her friends. Friedrich Weinreb who wrote about the same event gives a different glimpse of Etty:

> The people from the camp [Westerbork] were deeply shocked, especially those who assisted the miserable prisoners out of the train. ... The whole morning was almost hysterically busy. It was as if now, for the first time, people realized what the Nazis were up to. ... Then Etty Hillesum arrived with her dispatch bag—she couldn't speak a word, only cry. She sat on a chair between Weyl's bed and mine, with her face buried in a handkerchief. Loonstijn called out: "My good girl, for heaven's sake stop, we have troubles enough, we don't need any wailing women around." This helped a bit, and Etty started telling us what she'd seen. She said that some of the people from Vught looked fairly healthy, and someone else said, "Those must've been the ones from the Jewish Council or from the registration there." But Etty said, presumably to make amends for her tearful beginning, that some of the prisoners were also smiling, and were feeling hopeful now that they had left from Vught. However, Etty soon started crying again. We let her do so, and it did help—at least then you don't have to cry yourself. (Weinreb 1969, 1082f)

This is a rare occurrence, seeing and hearing Etty's unbridled emotion. It had to arise occasionally for Etty as distinct from, but part of, her equanimity and presence, the part of that "heart that is the fiery furnace in which everything must be felt and suffered intensely," the same thinking heart that prayed:

> At night as I lay in the camp on my plank bed surrounded by women and girls, gently snoring, dreaming aloud, quietly sobbing, tossing and turning, women and girls who often told me during the day, "We don't want to think, we don't want to feel, otherwise, we are sure to go out of our minds," I was sometimes filled with an infinite tenderness, and lay awake for hours ... and I prayed, "Let me be the thinking heart of these barracks." (ET 2002, 543)

Etty Hillesum's relatively short back and forth time to Westerbork within the period of a year was when she faced many people forced into desperation who did not have any inner reference point, whether the very young, very old, the disabled, or the very rich wanting to be separated from everyone else in their own barracks. She gives an example of a young girl who was partially paralyzed and had just been learning to walk again. Etty describes the encounter. These quotes are part of her final letter from Westerbork noted in the Appendix; August of 1943:

> The girl says to Etty "Have you heard? I have to go." We look at each other for a long moment. It is as if her face has disappeared; she is all eyes. Then she says in a level, gray little voice, "Such a pity, isn't it? That everything you have learned in life goes for nothing. And, how hard it is to die." ... She looks at me for a long time in silence, searchingly, and then says, "I would like, oh, I really would like to swim away in my tears." (ET 2002, 646, 648)

And another:

> She grabbed hold of me; she looked deranged. A flood of words poured over me: "That isn't right, how can that be right? I've got to go, and I won't even be able to get my washing dry by tomorrow. And my child is sick, he's feverish, can't you fix things so that I don't have to go? ... Can't you take my child for me? Go on, please, won't you hide him; he's got a high fever, how can I possibly take him along?" She points to a little bundle of misery with blonde curls and a burning, bright red little face. "... my child," and then she sobs, "They take the sick children away, and you never get them back."
> *God Almighty, what are You doing to us? The words just escape me.* (ET 2002, 646–647; italics added)

In the midst of the sorrow she stays connected to her experience of a loving commitment to others as well as to her hope about being a chronicler, having the right and freedom to have a "say" about what happened in twentieth-century Europe.

But I am digressing and all I wanted to say was this:

    The misery here is quite terrible; and yet, late at night when the day has slunk away into the depths behind me, I often walk with a spring in my step along the barbed wire. And then, time and again, it soars straight from my heart—I can't help it, that's just the way it is, like some elementary force—the feeling that life is glorious and magnificent, and that one day we shall be building a whole new world. Against every new outrage and every fresh horror, we shall put up one more piece of love and goodness, drawing strength from within ourselves. We may suffer, but we must not succumb. And if we should survive unhurt in body and soul, but above all in soul, without bitterness and without hatred, then we shall have a right to a say after the war. Maybe I am an ambitious woman: I would like to have just a tiny little bit of a say. (ET 2002, 616)

Again, in phase four, where her evolving consciousness meets the human reality of her time, "facing every fresh horror, we shall put up one more piece of love and goodness" with the "elementary force soaring straight from her heart—the feeling that life is glorious and magnificent" and that she is "an ambitious woman and wants a say," we see such an integration of her humanity and transcendence.

Etty's work at Camp Westerbork was multifaceted; she had solid friends and colleagues, like Osias Kormann and Jopie Vleeschhouwer and, eventually, Philip Mechanicus, the well-known Dutch journalist. According to Gerrit van Ord (2010), it should not be a surprise that Etty Hillesum would resonate with Philip Mechanicus, given their shared intelligence and writing being primary for both of them. It would be a surprise, however, that she purportedly worked on a clandestine project with another Jewish Council member, Ies Spetter, who survived Auschwitz.

Etty Hillesum and Ies Spetter at Westerbork

Recently, Bettine Siertsema has shared a surfaced text revealing the potential of Etty Hillesum's additional clandestine actions while at Westerbork. It is a text written in the fall of 1945 by Ies Spetter, later known as Matthew Ies Spetter, who survived Auschwitz and the death marches. Spetter was one of Etty Hillesum's colleagues on the Jewish Council in Camp Westerbork. This text is kept in the archive of the NIOD, or The Dutch Institute for War, Holocaust and Genocidal Studies, and had gone unnoticed for years until it was published in 2018 by Siertsema (Spetter 2018, 395–453).

    Spetter's name appears only once in Etty's letters. In Amsterdam, in February 1943, Etty's friend Jopie Vleeschhouwer, asks in passing about this person: "Do let me know some more news about Ies Spetter. Everyone here says that he is getting divorced, and I'd be interested if that's true" (ET 2002, 665). This was a curious question; who was he?

    Ies Spetter, born into a liberal Jewish family, studied psychology in Amsterdam and married Suze Turksma. Siertsema says that one day, when he saw how children from the Jewish orphanage were thrown into a truck, he decided to join the resistance. He became involved with the Westerweel group, which smuggled people to Spain.

Spetter's intentions were to continue his illegal work when he was offered a position on the Jewish Council at the end of March 1942, to begin the task of administering deportation of sixteen- to forty-five-year-old Jews for labor in Germany. According to Siertsema, it was the first time deportation had been mentioned. At first, Spetter refused to do this task, but then he was convinced by a resistance leader to do it, and in July 1942 he left for Camp Westerbork. At this juncture, he had the same privileges as Etty Hillesum and was able to travel back and forth to Amsterdam. He also had a fake personal identification card as extra security (Siertsema 2019, 344, 345).

At Westerbork, together with four others, presumably including Etty Hillesum, Spetter founded a social department (SD) "fully intent on helping as much as possible without lifting a finger for the SD's administration machine" (; quoted in Siertsema 2019, 345). The social department collected clothes or items from people with anything extra to give to those arriving who had nothing. Spetter's wife, during this time outside of Camp Westerbork, was able to find safe addresses for about one hundred children. Much like Etty's experiences of assisting transports both in and out of Westerbork, Ies was also a "bewildered" witness to the horrific chaos wrought by the mass transport of October 3, 1942. His description, says Siertsema, was similar to Etty Hillesum's view of Westerbork in tone and vision. Etty herself was in Amsterdam on that date and did not describe that particular event:

> Who will describe the suffering of all these mothers, children who have been picked up on their own, pregnant women and men who have been beaten up, psychologically broken, desperately clinging to what's left of their possessions, cold and hungry, dully bearing their fate, but actually unaware of the terrible end awaiting them. (Spetter; quoted in Siertsema 2019, 345)

In a few lines Ies Spetter described the deportees' anguished state of mind, and desperate mood that Etty also described and understood, and after those lines—and an added line space—Spetter continued with a sentence of particular importance to research about Etty Hillesum:

> Together with a friend, Mr. Hillesum, I managed to smuggle some children out of the camp. My wife went to pick them up and deliver them elsewhere. (Spetter; quoted in Siertsema 2018, 406)[1]

This line sheds new light on Etty Hillesum's additional activities in the camp and can easily be missed because Spetter addresses her as "Mr." In Dutch, *Meester,* abbreviated as *Mr.,* is an academic title used for persons who graduated in law. Siertsema concludes:

> In the margin of the typeset of Spetter's text in the NIOD archive, a handwritten note was scribbled: "by ambulance to Groningen." Apparently indicating the method by which this smuggling had been accomplished. (Siertsema 2019, 347)

Spetter does not say another word about it ...

Although neither the date nor time nor any of the details are known, or whether such attempts to smuggle children out of Westerbork were successful, we can surmise, because of Spetter's note about Mr. Hillesum, that Etty was involved. It seems, according to Siertsema, that Etty Hillesum's acceptance of her fate, for which her friends and some of her later readers criticized her, did not lead to passivity at all. Instead, it seems she committed herself to actively helping these children, both supporting them within the camp and, allegedly, when possible, helping them escape the same fate that she accepted.

Etty Hillesum, Philip Mechanicus, and the "Gentleman" Commander, Albert Gemmeker

> The terrifying thing is that systems grow too big for men and hold them in a satanic grip.
>
> Etty Hillesum (ET 2002, 259)

Etty and Phillip were both at Westerbork during the summer of 1943 and became fast friends. Although they had opposite social beginnings and their careers and experiences around travel were vastly different, they connected quickly. Mechanicus, a journalist, was twenty-five years Hillesum's senior, with much more life lived (not unlike Han and Spier), yet they shared strong intellectual development, skills of observation, and writing; his veered toward a socioeconomic, political, and historically oriented worldview whereas Etty's was in the arena of spirituality and psychology, with an ontological emphasis on the spiritual being and Jungian oriented self-realization. Gerrit van Ord reminds us that poetry and literature were exponentially more important to Hillesum than Mechanicus. His was all about an objective reporting of the events as they happened. Each of their styles complemented the other's (van Ord 2010, 318).

One can see this quite clearly when placing their diaries side by side; ironically, they often wrote side by side in the camp and shared many of Westerbork's small triumphs and overall tragedy. In fact, at one point in July 1943, both Mechanicus and Etty's parents were on the list for deportation and Etty intervened to get all three off the list:

> Yesterday was a day like no other. Never before have I taken a hand in "fixing" it to keep someone off the transport. I lack all talent for diplomacy, but yesterday I did my bit for Mechanicus. What exactly it was that I did, I'm not sure. I went to all sorts of officials. ... As far as Mechanicus was concerned, things were in doubt until the very last moment. I helped him pack his bags, sewed a few buttons on his suit. ... Jopie came by ... Mechanicus is *not* on transport. (ET 2002, 618)

The truth of Westerbork becomes clear to the underground resistance and to history based on letters that both Etty and Philip smuggled out of the camp in addition to both of their diaries, which survived the war and were later published. It is also true that they both experienced a privileged position in the camp: Etty's position was to offer the deportees concrete help with packing and preparation, and she also gave moral support and empathy.

Westerbork's "big lie" provided support for Hitler's ongoing deceit in regard to his full extermination plans for the Jews. Westerbork's own German demagogue, Albert Gemmeker, was tasked with carrying out that deceit. He was charismatic, cordial, promising everything to everyone and emphasizing law and order, discipline, and loyalty. Westerbork was a "model camp," a well-oiled machine managed almost entirely by the German-Jewish camp inmates themselves.

> The organizers tried to make themselves useful in the eyes of their oppressors, hoping this might put a brake on the deportations, which, of course proved illusory and the siphoning off went on week after week since the extermination of the Jews had absolute priority in Berlin. (Presser 1968, 6)

Hillesum and Mechanicus played a part in exposing the big lie of the model camp, as they both wrote about walking through the camp together on August 24th for the preparation for the deportation of August 25, 1943, to "Poland." They conveyed this experience in very different ways: Mechanicus as an objective reporter and Hillesum as an empathic storyteller, giving expression to the incomprehensible fear and despair of the women and girls and in one of the cases the suicide of the mother of one of Etty's female colleagues. Etty includes a description of Commander Gemmeker during his "performance" just before a transport[2]:

> He appears at the end of the asphalt path, like a famous star making his entrance during a grand finale … He walks along the train, his gray, immaculately brushed hair just showing beneath his flat, light green cap. That gray hair, which makes such a romantic contrast with his fairly young face, sends many of the silly young girls here into raptures—although they dare not, of course, express their feelings openly. On this cruel morning his face is almost iron gray. It is a face that I am quite unable to read. Sometimes it seems to me to be like a long thin scar in which grimness mingles with joylessness and hypocrisy. And there is something else about him, halfway between a dapper hairdresser's assistant and a stagedoor Johnny. But the grimness and the rigidly forced bearing predominate. With military step he walks along the line of freight cars, bulging now with people. (ET, 652, 653)

In the same letter, she notes how she heard someone behind her, just before a transport departed, remarking, "Once upon a time we had a commandant who used to kick people off to Poland. This one sees them off with a smile."

Both Phillip's and Etty's reports were smuggled out of the camp at great risk and remain invaluable documents describing Westerbork during the war. According to

Jacob Presser, who wrote the foreword to Mechanicus's diary: "These are irreplaceable documents, because the German authorities, toward the end of the war, did their best to wipe out every trace of their misdeeds" (1968, 10).[3]

As part of the Jewish Council, Etty had contact with Gemmeker as she advocated for certain Jewish inmates to be removed from the deportation list. Living from week to week in Camp Westerbork was a debilitating experience because of the transports.

> people lived from one Tuesday to the next, for that was the day on which, again and again, the infernal train swallowed up its thousand victims bound for a destination that people hardly dared to think about and yet thought about it all the time, about which people could say nothing and yet spoke of incessantly. Every week the emotional curve showed the same pattern—moving rapidly upwards from dejection and utter weariness to a peak, followed by a gradual decline, passing through uneasiness, alarm, agitation, till it reached a panic. For months on end. (Presser 1968, 7)

This was the excruciating and wildly beating heart of Camp Westerbork—the weekly transports whose purpose was to send the Jews to "work" in "Poland" when in actuality they were sent to a couple of adjunct locations: to the old concentration camp of Sobibor and Auschwitz, and now Auschwitz-Birkenau. The newly completed death camp, finished in March 1943, was equipped with four more crematoria, which included the gas chambers and dressing rooms with hooks for clothes and finally ovens to incinerate the bodies. The hoax was kept up until the last moment, the crematoria covered by trees and bushes with much underground so no one would see or panic, so a riot or hysteria would not happen to spoil the ruse and create mayhem in the rest of the camp.

This was Gemmeker's real commitment to Berlin (Hitler), regardless of the more livable environment of Westerbork compared to other camps, with its excellent hospital facilities and ongoing entertainment by Jewish camp musicians and actors and comedians whom Gemmeker took such an interest in and was greatly entertained by. He made sure he did everything possible to give off an air that he "took care" of the Jews and understood them and treated them well, much like Eichmann professed to do. In fact, he was nicknamed "the Gentleman-commander."

> The health services at Westerbork were also quite sophisticated: … at its peak the hospital had 1,725 beds, 120 doctors and a staff of over 1,000. And all of the specialties you can think of … an operating theater, … an x-ray scheme to test all camp residents for tuberculosis, immunization against typhoid and paratyphoid, the testing of bool groups. The doctors held weekly meetings to deal with scientific and clinical subjects. And this whole organization was for the benefit of people who were to be destroyed a little later on! (Presser 1968, 7)

Clearly this was part of a strategy to maintain the prisoners' belief that they were residents rather than prisoners. They were cared for so well by the Germans, how could they possibly have "evil intentions" toward them in "the east." The commandant's seeming interest in and support of children at the camp even allowed a Student's Circle to be taught religion, culture, and Zionism.

A story about Gemmeker reveals his true commitment to Berlin's orders however. Lotte Bergen has written a book about Albert Gemmeker. In it, she tells the story of baby Machieltje. The most conspicuous example of this public relations scam of Albert Gemmeker's Westerbork was his interest in the fate of the baby who came from Camp Vught. The premature infant needed medical care. Gemmeker arranged not only for the Jewish professor of pediatrics, Van Creveld, to come to Camp Westerbork but also for an incubator to be sent from a nearby hospital.

> The commander ensured that the infant received a drop of brandy in his bottle to gain strength. He regularly visited the maternity ward to inquire about the health of the little boy. Machieltje's condition improved slowly and once he reached six pounds, he was found strong enough to be transported to the East. (Bergen 2019, 66)

Etty saw through the "Gentleman-commander," as can be seen from her letters. She knew that Gemmeker, such a charismatic and sociopathic type, much like all of the Nazi leadership, was an executor of the system that was spreading through Europe. And even though by 1943 the war was on its way to being lost by the Germans, Hitler was determined to exterminate as many Jews as possible by the end of the war, even if it was lost, as then his primary mission would be accomplished.

Etty Hillesum's presence of mind, her self-realization, and her equanimity allowed her to use her gift of writing to inform the resistance and underground efforts in Holland of the true actions of Camp Westerbork. She was most likely involved with resistance efforts, such as smuggling out small numbers of children with Ies Spetter, who with his wife had the connections to make this happen. Her choice of the Jewish Council presumed she had enough of a leadership position to carry out these actions as well as being a witness and spiritual guide to those who suffered from transport to transport, until she herself suffered the same fate. Because her diary was saved, she became not only a chronicler, but also a catalyst for spiritual transformation and humanist action for generations to come.

Etty Hillesum—Deportation to Auschwitz, September 7, 1943

> It came without warning, orders from The Hague.
> Mr. Wegerif, Hans, Maria, Tide and everyone else I may not know so well.
> It is not going to be easy for me to tell you this. It all happened so suddenly, so unexpectedly. Odd, isn't it, it seemed unexpected even *now*, it seemed sudden

even *now*, although we had all been ready and waiting for such a long time. So when it happened she too was ready and waiting. And, alas, she too has gone. ... After the leaders of the J.C. had declared that nothing could be done for her, we wrote a letter as a last resort to the 1st *Dienstleiter*, or in this case Commandant Gemmeker requesting that he intervene personally.

We felt that something might still be arranged on the train. But that meant getting everything ready before she left, and so the parents and Mischa went off to the train first. And I brought up the rear trundling a well-filled rucksack and a wicker basket with a bowl and cup dangling from it along to the train. And there she set foot on the transport "boulevard," which she had described just fourteen days earlier in her own incomparable manner. Talking gaily, smiling, a kind word for everyone she met on the way, full of sparkling good humour, perhaps just a touch of sadness, but every inch our Etty, the way you all know her. "I have my diaries and my small Bibles and my Russian grammar and Tolstoy with me, and I have no idea what else there is in my luggage." One of our leaders came up to say good-bye and to explain that he had put forward all the arguments he could, but in vain. Etty thanked him "for putting forward the arguments all the same" and asked me to tell you all how everything went. And what a good departure she and her family had.

So here I sit now, a little sad, certainly, but not sad for something that has been lost, since a friendship like hers can never be lost; it *is*, and it endures.

Jopie Vleeschhouwer (ET 2002, 666, 667; original italics)

As the train left Westerbork, as they cleared the doors, the prisoners always sang Jewish songs, particularly the Jewish anthem from Palestine/Israel, the *Hatikvah*. Most knew they were going to their deaths. Etty also wrote about this, that only in the train could you sing the Jewish anthem. She knew this because no other people were allowed on the platform, only Etty (or someone else from the Jewish Council) when they brought people to the train.

Etty threw a postcard out of the train window on September 7th, where it was found by farmers and posted by them, postmarked September 15, 1943:

Christine,
Opening the Bible at random I find this: "The Lord is my high tower." I am sitting on my rucksack in the middle of a full freight car. Father, Mother, and Mischa are a few cars away. In the end, the departure came without warning. On sudden special orders from The Hague. We left the camp singing, Father and Mother, firmly and calmly, Mischa, too. We shall be traveling for three days. Thank you for all your kindness and care. Friends left behind will still be writing to Amsterdam; perhaps you will hear something from them. Or from my last letter from camp. Goodbye for now from the four of us Etty (Etty 1996, 360)

According to the Red Cross, Etty Hillesum was killed at Auschwitz on November 30, 1943.

Camp Westerbork: Her Choice 75

Figure 4.3 Portrait of Etty Hillesum, date unknown. From the collection of The Jewish Historical Museum, the Netherlands.

Kaddish for Etty Hillesum

She praised Your Great Name from the unsullied corners
Of her soul. Sifted silence for words,
Weaved them to the sky within.
She insisted on God, demanded dignity,
We can pray anywhere. In a wooden barracks,
In a stone monastery, God is everywhere.

She guarded the inner temple where God
Patiently waited. She lifted and cradled and brought forth
The God who needed us as much as we needed him.
Broken, helpless God in the rubble. God
She would not abandon even when he'd abandoned her.
She praised the God she dug up from her gut
Rooted in stubborn trust. She saved herself.
She saved God. She made God
Possible. She led God through the darkness
And would not let him go. Dragged his hand
Through the ash, turned his face to his people,
Said, *look*. Said, *stay*. The ghosts
Of Auschwitz said to God, *You shall not see us*
And live. But she held God's hand,
traced the lines on his palm, said, *This*
Is your lifeline. Some of us will live.
Some of us will praise Your Name, forever and ever.

                 Hila Ratzabi[4]

Notes

1. Because Etty had a law degree, this title, Mr. Hillesum, was the appropriate one chosen by Spetter.
2. Hillesum's letter is reprinted and paraphrased in Appendix A.
3. The Imperial Institute of War Documents in Amsterdam has collected a large number of testimonies from camp inmates; among these are the letters of Etty Hillesum, which are incomparable documents of their kind. Etty's letter of August 25th is included in full in Appendix A.
4. Hila Ratzabi is the author of the poetry collection *There Are Still Woods* (June Road Press, 2022). Her poetry has been published widely in literary journals and in *The Bloomsbury Anthology of Contemporary Jewish American Poetry* and *Ghost Fishing: An Eco-Justice Poetry Anthology*. She lives outside Chicago with her spouse and two children.

Chapter Five

Our Time: 2016–2024

It is the problem of our age...hatred of the Germans poisons everyone's mind ... If there were only one decent German, it is wrong to pour hatred over an entire people.
(ET 2002, 18)

The terrifying thing is that systems grow too big for men and hold them in a satanic grip.
(ET 2002, 18)

What are the contours of our time? After centuries of colonialism, wars of conquest, and slavery, many countries embarked upon a slow and inherently flawed trajectory toward more freedom, more empathy, more inclusion, and greater understanding of the differences among the groups of people that exist in the various societies of our world. Yet some Western democracies have discarded the basic fabric underlying democracy itself, in favor of authoritarianism, exclusion, fearmongering, and hatred. Some countries are blatantly building walls, cataloging their "enemies," and rejecting the vulnerable and helpless. How can Etty Hillesum's insights and practices help us navigate these complexities of contemporary authoritarianism and the psychological challenges they present?

Authoritarian politicians worldwide consistently double-down on their lies. Compared to the dictators of Etty's time, today's strongmen are better considered as personalist dictators: Victor Orbán, in Hungary; Trump in the US; formerly, Bolsonaro in Brazil; Netanyahu in Israel; and Erdogan in Turkey, to name a few. The central goal of this kind of personalist authoritarian is to gain more and more power, but instead of terrorizing people physically, this kind of ruler reshapes their citizens through charisma, enthusiasm for pitting people against each other, banning a free press, taking away women's choices, injecting fear of losing what one has accumulated to "the woke left," and promising a return to an idealized past, which is always safe, secure, and free from the unwanted other.

Our times have echoes of the 1930s and 1940s that my generation (the Baby Boomers) thought we would never see in our lifetimes. "Never again" and "history repeats itself," like most opposites, can reside in the same sentence, never mind the very next century. What would Etty have thought, in 1939, as she probably read in the newspaper about Hitler's takeover of Czechoslovakia and then Poland? Hitler claimed that millions of ethnic Germans were being persecuted there and had already chopped off parts of the country for that reason, and incorporated them into Nazi Germany. With no pushback from a Europe wishing to avoid war, six months later, Adolf Hitler was threatening Czechoslovakia, on the pretense that it was a threat to German national security, and he demanded its surrender, or face the Blitz. The Czech president capitulated, and German troops occupied the country from that point forward (Ruane 2022).

These problems with authoritarianism have resurged in the twenty-first century. Under the guise of populism, nativism, "freedom" parties, and "making America great again," the souls of democratic institutions around the world are being replaced by misguided versions of Christian Nationalism, or at least the nascent forms of authoritarian regimes. This is happening here in the United States, in the far right's desire to return to a quasi-Confederacy, where states' rights would supersede federal laws. This was the same rationale promoted by the southern states before the Civil War in an effort to preserve slavery.

The Contours of Our Time

Scholars point to a number of specific events as the harbingers of this resurgence: the rise of the Austrian Freedom Party; the Brexit vote in the UK; the early and current successes of Geert Wilders in the Netherlands; Marine Le Pen's National Front in France and now Macron joining with Le Pen against immigration; and for many, most shockingly, the election of Donald Trump in 2016. These political events share common underlying themes, always beginning with a fear of the "other," who is blamed for the ills of contemporary society. Regardless of how the "other" is articulated in any given context, the message is the same: we are now engaged in an existential struggle, a zero-sum game, in which one segment of the population (often white and Christian), sees itself in opposition to the "other" taking what is "theirs," or destroying their traditional culture and values.

Trump's worldview substantively overlaps with his authoritarian cohorts in Europe. Hitler, and Putin are of a similar kind of ruthless and totalitarian tyrant. Hitler, in the 1930s and 1940s, while Putin, still in power for life, comes from a Stalinist Russian tradition, including KGB training. Anyone who opposes him disappears, even outside of Russian borders.

Dr. Anna Orenstein, a psychoanalyst, psychiatrist, and a survivor of several concentration camps, wrote an article entitled "The Relativity of Morality in the Contemporary World" for *Psychoanalytic Inquiry* (2020). She says as part of her introduction:

> Living in close proximity with Germans soon after the war and having survived concentration camps a year earlier, gave me an opportunity to recognize just how profoundly the sense of morality is affected by the political and social

circumstances in which one lives. On the side of the perpetrators, I experienced the ruthlessness and cruelty of a political system completely void of moral considerations. On the side of the victims, I witnessed the attempts that we made to hold onto our values by behaving with consideration for others whenever we could. This was not always possible and I believe that the often cited "survivor guilt" is frequently related to the guilt the survivors experienced for not being able to reconcile their behavior in camp with their standards and values under civilized conditions. (Orenstein 2020, 223)

What was remarkable about this part of her life is what came next: during the forty-five years of Dr. Orenstein's professional life in the US, she had not been concerned about morality questions. Of course, there have been plenty of them in the US during this time period, but none that reminded her of the increasing signs of a collapsing moral social order that she experienced under totalitarian Germany—until now:

Today, in 2019, as America is experiencing another political crisis, I had returned to these questions. It appears we had become more keenly aware of the impact that political and social forces have on mental life, how corrosion and the gradual disappearance of moral principles in business and in politics are affecting our daily lives. (Orenstein 2020, 223–224)

Orenstein does not believe that what happened in Nazi Germany could happen here, as she indicated that Black Americans suffer more from institutionalized racism in this country than Jewish people, yet since this writing, antisemitism is on the rise in the United States. However, she feels there are good reasons why many Americans are comparing Germany in the 1930s to our current situation, as "Germany's slide into a popular embrace of authoritarianism that ended in tyranny offers a frame of understanding how liberal democracies can in a relatively short period be totally destroyed ..." (Orenstein 2020, 232) She goes on to say:

As with Hitler, after the first shock of a Trump presidency, many tried to dismiss him as an ineffectual puppet until he proved his ability to hold onto a loyal political base and to succeed in seducing his party to go along with many of his un-democratic and destructive ideas. We have to take note and be concerned about the fact that the normalization and gradual acceptance of anti-democratic behavior has been underway in the first years of his presidency ... *The danger, I believe is the gradual and steady "caving in" of the elected officials who, fearful of losing their positions, appear to follow the leader regardless of how destructive his policies may be to our democracy.* (Orenstein 2020, 232; italics added)

Mirroring Hitler's promise of a return to a mythical German past, Trump, too, announced in July 2016 at the Republican National Convention that "I am your voice ... and I alone can fix it." He harkened to an antebellum America when the brutality of slavery and the destruction of Native American culture were sublimated in favor of a more heroic American self-image.

In an effort to understand our time, along with Dr. Orenstein, I also turned to Heather Cox Richardson, a historian, author, and professor at Boston College in Chestnut Hill, Massachusetts, to try to understand the contours of our time. In September 2019, she began writing an online newsletter entitled *Letters from an American*. Published on Substack, it has served as a straightforward and clear transmission of her own research of current events without hyperbole. She started writing in response to Trump's first impeachment. Her commitment to truth and fact-finding to uncover disinformation, which has been rampant since 2016, has attracted an extensive following.

> "We're in an inflection moment of American politics, and one of the things that happens in that moment is that a lot of people get involved in politics again," she said. Many of those newly energized Americans are women around Dr. Richardson's age, 58, and they form the bulk of her audience. She's writing for people who want to leave an article feeling "smarter not dumber," she says, and who don't want to learn about the events of the day through the panicked channels of cable news and Twitter, but calmly situated in the long sweep of American history and values. (Smith 2020)

I can imagine Etty Hillesum would be drawn to Heather Cox Richardson, as the former tried to sort through the conflicting voices of her day. Etty was just as passionate about what was true. And her frustration was particularly acute around her perception that there was no earnest attempt to search for or clarify the significant historical trends in Dutch and European history. She especially disliked the "acrimonious discussions" that keep cycling around the small international community of her household when they begin to talk about their hatred of the Germans. Etty describes these polarizing discussions in her times:

> These discussions are hardly ever concerned with real politics, with any attempts to grasp major political trends or to fathom the underlying currents. On the contrary, everything looks so clear-cut and ugly, which is why it is so unpleasant to discuss politics in the present climate. (ET 2002, 20)

The polarization of our times has reached this same frenzy between Republicans and Democrats, particularly on the far right or far left. Even vaccines and masks became highly politicized around party lines, with fights breaking out in public places, particularly in enclosed spaces like airplanes. Extended families have split, unable to celebrate Thanksgiving or other holidays together, given the extent of political polarization in families.

The problems of disinformation, propaganda, and conspiracy theories fuel this polarization, and are age-old, hugely layered, and complex. As Dan Pfeffer speaks of in his most recent book, *Battling the Big Lie: How Fox, Facebook, and the MAGA*

Media Are Destroying America (2022), he wrote it as a "wake-up call and a call to arms for the Democrats sick of losing the message wars" (xv). I think most would agree that the internet has expanded our universe, and at the same time it has addicted us, distracted us, increased our materialism, disconnected us from the earth, and created a great deal of comparison with others. I have heard these fixations in my private practice over the years, about the need to share the same number of photos, travels, and events as their peers, or one does not feel as if "they have a life." Social media has certainly excited us, challenged us, and brought us together, as well as torn us apart.

Trump's claims about the free press being an "enemy of the people" and "fake news" have been heard hundreds of times. Steve Bannon became the chief executive officer of Trump's 2016 presidential campaign, and then was appointed chief strategist and senior counselor to the president, following Trump's election. Bannon, the architect of Trump's victory, described his strategy to journalist and author of the *Big Short*, Michael Lewis, as follows: "The Democrats don't matter. The real opposition is the media. And the way to deal with them is to flood the zone with shit" (Stelter 2021).

No wonder Jonathan Greenblatt of the Anti-Defamation league on a recent newscast called social media "an unfettered flow of sewage from the margins into the mainstream." I looked at Breitbart News in writing this piece, and I was in disbelief at the cartoonish headlines that seemed so obviously exaggerated or, in fact, had no basis in truth. This is what I saw on July 7, 2023, on Breitbart: "President Joe Biden's administration sold 950,000 barrels of oil from the U.S. Strategic Petroleum Reserve to a Chinese state-owned gas company that has financial ties to a private equity firm cofounded by Hunter Biden." Or this headline from August 5th: " 'Don't Test, Don't Tell': Senate Democrats Cancel Covid Policy to Ram Through Reconciliation Bill," or "Biden's Contribution to Lowering Gas Prices Is Causing a Recession."

It reminded me of the much more heinous Nazis propaganda cartoons, in which they often portrayed Jews as engaged in a conspiracy to provoke war. In one 1942 cartoon, a stereotyped Jew conspires behind the scenes to control the Allied powers, represented by the British, American, and Soviet flags. The caption reads, "Behind the enemy powers: the Jew." Or a Nazi German cartoon, circa 1938, that depicts the Jews as an octopus encircling the globe. Conspiracy is as alive at this time in our history, more than we have ever known, given the speed at which they travel around the globe via the internet.

Trump's Big Lie

The events following the first impeachment of President Trump in 2019 and Dr. Orenstein's reflections have a great deal to do with a basic tenet of democracy—the peaceful and orderly transfer of power. In his first inaugural address, on January 20, 1981, President Ronald Reagan praised our collective achievement:

> To a few of us here today this is a solemn and most momentous occasion, and yet in the history of our nation it is a commonplace occurrence. The orderly

transfer of authority as called for in the Constitution routinely takes place, as it has for almost two centuries, and few of us stop to think how unique we really are. In the eyes of many in the world, this every 4-year ceremony we accept as normal is nothing less than a miracle. (Iannacci 2016)

The 2020 US presidential election, a race between Donald Trump and Joseph Biden, took place on November 4, 2020. Several days later, Biden was declared the winner. He won the popular vote by more than seven million, and the Electoral College 306 to 232. Yet, Trump contended that he won the election in a "landslide," claiming massive "fraud" on the part of Democrats. His campaign filed and lost at least sixty-three lawsuits, going all the way to the Supreme Court.

Trump tried to force the Justice Department to support false allegations of election fraud; he pressured state lawmakers and election officials to "find more votes"; he tried to send alternate or fake electors to Congress. Even then he wouldn't stop. He incited a mob to attack the US Capitol and disrupt the certification of the election results. That day, January 6, 2021, will long be remembered as countering, in a radical way, that very article in the United States' Constitution that Reagan celebrated.

January 6, 2021 was the day set aside for Congress to certify the results of the election, formalizing Joseph Biden's victory. Trump demanded that Mike Pence, who as vice president presides over the certification, refuse to count the Electoral College votes and certify the election. Bob Woodward and Robert Costa reported that when Pence informed him that this was not legally permissible, the president told him, "You can do this. I don't want to be your friend anymore if you don't do this." This plays like a slow-motion coup, yet the words uttered by Trump are both demanding and as sophomoric as a playground threat.

Maggie Haberman (2022) reported that on January 5th, Pence's chief of staff, Marc Short, called the Secret Service to inform them that "the president was going to turn publicly against the vice president, and there could be a security risk to Mr. Pence because of it." And this is, indeed, what happened. At Trump's January 6th rally on the mall, the president told his audience, "You're never going to take back our country with weakness." He said he hoped Pence would "do the right thing" by not certifying the election.

After the mob stormed the Capitol, Trump tweeted, "Mike Pence didn't have the courage to do what should have been done to protect our Country and our Constitution." It was around this time that some of Trump's supporters built a gallows outside the Capitol building. Other Trump supporters attacked police, breached the building, and roamed the halls chanting "Hang Mike Pence." Five people died as a result of this attack (Last 2022). If former Vice President Pence had agreed with Trump's demands, we would be in a very different place today. In this instance democracy worked. It was an unlikely heroic act, as until this point Pence had been seen by most as a loyal acolyte to Trump.

The Select Committee to Investigate the January 6th Attack on the US Capitol held eight televised hearings for the American public laying out the findings of their investigation into the attack. There were only two Republicans on the committee: Liz Cheney and Adam Kinzinger, both of whom have been shunned by the GOP for not supporting the "big lie." Cheney, whose father, Richard Cheney, was vice president under George W. Bush, was disowned by Republicans, as she voted for Trump's impeachment and for Biden to be certified. Kinzinger announced he would not seek reelection, and Cheney lost her primary to a Trump supporter, Harriet Hageman. As Liz Cheney said right after the election, she will continue the fight to keep Donald Trump out of the Oval Office. She also said that it is too early to think about running for president of the United States, but she will be thinking about it.

Cheney paid a price for her courage in voting to impeach Trump after January 6th, as well as for her work co-chairing the January 6th committee. Trump still has a powerful hold on the Republican Party: so far eight of the ten House Republicans who voted to impeach him have lost their primary elections, as a result of his revenge.

To this day, Trump continues the big lie of having won the election, claiming it was stolen by Democrats. Although he was impeached again in January 2021 for his role in trying to overturn the election, once again, he was acquitted by the Senate. At this moment in time, Trump is poised to become the Republican nominee in 2024, and the House has gone to the Republicans, with many vying for the speaker position, promising the most radical group of the House, the election deniers, every wish of opposing the rule of law. We continue to watch the brinksmanship of this live grenade at this writing, with the distinct feeling that groups on the far right in the House aim toward the destruction of our economic stability, democracy, with a will toward anarchy.

And most of those Republicans who backed away from Trump after January 6th have returned to the fold. I am reminded of Dr. Orenstein's article on morality cited earlier, that "the danger, I believe is the gradual and steady 'caving in' of the elected officials who, fearful of losing their positions, appear to follow the leader regardless of how destructive his policies may be to our democracy" (2020, 232).

As of this writing, an Associated Press study showed that more than 120 January 6th defendants have pled guilty or been convicted at trial for rioting, arson, and conspiracy and that they are from all over the political spectrum, with many of them far-right extremists who traveled across state lines to join the protests. And the January 6th attack was hardly victimless: nine people died at the Capitol riot, or just after it; more than a hundred law enforcement officers were injured, "attacked with cudgels and bear spray"; and the rioters did more than $1.5 million in damage to the Capitol (Associate Press news study cited in Richardson, *Letters from an American*, June 6, 2022).

Unfortunately, the United States is not alone in this slide toward authoritarian thinking and action. Countries such as Hungary, Poland, Turkey, Venezuela, and the Philippines have been moving in this direction for some time and, of course, it goes without saying, China and Russia.

It is popular knowledge in the United States that Vladimir Putin aided Donald Trump's campaign against Hillary Clinton in 2016. Clinton had, during her tenure as United States Secretary of State, drawn controversy by using a private email server for official public communications. The Democrats were hacked several times by the Russians, Chinese, and other countries, and Donald Trump said at a rally in front of 25,000 people and telecast to the world: "Russia, if you're listening—I hope you are able to find the 30,000 emails that are missing. I think you will probably be rewarded mightily by our press. Let's see if that happens."

In addition, on July 25, 2019, Donald Trump had a call with the new president of Ukraine, Volodymyr Zelensky. Zelensky asked for an increase in military aid for the ongoing conflict with Russian-backed separatists in eastern Ukraine. Former President Trump conditioned military aid to Ukraine on the country's willingness to investigate his domestic political enemies, specifically Joe Biden's son Hunter's allegedly corrupt dealings with a Ukrainian prosecutor, a quid pro quo for Trump's political agenda. Thankfully, this deal did not come to pass. As a result of his actions, Donald Trump was officially impeached by the House of Representatives on December 18, 2019. However, on January 31, 2020, Donald Trump was acquitted by the Republican-controlled Senate.

Russia's mission was not only limited to assisting Trump but also to sowing seeds of controversy, chaos, and disinformation to destabilize American politics. Trump has always been seen as having an affinity for the world's strongmen: Putin, Kim Jong Un, Viktor Orbán, and Xi Jinping to name a few. As Etty would say, there will always be an Ivan the Terrible, or a Hitler ... and for us in today's world, a Vladimir Putin.

Now in 2022, Putin has stepped onto the world stage as one of these genocidal conscience-free "strongmen," when on February 24, 2022, he attacked Ukraine, an independent democratic nation, just as he had done with Crimea in 2014, and Georgia in 2008. On February 23, 2022, Heather Cox Richardson shared the following:

> Today, Ukraine president Volodymyr Zelensky made a passionate plea to the people of Russia to avoid war. He gave the speech in Russian, his own primary language, and, reminding Russians of their shared border and history, told them to "listen to the voice of reason": Ukrainians want peace. "You've been told I'm going to bomb Donbass," he said. "Bomb what? The Donetsk stadium where the locals and I cheered for our team at Euro 2012? The bar where we drank when they lost? Luhansk, where my best friend's mom lives?" Zelensky tried to make the human cost of this conflict clear. ...
>
> Tonight in America, but early Thursday in Ukraine, Russian president Vladimir Putin launched a "special military operation," claiming, quite transparently falsely, that he needed to defend the people in the "new republics" within Ukraine that he recognized Monday from "persecution and genocide by the Kyiv regime." (Richardson, *Letters from an American*, February 23, 2022)

Putin, it seems, is out to re-create the Stalinist methods of repressing political opponents and now has started an unwinnable imperialistic war causing massive carnage and a huge loss of life, not only to soldiers, but consistently to innocent civilians. The estimates of death and destruction are tremendous and constantly increasing after the first year of the war.

Ukraine has fought valiantly now for close to two years. The death tolls have been staggering for both Ukrainian and Russian soldiers. As the war has gone on, the more brutal and grotesque these crimes have become, particularly to Ukrainian civilians. Russians have begun to attack the electrical systems of Ukraine, which dramatically impacts light and heat for innocent people in the freezing time of winter. The war rages on, causing financial havoc, and both grain and energy shortages throughout the world. Here in the United States, gas prices have skyrocketed.

Speaking with a group of young Russian entrepreneurs in Moscow on June 10, 2022, Putin compared himself to Peter the Great, Russia's modernizing czar and the founder of St. Petersburg, Putin's own birthplace. According to Nathan Hodge from CNN, Putin has often argued that "Ukrainians do not have a legitimate national identity and that their state is, essentially, a puppet of the West. In other words, he thinks Ukrainians have no agency and are a subject people." By summoning Peter the Great, he makes it quite clear that his goals are catalyzed by a drive toward historical destiny.

Most of us can't help but feel the forces of evil at work when Putin likens Ukrainian leaders to Nazis. Heather Cox Richardson lays out the facts—the reality:

> He also promised to provide for the "denazification" of Ukraine, a harking back to the period after World War II when Nazis and those who had worked with them were purged from society. Putin has repeatedly referred to Ukrainian leaders as Nazis, a charge Zelensky, who is of Jewish heritage, has pleaded with Russians to reject, citing Ukraine's losses in World War II and his own grandfather's service in that war. Putin's chilling word here suggests that he intends to purge from Ukraine all those who worked with the Zelensky government. (Richardson, *Letters from an American*, February 23, 2022)

Ukrainian President Volodymyr Zelensky has often compared his country's struggle against Russia to World War II, a fight between a free people and a barbaric invader. So very tragically, he is right. In early 2023, an agreement was reached by the US President (Joe Biden) and the German Chancellor (Olaf Scholz) to send their most formidable battle tanks to President Zelensky in Ukraine. While NATO countries have given Ukraine significant military aid, it has not been enough to drive Russian forces out of Ukraine, including the Crimea.

It was not until four Nordic countries (all geographically close to Russia)—Finland, Sweden, Denmark, and Norway—put tremendous pressure on NATO to take the next step, before the next offensive from Russia (O'Brien 2023). It is a stretch of the imagination to think of Putin stopping the destruction unless his own country's citizens turn against his policies, or he dies in the process. This type of Hitleresque dictator does not stop his rampage using peaceful means.

As of this writing Ukraine continues to fight, although the Republican House has been blocking funding to Ukraine. If Trump wins the presidency, in '24 we imagine his favoring of Putin will cause some kind of land agreement in the name of peace in Russia's favor, and an end to support for Ukraine's democratic independence.

Normalization of Hatred and Violence

Our country, on the whole and over time, has become sensitized to the racist symbol of the Confederate flag. However, the flag that was raised at the attempted coup by armed insurgents on January 6th was the Confederate flag, the symbol of the south that empowered slavery. Although never the official flag of the Confederacy, it served as the battle flag since the period of secession and has since been claimed by white supremacists and mythologized by others as a symbol of racism. Why the Confederate flag yet again?

Heather Cox Richardson has tracked the beginning of the shift back to "confederacy" thinking to a moment in July 1964, in California, when Barry Goldwater took the stage after Republicans had nominated him as the Republican candidate for president and delivered the line "Extremism in the defense of liberty is no vice … and moderation in the pursuit of justice is no virtue." Goldwater lost to the incumbent, Lyndon B. Johnson, by a landslide in 1965; however, his words "became a rallying cry for a rising generation of conservatives. His nomination marked the resurrection of an old political movement adopted by a modern political party. They called themselves 'Movement Conservatives.' A century before, their predecessors had called themselves 'Confederates'" (Richardson 2020, xiii).

Her next comments bring me back to today:

> "Movement Conservatives" maintained that the liberal consensus was destroying America. People should be free to operate however they wished, without interference from government bureaucrats and regulations. They hated that the government had taken on popular projects since the 1930s. Highways, dams, power plants, schools, hospitals, social welfare legislation cost tax dollars. This, they warned, amounted to a redistribution of wealth from hardworking white men to the poor, often to poor people of color. Such a dangerous trend toward an activist government, had to be stopped before it destroyed the liberty on which America was based. (Richardson 2020, xiv)

This perfectly describes the current 2022 stance of the Republican Party. But instead of coming from the Western cowboy tradition, like Andrew Jackson or Barry Goldwater did, this era's frontman is a very different and flamboyant real estate developer and TV "strongman," who became famous in America for a show called *The Apprentice*, where his popularity for budding ruthlessness was centered on the phrase "You're Fired!" when a budding apprentice didn't cut it.

Trump reflects the drivenness of our time—around status and image, material accumulation, the need for obscene wealth, and for power. He invokes the rage and hate simmering beneath the surface, about having to take on three jobs to survive, against any real or perceived blocks to get ahead, the collapse of manufacturing jobs, the middle class being unable to keep up. With his constant refrain of "fake news" about anything he disagrees with, he has focused suspicion and paranoia on the press. Fox News has become its own country of news, serving the conservative, and the radical right. We're in a perfect storm to ignite the extreme polarization this country knew during the secessionist time prior to the Civil War.

What is also true at such a charged time is the extraordinary tension between fundamental Christian religion and its patriarchal treatment of women, generally, as well as women of color, specifically. On one side, religious thought determines what a woman chooses to do with her own body in terms of her age, family management, socioeconomic reality, and in the worst of situations, sexual assault, rape, or incest. On the other, we have a range of people in this country with a variety of spiritual, religious, and secular views who have different viewpoints about when life begins and who becomes most important—the woman or the fetus—when a major dilemma presents itself for a pregnant woman.

When Etty Hillesum was growing up, she would have fallen under the Reform umbrella of Judaism. Although her family was not religious, her father was quite intellectually interested, modern, and perhaps religion offered him ethical guidance. In reproductive matters, that meant life starts at birth. Etty's spirituality was modern, and she held neither to dogmas nor rituals, yet she deeply honored the "God within," this sense of "reposing" in herself, as well as a deep love for the "other." As mentioned, this presence offered her an inner freedom in the worst of times, and this freedom allowed her to make decisions based on love. The deeply conservative or fundamental Christians hold tightly to an absolutism rather than a pluralism of thought, because they believe that society is morally corrupt, and the answer lies in the imposition of their beliefs onto others. These religious beliefs have begun to impact political decisions. How did we get here?

Donald Trump nominated three right-wing activist judges to the Supreme Court. Now there are six conservative justices to the three liberal justices. Not only has this Supreme Court come down firmly on the side of prayer in school settings (Kennedy v. Bremerton School District), but they also overturned, on June 24, 2022, Roe v. Wade, a Constitutional protection that generally protected a pregnant woman's right to privacy and to choose to have an abortion. Rather than bestowing a right, this ruling has taken away a fundamental right that affects women, LGBTQIA+ individuals, people of color, Jews and Muslims, or any indigenous groups of people with varying sets of beliefs.

Although the Supreme Court's decision to overturn Roe v. Wade was written by Justice Samuel Alito, a concurring opinion in favor of the conservative majority by Justice Clarence Thomas raises fears that rulings protecting contraception and same-sex marriage could also be overruled in the near term. Clarence Thomas, one of two African Americans on the current court, and possibly the furthest to the right, is a controversial figure. During his confirmation hearings for the Supreme Court, Anita Hill made history in 1991 when she testified before Congress about the sexual harassment she alleged she had experienced while she was an aide to Clarence Thomas, who had been her supervisor at the Equal Employment Opportunity Commission. In spite of this, he was confirmed by the US Senate 52–48.

Further, even with the advent of the MeToo movement, when it seemed that women were finally being heard, Brett Kavanaugh was sworn in as a Supreme Court justice, in spite of being accused of sexually assaulting Christine Blasey Ford when they were teenagers. This overturning of Roe v. Wade feels like a regression to an earlier time in history, where there was no separation between religion and state, when patriarchy and privilege reigned supreme, and fear and religious righteousness predominated. Already this decision has caused untold harm, with a ten-year-old rape victim being forced to cross state lines to receive an abortion and women being denied life-saving treatment, because doctors are afraid.

Etty herself self-induced an abortion in 1941 with "12 quinine pills" and "blood-curdling instruments" a month or so after her missed period, at another tumultuous time in history. She was not yet fully aware that her life was so threatened by the debacle to come, but because the mental illness in her family was so severe, she felt she must act on getting pregnant. In her time, there was no such thing as modern contraception. Emma Garman, as recently as 2019, shared Etty Hillesum's experience in *The Paris Review* for a monthly column called "Feminize Your Canon":

> Hillesum hankers after neither marriage nor children. Mainly, she's wary of passing on her family's "taint": the psychiatric problems suffered by her two younger brothers. Like their sister, both are geniuses. Mischa, a classical pianist, did a public performance of Beethoven at age six, and Jaap is a doctor who discovered new vitamins while still in his teens. But Jaap's severe depression has led to several stays in hospital, and Mischa has schizophrenia. Hillesum writes: "When Mischa got so confused and had to be carried off to an institution by force and I was witness to the whole horror of it, I swore to myself then that no such unhappy human being would ever spring from my womb." On realizing she's pregnant, she doesn't hesitate to self-abort by taking twenty quinine pills, supplemented "with hot water and blood-curdling instruments." She tells the embryo: "I shall bar your admission to life, and truly you should have no complaints." (Garman 2019; ET 2002, 168)

Women of child-bearing age suffered extensively at Auschwitz because of eugenics along with the scientific research that was done in this new "laboratory" of women who had heinous acts performed upon them daily. Dr. Carl Clauberg came to Auschwitz in December 1942, just nine months before Etty's arrival, and had part of Block No. 10 in the original camp put at his disposal. Looking for a "cheap and efficient" method to sterilize women, he injected acid liquids to their uterus without anesthetics. Thousands of Jewish and Gypsy women were subjected to this treatment. They were sterilized by the injections, producing horrible pain, inflamed ovaries, bursting spasms in the stomach, and bleeding. The injections seriously damaged the ovaries of the victims, which were then removed and sent to Berlin to be studied. Clauberg's experiments killed some of his subjects, and others were put to death so that autopsies could be performed.

We do not know what Etty Hillesum experienced at Auschwitz, whether she succumbed from illness, or had to face reproductive experimentation, because it is likely she could have been grouped with other childless women. She could have been gassed along with her parents, who were immediately sent to the gas chambers. According to Judith Koelemiejer's research at Auschwitz, there was a 75 percent chance that she was integrated into Auschwitz-Birkenau for some period of time.

We don't even know whether she even made it to November 30, 1943, which is the date the Red Cross had printed on her death certificate. It seems likely that, given her age, she would have survived for at least a time. Most in the Hillesum research world guess she may have survived for a month or possibly six weeks because of her fragile health (Koelemiejer 2022, 451–456).

Clauberg's former victims, survivors of Block 10, who have been interviewed over the years emphasize that it was Himmler who personally brought Carl Clauberg the means he was asking for. In 2017, I traveled to Auschwitz with a group led by Armand Volkas a drama therapist, professor, and founder of Playback theater in Berkeley, California. We stayed at a retreat center nearby for more than five days. We took a variety of tours and had time on our own to process our experiences with a variety of drama therapy methods.

It was an overwhelming, challenging, and profound experience. The Germans bombed all but one of the crematoria and "faux shower" gas chambers, as they knew these would be seen as crimes against humanity. Those structures, left in the same form as when they were bombed, were a chilling reminder of the factory-like nature of the killing machines, and the Nazis' continuation of the "big lie" to the very end.

We visited Block 10 purposely because Armand's mother was a victim of the sterilization experiments. It was a miracle that Armand's mother survived Auschwitz and Block 10, because one of the women physicians, a political prisoner herself, aiding Clauberg, did not actually do the acid experiments on her group of eight to ten women. That physician paid for it with her life. Armand's mother and father actually met at Auschwitz, if that can even be imagined.

A good friend of mine, as well as colleague at CIIS, Theresa Silow, of German descent, was also visiting her family of origin in Germany that summer and joined me at Auschwitz at the end of my retreat there, and for a tour of parts of Poland. We performed a ritual for Etty Hillesum at one of the ponds there where all the ashes of murdered Jews were distributed. We could look across the pond to the preliminary processing center where prisoners were registered, shaved, tattooed, and showered for real. I can only speculate, but likely, Etty had been there. Historians estimate that around 1.1 million people perished in Auschwitz during the less than five years of its existence. The vast majority, at Auschwitz-Birkenau, around one million people, were Jews. We honored Etty and the million plus we did not know by name.

Antisemitism, Past and Present

In Dara Horn's provocative book, *People Love Dead Jews: Reports from a Haunted Present*, she makes a searing point in her investigation of modern-day antisemitism, when she says, "people love dead Jews, living Jews not so much" (2021, 1). She begins the book with the "world's second favorite dead Jew," Anne Frank. The world's affection for her is well known, given her wisdom, innocence, goodness, and hope. The line most often quoted from Frank's diary are her famous words, "In spite of everything, that people are good at heart" (Frank 1952). Horn gives us something to think about when she says:

> These words are inspiring by which we mean they flatter us. They make us feel forgiven for those lapses of civilization that allow for piles of murdered girls—and if those words came from a murdered girl, well, then we must be absolved, because they must be true. That gift of grace and absolution from a murdered Jew (exactly that lies at the heart of Christianity) is what millions of people are so eager to find in Frank's hiding place in her writings, in her "legacy." It is far more gratifying to believe that an innocent dead girl has offered us grace than to recognize the obvious: Frank wrote about people being "truly good at heart" before meeting people who weren't. Three weeks after writing those words, she met people who weren't. (Horn 2021, 9)

As I move to more current examples of twenty-first-century antisemitism, with its unconscious biases, disguises, and blatant insensitivities, all the way to murderous hate crimes, I will begin with an example from 1989.

The Auschwitz Cross Controversy

In 1989, to commemorate Polish prisoners killed by the Nazis in 1941, a 26-foot-high cross was erected on the grounds of the base camp at Auschwitz behind Block 11. Ever since, this cross has been the source of controversy and criticism from many Jewish groups. Ten years later, in 1998, hundreds of smaller crosses were placed around it, triggering condemnation from both Catholic and Jewish leadership, and pressuring the Polish government to order their removal. In 1998, however, Pope John Paul II was on the other side of that controversy, after the beatification of Edith Stein, a German Jewish philosopher who had converted from Judaism to Catholicism, and was killed at Auschwitz on August 9, 1942.

The Auschwitz Cross still stands today, and the conversation over what role the Church should play at the Auschwitz Memorial is a prominent example of a long and oftentimes contentious dialogue about Catholic-Jewish relations in the country of Poland and beyond. The central issue in the controversy over the Auschwitz

Cross was articulated by the author and former Catholic priest James Carroll, author of many books. In particular, he garnered fame and praise from Jewish leadership for his book *Constantine's Sword: The Church and the Jews*, published in 2002. James Carroll, who visited Auschwitz in 1995, shared his views in a podcast from the United States Holocaust Memorial Museum:

> The last thing I expected to find when I went to Auschwitz was looming at the wall, Polish Catholics had erected a very large, stout wooden cross. And I associate myself with Jews who find it offensive. For Auschwitz to be in even the most implicit of ways claimed by Christians is something deeply wrong.

What are Christians saying to Jews? asks Carroll, Are Christians saying that the deaths of those who were murdered at Auschwitz are somehow redemptive, in the way that Christians believe that the death of Jesus was redemptive? If that's what's being said, it is insensitive and offensive. There is no redeeming the deaths of people who died in Auschwitz—period. There must be no diminishment of the horror, no overlay of Christian piety on it he stresses. These actions become our cultural and religious complexes, when any of us project what we consider as "right" onto a group different from our own is an important part of our collective shadow work.

The question has to be asked, "what is being said about Jesus Christ by having this symbol that we associate with him, this device on which he died? What is it saying? Jesus of Nazareth at Auschwitz? If he had been at Auschwitz, he would have been there simply as a Jew, one of the Jews who died with a number instead of a name" (Greene 2008).

And what would Etty have thought if she had lived and seen that cross at some point in her later life? Of course, we will never know, as she would have had her own experience at Auschwitz to contend with. But what we do know is what she wrote about when she crossed paths with Edith Stein, the saint at the center of the Auschwitz Cross controversy. At Westerbork in early August 1942, when Etty describes the arrival at camp of a group of Jewish Catholics, among them Edith Stein, now known as St. Teresa Benedicta of the Cross, after the beatification by John Paul II previously mentioned. The group arrived at Westerbork on August 2, 1942.

> There was a remarkable day when the Jewish Catholics or Catholic Jews—whichever you want to call them—arrived, nuns and priests wearing the yellow star on their habits. I remember two young novices, twins with identical beautiful, dark ghetto faces and serene, childish eyes peering out from under their skullcaps. They said with mild surprise that they had been fetched at half past four from morning mass, and that they had eaten red cabbage in Amersfoort.
>
> There was a priest, still fairly young, who had not left his monastery for fifteen years. He was out in the "world" for the first time, and I stood next to him for a while, following his eyes as they wandered peacefully around the barracks where the newcomers were being received. ...

I looked at the priest who was now back in the world again. "And what do you think of the world now?" I asked. But his gaze remained unwavering and friendly above the brown habit, as if everything he saw was known, familiar from long ago. That same evening, a man later told me, he saw some priests walking one behind the other in the dusk between two dark barracks. They were saying their rosaries as imperturbably as if they had just finished vespers at the monastery. And isn't it true that one can pray anywhere, in a wooden barracks just as well as in a stone monastery, or indeed, anywhere on this earth where God, in these troubled times, feels like casting his likeness? (ET 2002, 585)

Antisemitism, White Supremacy, and Hate Rallies

The Anti-Defamation League's Oren Segal says it's really not important which side of the political aisle is instigating the anti-Jewish movement:

> Anti-Semitism is not a right-wing issue. It's not a left-wing issue. It's a problem in and of itself. It's unique, in that no matter where someone is on the ideological spectrum, they're able to manipulate anti-Semitic tropes to make a point if they want to. Sometimes it's not necessarily coming from an extreme left or an extreme right, but it's just an anti-Semite. (Matza 2021)

Marjorie Taylor Greene, a representative from Georgia in the US House, has likened coronavirus-masking measures to the Holocaust, which killed six million Jews. Public figures like this have played a major role in the general rise of antisemitism in the US. "Any public official, whether left or right, who is normalizing tropes commonly used by anti-Semites, that's a problem," Segal adds. And I can say that Greene received very little reprimand or consequences of any kind for making that statement; in fact, she easily won the 2022 Republican primary in her district. "Normalizing anti-Semitism, I think, has more to do with the rise in anti-Semitism than people might think" (Matza 2021).

Consider the images, chants, and violence at the "Unite the Right" rally in Charlottesville, Virginia on August 12, 2017. It was a tense moment for the Jewish faculty at the graduate school where I teach, to hear the chant: "Jews will not replace us" in a rally of far-right groups, including the alt-right, neo-Confederates, neo-fascists, white nationalists, neo-Nazis, Klansmen, and various right-wing militias, along with various anti-Islamic and antisemitic groups. The organizers' stated goals included the unification of the American white nationalist movement and opposition to the proposed removal of the statue of Robert E. Lee from Charlottesville's former Lee Park. Clashes broke out between the marchers and counter-protesters. At one point a car drove through a crowd of counter-protesters, killing one and injuring more than a dozen.

US President Donald Trump's remarks about Charlottesville generated an avalanche of negative responses. Trump initially criticized the "display of hatred, bigotry, and violence on many sides." When he tried to defend his statement, he also noted "very fine people on both sides," (Trump in continual newscasts during the Charlottesville event) which was widely criticized as implying a moral equivalence between the white supremacist protesters and the counter-protesters.

The October 7, 2023 Attacks on Israel

On October 7, 2023, Hamas militants broke out of the Gaza Strip, where close to two million Palestinians live and are unable to leave because of the restrictions Israel has imposed for many decades. It can be called nothing short of a massacre by Hamas, as the final tally of dead in Israel is 1,400, and 240 civilians taken as hostages. The US called leaders of France, Germany, Italy, and the United Kingdom to issue a rare joint statement expressing "our steadfast and united support to the State of Israel, and our unequivocal condemnation of Hamas and its appalling acts of terrorism." There is never justification for terrorism. The world has watched in horror as Hamas terrorists massacred families in their homes, slaughtered over 200 young people enjoying a music festival at the end of the Jewish high holy days. It is important to remember that it is the supreme mission of Hamas to rid the world of Jews.

Retaliatory strikes on Gaza have killed approximately 30,000 (Al Jazeera, As of February, 2024) and displaced millions. The Biden administration has been stressing diplomacy to stop the crisis from spreading. The US has stressed it would "stand for it [Israel] today, tomorrow and every day … in word and in deed." But, Blinken, Secretary of State, added that Israel "has the right—indeed it has the obligation—to defend itself," and "it needs to do it in a way that affirms the shared values that we have for human life and human dignity, taking every possible precaution to avoid harming civilians" (A. Blinken; quoted by Richardson, *Letters from an American*, November 15, 2023).

And, overall, says Heather Cox Richardson, "the conflict is steeped deeply in centuries of history, both in the region and elsewhere as well as in longstanding cultural antisemitism which has been on the rise and which is now, in some countries, at a fever pitch" (Richardson, *Letters from an American*, 2023). Clearly, this is true regarding antisemitism in the United States toward Jews, as well as Trump the candidate wanting another ban on Muslims entering America (Richardson, *Letters from an American*, October 7, 9, 15, 2023).

Nicholas Kristof of the *New York Times* has tried to educate readers about the myth that there is complete "right" on one side and "wrong" on the other—which will always echo Etty Hillesum's deepest sentiments. He gets at the truth of each side by first, recognizing that Israel is a sovereign state and that "Israelis deserve their country, forged by refugees in the shadow of the Holocaust," and they have built a creative and sophisticated high-tech economy that "largely empowers women and respects gay people, while giving Palestinians more rights that most Arab nations give their citizens." Israel's legal system, and its free press models a civil society for the region (Kristof 2023).

In the same vein, Kristof goes on to say that "the Palestinians deserve a country, freedom and dignity"—and they shouldn't be expected to bear collective punishment. They too, have their "coming into being" stories, their myths of heroism, and connection to the land. Palestine has not had consistent representation, and Hamas has not been good at governance, and in this October 7th massacre, it has reverted to what it knows best—terrorism—to preserve its identity. Kristof maintains "that the best way to ensure its security may be not to defer Palestinian aspirations, but to honor them with a two-state solution. This is not just a concession to Arabs but a pragmatic acknowledgement of Israel's own interest—and the world's" (Kristoff 2023).

The Collective Need for Shadow Work

The authoritarians considered so far are exemplified by their inability to admit error or shame, and they stand in direct opposition to Etty Hillesum's openness and willingness to have compassion for the "other." Trump reflects the personality type that personifies hatred and, in extreme cases, evil. According to M. Scott Peck, "The imposition of one's will upon others by overt or covert coercion is done in order to avoid spiritual growth" (Peck 1983, 74). In other words, evil turns outward and attacks others, instead of the far more difficult process of turning inward to engage one's own shadow material and, over time, to transform it.

Jungian psychology is very much concerned with shadow work, both of the individual, which Etty was drawn to, and also of the group psyche. Thomas Singer, a Jewish American Jungian analyst and psychiatrist, along with Samuel Kimbles, an African American Jungian analyst and psychologist, have developed a working model of the theory of cultural complexes (2004). This theory is helpful in understanding the psychological elements of Trumpism and today's changing societal norms.

Since the 2016 election, Americans have had to come to terms with the ways in which Trump reflected our materially oriented, achievement-focused, white, primarily Christian, privileged, individualistic, and self-absorbed culture. He both mirrored it and greatly amplified it. Trump seems to have tapped into the severely wounded unconscious of a portion of the American electorate, who felt left behind by the technological revolution propelling both coasts forward. This has caused structural changes in our social mores, including, but not limited to, affirmative action and the legalization of same-sex marriage. Many have been able to openly articulate their pent-up frustration and anger under the cover of a Trump presidency that neither discouraged racism nor homophobia (Singer 2017).

Contrast this with Etty's reflections in her diaries on polarization and hate. In many instances, she writes of not adopting binaries, or getting caught in the cultural complexes of her time, whether German and Jew, or Jewish and Christian. In the matter of the Germans, she does not condemn them as a people, aware that there are good Germans and that German mothers grieve just as much for the loss of their sons:

> It is the problem of our age: hatred of Germans poisons everyone's mind. "Let the bastards drown, the lot of them"—such sentiments have become part and

parcel of our daily speech and sometimes make one feel that life these days has grown impossible. Until suddenly, a few weeks ago, I had a liberating thought that surfaced in me like a hesitant, tender young blade of grass thrusting its way through a wilderness of weeds: if there were only one decent German, then he should be cherished despite that whole barbaric gang, and because of that one decent German it is wrong to pour hatred over an entire people. (ET 2002, 18)

In a similar way, I believe Etty Hillesum would have compassion for Donald Trump, given his childhood trauma that has a great deal to do with his self-absorption and winning at all costs. Trump's niece, Mary Trump, has written a great deal about this in her book: *Too Much and Never enough; How My Family Created the World's Most Dangerous Man* (2020). Failure was not allowed by his father, Fred Trump, the original real estate mogul that gave Donald the financial backing to get him started. Mary Trump's father, on the other hand, died an alcoholic because of the family's abuse, and because of Fred's own failings in not stepping into the family's pattern—he was routinely mocked. Mary says: "the only reason Donald escaped the same fate is that his personality served his father's purpose" (Trump 2020, 30)

She goes on to say that is what sociopaths do, "they co-opt others to use them toward their own ends—ruthlessly and efficiently, with no tolerance for dissent or resistance" (Trump 2020, 41, 43). Etty Hillesum knew this personality disorder up close with Commandant Gemmeker. Still, while she saw through him, and could see the tremendous damage unleashed by such a person, she refused to hate as it would cause the harm and frozenness to herself. She chose instead to give to those who most needed her energy.

She was also realistic about what was going on in Europe. A big part of her inner work was to root out first the "rottenness" in herself:

That doesn't mean you have to be halfhearted; on the contrary, you must make a stand, wax indignant at times, try to get to the bottom of things. But indiscriminate hatred is the worst thing there is. It is a sickness of the soul. Hatred does not lie in my nature. If things were to come to such a pass that I began to hate people, then I would know that my soul was sick and I should have to look for a cure as quickly as possible. I used to believe that my inner conflicts were due to a particular cause, but that was much too superficial an explanation. I thought that they simply reflected a clash between my primitive instinct as a Jew threatened with destruction and my acquired, rationalist and socialist belief that no nation is an undifferentiated mob.

But it goes deeper than that. Socialism lets in hatred against everything that is not socialist through the back door. That is crudely put, but I know what I mean. (ET 2002, 18, 19)

Etty expresses here what is true for us today: radical progressives on the left have become just as prone to hatred in the form of cancel culture, which does not accept anything with a differing viewpoint. Etty, along with Spier and Jung, believed that all we could do for deep change is to work on ourselves; over time that is what can make a true difference collectively.

Jung was not exempt from the need for shadow work himself, especially when it came to antisemitism. Both Etty Hillesum and her analyst, Julius Spier, would have recognized both Jung's shadow and his owning of it, when he was asked after World War II about his seemingly antisemitic behavior during the war. Rabbi Leo Baeck met with Jung in 1946 and asked him about it. Jung said, "Well, I slipped up" (Jaffé, 1971, 97–98). Jung was referring to 1933, when he took on the role as president of the General Medical Society, an international body based in Germany. This organization was dominated by Germans at that time and was gradually coming under Nazi control. Further, Jung's writings of the period focused on questions of differing racial psychologies and contained generalizations about Jewish culture and psychology. These writings seemed then, and later, misguidedly published. "For they could easily be understood as supporting Nazi racial ideology" (A. Samuels, vii in Foreward of Jung 1946/1989, CW 10 & 16).

It became a time of seeing the shadow of Jung's reputation. *Shadow* is the appropriate word to use, for it is one of the key terms in analytical psychology. The shadow, wrote Jung, is "*the thing the person has no wish to be and yet, in some way, is*" (1946/1989, CW 10 & 16, para. 470). In other words there is a negative side to every personality, Jung's included. It is the belief of Andrew Samuels, who wrote the foreword to Jung's *Essays On Contemporary Events: The Psychology of Nazism* (1946/1989, CW 10 & 16) that this slim volume, published in German right after the war in 1946, represents a part of Jung's own attempt to integrate his personal shadow.

It was Jung's belief, as expressed in this essay, that Germany had fallen prey to a mass psychology, or today, what we could call a collective complex:

> Hitler was an exponent of a new order, and that was the real reason that practically every German fell for him. The Germans wanted order, but they made the fatal mistake of choosing the principal victim of disorder and unchecked greed for their leader. [...] He symbolized something in every individual. He was the most prodigious personification of all human inferiorities. He was an utterly incapable, unadapted, irresponsible, psychopathic personality, full of empty, infantile fantasies, but cursed with the keen intuition of a rat or a guttersnipe. He represented the shadow, the inferior part of everybody's personality in an overwhelming degree, and this was another reason they fell for him. (Jung 1946/1989, CW 10, 6)

And we could also imagine that Jung, at the very beginning, fell for him as well, possibly as that archetypal symbol of a "new order." After the war, Jung recognized this figure as "Wotan," the Supreme God from Germanic mythology—an ancient god of "storm and frenzy" that awakened a new, dark activity in a civilized country. "Wotan is a restless warrior who creates unrest and stirs up strife, now here, now there, and works magic . . . The Hitler movement literally brought the whole of Germany to its feet, from five year olds to veterans" (Jung 1946/1989, CW 10, 11).

We are in such a time in the United States, a time of either the painstaking work of the reconstruction of democracy or burning it all down for a more regressive model of "safety," meaning exclusion, patriarchy, and autocratic rule. Trump's speech on Veteran's Day of 2023 speaks to how far he has come from "authoritarian bluster," as Tom Nichols put it in *The Atlantic Daily*, to "recognizable fascism":

> We will drive out the globalists, we will cast out the communists, Marxists, fascists and the radical left thugs that live like vermin within the confines of our country, that lie and steal and cheat on elections and will do anything possible … legally or illegally, to destroy America and to destroy the American Dream. (Nichols, *The Atlantic Daily Newsletter*, November 16, 2023).

The Contours of our Time: "Malignant Normality"

Trump's charged rhetoric has created a space for the public airing of racist, homophobic, and misogynist rhetoric, creating what Robert J. Lifton (1986) referred to as "malignant normality," in his study of the German medical profession's role in the Final Solution. Lifton notes that normality is fluid and "can be much affected by the political and military currents of a particular era" (Lifton 2017, xv). The Trump presidency will probably be considered one of the most chaotic periods in modern times, perhaps a time of "malignant normality," that have shaped the contours of our time since at least 2014.

This period has included heightened polarization between Democratic and Republican agendas enhanced by the rhetoric of both the far left and the far right, social media gone awry, and rampant disinformation. Trump's own predilection for "ruling" by Twitter was a deep aberration of leadership to Democrats and a source of ongoing irritation even to Republicans. The last year of his presidency was marked by the beginning of a worldwide pandemic that took more than six million lives (over a million in the US).

Here in the United States even mask-wearing and vaccines became politicized, causing more fear and confusion and deepening anger that turned to rage in significant swaths of the population. It's quite apt that the famous journalist Bob Woodward wrote three books about Trump and his administration called *Fear* (2018), *Rage* (2020), and *Peril* (2021) in that order, with the last book being about the transition of power after Joe Biden won the presidency in 2020. Donald Trump seemed to have a visceral awareness of how to pick up on and then fuel the fear that leads to resentment and ultimately hatred.

For African Americans, the climb toward justice has been a centuries-long agonizing climb. They have held the place in this country that the Jews held in Europe, with both being deeply affected by the archaic pseudo-science of eugenics. Eugenics is an inaccurate theory to arrange reproduction to increase the occurrence of desirable human traits. It is linked to historical and present-day forms of discrimination, racism, ableism, and colonialism. It has persisted in policies and beliefs around the world, including the United States. Police brutality toward African Americans has existed as long as racism has existed, and is malignantly normal in the United States.

Elizabeth Alexander, a poet who spoke at Barack Obama's first Inauguration, wrote a book entitled *The Trayvon Generation*, based on *The New Yorker* article of the same title, and she says it best:

> This one was shot in his grandmother's yard. (Stephon Clark) This one was carrying a bag of Skittles. (Trayvon Martin) This one was playing with a toy gun in front of a gazebo. (Tamir Rice) Black girl in bright bikini. Black boy holding cell phone. This one danced like a marionette as he was shot down in a Chicago intersection. The words, the names: Trayvon, Laquan, bikini, gazebo, loosies, Skittles, two seconds, I can't breathe (Eric Garner), traffic stop, dashboard cam, sixteen times. His dead body lay in the street in the August heat for four hours. (Laquan MacDonald) He was jogging, was hunted down, cornered by a pickup truck, and shot three times. One of the men who murdered him (Ahmaud Arbury) leaned over his dead body and was heard to say, "Fucking nigger." I can't breathe, again. Eight minutes and forty-six seconds of a knee and full weight on his neck. "I can't breathe" and, then, "Mama!" George Floyd cried. George Floyd cried, "Mama ... I'm through!"
>
> His mother had been dead for two years when George Floyd called out for her as he was being lynched. Lynching is defined as a killing committed by a mob. I call the four police officers who arrested him a mob. (Alexander 2022)

White institutionalized racism has been in place since the institution of slavery in this country, systematically affecting everything from housing, voting, health, finance, police violence, and general opportunities for African Americans as well as for Latin Americans. On May 25, 2020, George Floyd, a black man, was murdered in Minneapolis by a white police officer, Derek Chauvin. Three other officers just stood by to watch the murder of Floyd, who had been arrested on suspicion of using a counterfeit $20 bill.

His murder, and the murder of other Black Americans during the height of the pandemic, led to waves of widespread protests. Conviction, it seems, was only possible because a young woman, Darnella Frazier, filmed this act of murder on her iPhone. Because of this act of bearing witness—this positive use of technology—exposing the truth on camera for the country to see, Chauvin was brought to justice with a murder conviction of twenty-two-and-a-half years. Many felt the sentence to be too light, and sadly, a conviction for a police officer on duty is a rare conviction.

Conclusion: An Uncertain Future

History repeats itself. Again and again. I am reminded of Etty's encounter with her professor on the day the Dutch capitulated to the Nazis. She asked him about democracy and if it would survive:

It was that afternoon when people thought of nothing but getting away to England, and I asked, "Do you think it makes sense to escape?" And he said, "The young have to stay put." And I, "Do you think democracy can win?" And he, "It's bound to win, but it's going to cost us several generations." (ET 2002, 52; italics added)

Here we are, several generations later, and we are still faced with this question, "Do you think democracy can win?" The answer, at this point, is unknown. What we do know is that Donald Trump has been indicted four different times, as of September 2023, and one of those indictments is for the attempted overturning of the 2020 election that culminated in the January 6th attack on the US Capitol by a mob of his supporters. As of this moment, Trump is polling over 50 percent ahead of those Republicans running against him and is slightly ahead of Biden in swing states. Here we are, several generations later, and we are still faced with this question, "Do you think democracy can win?" The answer, at this point, is unknown.

Chapter Six

The Significance of Etty Hillesum's Writings in our Time and all Time

> Living fully, outwardly and inwardly, not to ignore external reality for the sake of the inner life, or the reverse—that's quite a task
>
> Etty Hillesum (ET 2002, 53)

This exploration of Etty Hillesum's exceptional poiesis—the activity in which she brought something into being that did not exist before, discovering the ground of her being—allowed her to live into and chronicle her own experience for almost three years during an unprecedented scientifically and psychologically calculated genocide of Jewish people in Eastern and Western Europe. Her diaries record her inner and outer journey of individuation, self-realization, and resistance in her time. For our time, her diary gives us, significantly, a historical, contemporary, psychological, and transcendent perspective of her radical evolution of consciousness, offering a glimpse of both beautiful and desperate historical "moments" in her time, that are, indeed, timeless. As I look through the lens of her "sacred resistance," a model of resistance that is meaningful today, I see not only those essential aspects of life and spirit that Etty discusses in her daily journal, but also a larger perspective of history, of its changing pendulum. She exposes the hatred and fears and reactions of her times as well as the losses and threats to existence, which are perceived and real in all times. Both her lived and written guidance has reinforced for me the essential aspects of potential that dwell within us in all times and where she turned for guidance and solace that still have meaning for our time: analytical psychology, including individuation, self-realization, and the union of opposites; truth and courage; spirituality, along with aspects of several religious traditions; beauty and poetry and writing as artistry and activism; the face of the "other"; and hope.

Analytical Psychology

Etty and Julius Spier were very influenced by Jung, and although *The Undiscovered Self* (1957) had not been published during the 1940s, another book that they read together, *Modern Man in Search of a Soul*, which was published in 1933, had similar themes and introduced them both to Jung's work. After Jung lived through two world wars, he felt that civilization's future depended on our ability as individuals to resist the collective forces of society. Only by gaining an awareness and understanding glimpses of one's unconscious mind and true inner nature—this "undiscovered self"—can we as individuals integrate the self-knowledge that is antithetical to ideological fanaticism. But this requires that we face our own primal capacity for evil, hatred, or that which is unilluminated, which Jung calls the shadow in every individual. Such an important reminder shortly after the war—when the recurrent question was "How could this have happened in a civilized and erudite country such as Germany?"—is critical today—when the question has become "How can the overt signs of the demise of democracy and being created equally, along with the unalienable rights of life and liberty, happen here in the land of the birth of democracy?" America as the so-called city on the hill from Jesus's Sermon on the Mount in the New Testament is a declaration of American exceptionalism. The noble experiment of a working democracy refers to the United States as a "beacon of hope" for the world. Idealism seems to pervade both sides of the opposites of good and evil as the shadow is that which is unilluminated. We can't see our own capacity for evil if it is projected out to the "other," and in the same way, we can't see our own goodness if it is projected out to the "other"—a lifetime of work is required, even when one is conscious of it!

Jung, Rilke, God, and Experience

Etty had a deep interest in Jung as well as the writer and poet Rilke, her mainstay "philosophers" throughout the period of writing her journal, somehow a fruitful and love-filled time even when the clouds of danger grew steadily heavier and darker:

> Slowly but surely I have been soaking Rilke up these last few months: The man, his work, and his life. And that is probably the only right way with literature, with study, with people or with anything else: to let it all soak in, to let it all mature slowly inside you until it has become a part of yourself.
>
> That too, is a growing process. And in between, emotions and sensations that strike you like lightening. But still the most important thing is the organic process of growing. (ET 2002, 315)

And then she would turn to Jung. "I keep being drawn towards Jung," said Etty in 1941 (ET 2002, 56). Early in her diary she wrote that she "hope[d] to make some progress with Jung this evening." Later that same evening she quoted Jung at length, including this:

> A high regard for the unconscious psyche as a source of knowledge is not nearly such an illusion as our Western rationalism likes to suppose. We are inclined to assume that in the last resort all knowledge comes from without. Yet today we know for certain that the unconscious has contents which would make an immeasurable increase of knowledge if they could only be made conscious. (Jung 1933, 185; quoted in ET 2002, 213)

And by knowledge, Etty includes the knowing of her own experience:

> As Jung says and I repeat "god" too is a theory in the most literal sense … an image which the limited human mind creates in order to express an unfathomable and ineffable experience. *The experience alone is real,* not to be disputed; but the image can be soiled or broken to pieces. (Jung, *The Importance of Psychology for the Present*, Lecture delivered in Rhineland in February 1933, included in his *Gesammelte Werke*; quoted in ET 2002, 227, 557; italics added)

Etty copied this quote, or parts of it, from Jung three different times in her diary as I have said previously.

Nadia Neri, author and Jungian analyst, was interested in what came before in Jung's conference and quote on the god-image, as it exposes an extraordinary harmony between them:

> But I speak not to nations, only to the individual few, for whom it goes without saying that cultural values do not drop down like manna from heaven, but are created by the hands of individuals. If things go wrong in the world, this is because something is wrong with the individual, because something is wrong with me. Therefore, if I am sensible, I shall put myself right first. For this I need—because outside authority no longer means anything to me—a knowledge of the innermost foundations of my being, in order that I may base myself firmly on the eternal facts of the human psyche. (Jung 1934/1968, CW 10, para. 329; quoted in Neri 2010, 423)

Etty had extensive dialogues with "God" as a relational experience, an essence that she wanted to protect within herself, the place she "reposes in." I am struck by her modernity, her eclectic integration of parts of religious traditions through reading and sharing with others—her own Jewish tradition that grounds her in existential reality and in Christianity around love as spoken by the "Jew Paul" (in his book of Corinthians in the New Testament) as well as tributaries of Buddhism in such practices as meditation and the notion of impermanence. But experience alone seems most real to her—"like some 'elemental force'" as she walks along the barbed wire. Yes, she was modern and assimilated, perhaps more mystical in her style, not unlike Jung who became far more mystical in his work after his own descent into the unconscious, which seemed like a mild psychosis, in service of the Self. Jung, after his break with Freud in 1913, began to write and paint his experiences in a huge red book from 1915–1930, which was published in our time (2009) as *The Red Book*.

As long as there will be humans on this planet, and we do not know how long that will be given the dire circumstances of the climate crises, there will be the continual clashing of power complexes, both individual and cultural, an "us versus them" at many levels, and the ultimate deconstruction or breakdown that comes from it. At the same time, there will be efforts toward compassion and love and continual healing, toward reconstruction or wholeness. Etty Hillesum's short life is a snapshot of a life determined to find meaning, beauty, and love in such an extreme time of rage, evil, and destruction. In fact, she resisted this demonic power to strip her of her worth, her birthright.

Genocide

There have been many genocides since the Holocaust and the crimes related to it such as the Nazis' crimes against the Polish and Russian people; the Cambodian, Rwandan, Armenian, Darfurian, Croatian, Yazidi, Uyghur, and Rohingya genocides all occurred after the Holocaust, in the twentieth and twenty-first centuries. The Genocide Convention of 1948 defines genocide as follows: "The intent to destroy, in whole or in part, a national, racial, or religious group" (Maritz 2012).

In the majority of genocides, the destruction of said groups, often begins with a steady and slow scapegoating of the group that evolves into a propaganda-fueled hysteria and hatred toward an ethnic or religious group. This hatred holds the unconscious, split-off projections of the majority, which could include envy, fear of being taken over, and deep paranoia or conspiracy theories carrying all kinds of terrifying, imaginative horrors allegedly perpetrated by the group under attack.

In the United States the election prior to 2020, that of 2016, held the conspiracy theory fantasies that Hillary Clinton, running for president against Donald Trump, was involved in a sexual trafficking and child sex ring. The hallmark of a conspiracy theory seems to be the more unfathomable the more believable. The 2016 conspiracy regarding Hillary Clinton was the beginning of QAnon, a conspiracy theory and political movement that believes Donald Trump is waging a secret war against a group of cannibalistic pedophiles within Hollywood, the Democratic Party, and the Deep State. There is an explicit as well as implicit message that "we" are "pure" and "you" intend to taint us to be impure, base, and evil. This idea is as old as civilization itself and played out on American soil in its most depraved way over several hundred years with the institution of slavery. And this sense of American white privilege and superiority, regardless of the level of material privilege, continues to this very day, in spite of the vast efforts by so many beginning with the civil rights movement in the 1950s and 1960s and the Black Lives Matter movement of the present day.

The Work

Etty Hillesum's work was to cultivate herself—and it remains as the significance of her work for our time. Not only was Etty Hillesum an individuated, creative, and astute thinker, but she also acted out of tremendous compassion and caring for others in their suffering. She became an activist both in the choice that she made to be at Westerbork, to be with her tribe, as well as in the use of her craft, her art, to continue to let others know the truth of what was happening there at the very time it was happening. The "work" that *Tikkun Olam* refers to is this very work of repairing the world with compassionate and spiritual acts.

I would add to this, as Etty did, the individuation "work" on herself as can be seen in the plethora of quotes from her diary in Chapter Three, as she grew in awareness, as her consciousness evolved, preparing her for what was to come. Long before the advent of psychoanalysis, "work" on oneself was limited; it was in fact up to the grace of the gods or prayer to a god, often more superstitious and without much understanding of the workings of the mind and emotions, about projection or conditioning or prejudice leading to institutionalized forms of racism, antisemitism, and hatred. Etty and Spier's moment in history, however, was *during* the birth of psychoanalysis and the advent of the construct of the unconscious. Rick Tarnas, author of *The Passion of the Western Mind*, says, so succinctly, that "Freud brought the fundamental recognition that the apparent reality of the objective world was being unconsciously determined by the condition of the subject" (Tarnas 1993, 422). Again, Etty quotes Spier who quotes Jung:

> What you expect from others, that is, from the outside, you carry unconsciously in you. Instead of expecting it from the outside, you ought to develop it in yourself, by making it conscious. The soul is not time bound, it is eternal. You must immerse yourself in it, raise it into consciousness, that is, develop yourselves. (ET 2002, 17)

So one of the primary ways in which Etty can help us deal with "our time" is for us to become conscious, to "develop ourselves," as she urges us throughout her writing. We must recognize in real time when the mind becomes sticky and then the thoughts become obsessive, compulsive, anxious, reactive, angry, impulsive, or rageful and create patterns within us that are difficult to break and easy to act out—unless one stops to experience, or gets help to sort through and experienc, the underlying feelings that are at the root of the driven emotions. She did that; her own inner witness could catch her and say, essentially, something like, "Oh Etty, Etty, don't let yourself down like that!" Whether we call it her critic or her shadow, it is her human vulnerability arising. She then rejoins her head to her heart in that inner workshop of hers as she sought to be the "thinking heart of the barracks," to stay present to herself and to the others in the most frightening of times:

> That's why it seemed such a great danger to me when all around one could hear, "We don't want to think, we don't want to feel, it's best to shut your eyes to all this misery."
> As if suffering, in whatever form and however it may come to us—were not also part of human existence. (Smelik, Brandt, and Coetsier 2010, xvi)

Etty felt accountable toward her victimized fellow Jews in two ways: "she had to give them empathic attention as well as ethical guidance." In other words, they must be comforted, but also must be invited to "make a connection to their own moral responsibility" (Brenner 2010 243). What does she mean by that in such a time of terror? Was it even possible? As Etty saw it, her task not only as a writer, but also as a budding psychological teacher, was to bring about her fellow Jews' fundamental change in their self-perception *as they faced destruction*. She would like to "*catch and stop them in their flight from themselves and then take them by the hand and lead them back to their own sources*" (ET 2002, 399; italics added).

This, to me, is what she gives back, whenever possible, this redeeming of her Westerbork imprisoned community's self-worth and dignity. It is one of her "actions" arising from her own self-realization. "It is not morbid individualism to work on oneself," she claimed (ET 2002, 434). On the contrary, it was absolutely essential to rub out the feelings of giving up, of self-hatred and debasement as well as the responses of hate and violence toward the "other" (Brenner 2010, 243). And from her cultivated artistry of writing, she sent perfectly crafted letters to others who sent them to the Dutch Resistance revealing the truth of the horrors of the transports every week to "the east" and the tragedy and pathos and the malignantly narcissistic leadership of Camp Westerbork ... in short, what was really going on at Westerbork transit camp. She did become a chronicler, not just of events, but also of the depth of her awareness of how she and others were experiencing those events.

Etty helps us in our times to see the importance of working on ourselves, standing for our truth, our dignity, and our awareness of our own sense of moral responsibility, when we are tempted to live in denial or become reactive, regressed, and fearful about the *right now* in the United States and the whole of the world community. We could also utilize the strength of will that Etty Hillesum possessed. Brenner reminds us that the Nazis' mission was to turn Jews into "self-hating creatures, to deprive them of the ability to reason." They knew, and Etty seemed to know, that once the prisoners or victims let go of their moral values, for the sake of staying alive, "they were bound to lose their humanity" (Brenner 2010, 245). We get a glimpse into Etty's will and indignant determination when she says:

> They can harass us, they can rob us of our material goods, of our freedom of movement, but we ourselves forfeit our greatest assets by our misguided compliance. By our feelings of being persecuted, humiliated, and oppressed. By our own hatred ... [The] greatest *injury* is one that we inflict upon ourselves. (ET 2008, 435)

Even though Westerbork was a continual challenge for Etty with the misery of those heading toward the transports, her arrival at Auschwitz had to be an utter shock to her system, one which could not be anticipated, could not even be imagined—such carnage—as her will and her love was of a higher order of development than the primal murderous hate of the Nazis. This hate was at its highest pitch in 1943 and 1944 when concentration camps became scientific factories— killing and torturing machines followed by the burning of those bodies as quickly as possible because they were running out of space to even bury them. At this point the war itself was being lost, but not Hitler's deadly primary purpose of exterminating Jewish human beings.

According to Rachel Brenner (2010), "Indeed, her real life took place in her inner space, where she worked very hard to actualize her artistic potential," and I would add the healing potential of her own true nature. It is through the exploration of our own souls that we might transform "our hatred for our fellow human beings of whatever race" into love. Etty was not a naive dreamer; she realized that asking for love at this time was "perhaps asking too much" and yet she did not retract her position. Love, she asserted, was "the only solution to the horrible situation of the world" (ET 2002, 435; Brenner 2010, 245).

Like Etty, most Americans have become much more politically informed during these last seven years as, for many of us, it has been absolutely necessary given the growing tumult in our country. The personal, at times such as ours, becomes political. The question is how to live an examined life without falling into unconscious despair or indiscriminate rage and bitter resentment and recognizing what arises that can become an action—growing compassion toward others, taking a stand that is unique to each one of us, building toward a reconstituted, caring society, a democratic future for all who come after us. All of this is about hospicing old forms of regressive colonial schemas of modernity on their staggering last legs. This is only one scenario, of course; we could also continue on the path that began with Trump and his covey of politicians and supporters in the next election. The midterms have happened in January '23 and while most of us thought, and the poll numbers at the time supported the notion, that the Republicans would win the midterms by a vast number, they did not. Sixty-four seats were available in the House to win yet the Republicans won the House by only nine seats and the *Democrats kept the Senate*, unimaginable in a year of a Democratic presidency, strengthened by winning Georgia in a contentious election. One reason that Democrats led in the midterms was due to many losses for Trump's endorsed candidates. Trump, it is important to add, although under multiple investigations, is still considered the leading candidate for the Republican nomination in 2024. Many others eventually filed to run against him, but none have confronted him, afraid to lose his faithful constituency. Ronald DeSantis and Nikki Haley are tied for second place and several have already dropped out, as Trump is far ahead. Haley and DeSantis eventually dropped out and Trump is the presumptive nominee of the Republicans.

The Union of Opposites

Etty's narrative reveals an emerging truth arising from her ongoing struggle between the opposing forces of light and dark. As Jung would say, "waxing and waning make one curve," and that wholeness is the result (1934/1969, CW 8, para. 800). What is remarkable about Etty is that she approached both the human and the divine aspects of human existence in the same way, with a sense of moving toward wholeness. She did not reduce experience to one or the other. She did not collapse the tension. A good example of this and her honest inner experience of resisting becoming a prisoner of ideologies or beliefs or individual, religious, or cultural complexes becomes clear in this passage:

> On Friday evening a discussion between S. and L. and W. L. about Christ and the Jews:
> Two philosophies, sharply defined, brilliantly defended, rounded off; defended with passion and vigor. But I can't help feeling that every hotly championed philosophy hides a little lie. That it must fall short of "the truth." And yet I myself will have to find a philosophy to live by, a fenced-in space of my own, violently seized and passionately defended. But wouldn't that be giving life short change? (ET 2002, 159)

"Having the courage to be oneself," she says, "a fine phrase, so often applied to mere trifles" (ET 2002, 158). Yet, in so many ways, she actually lives into the dynamic or tension of the union of opposites. Jung's transcendent function (the third position) is that which mediates the opposites, where there is not just a synthesizing of the attitudes or positions but a new psychological attitude emerging. As Jung says:

> Psychologically, we can see this process at work in the development of a lasting and relatively unchanging attitude. After violent oscillations at the beginning the opposites equalize one another, and gradually a new attitude develops, the final stability of which is the greater in proportion to the magnitude of the initial differences. *The greater the tension between the pairs of opposites, the greater will be the energy that comes from them ... [and] the less chance is there of subsequent disturbances which might arise from friction with material not previously constellated.* (Jung 1928/1969, CW 8, para. 49; italics added)

Etty's transformation had much to do with this tension, at first with the opposites she faced with her parents, Julius Spier, gender-oriented opposites, commitments to two very different partners, the opposites of age, and so on. And then, the radical, clashing larger forces of Jew and German, Christian and Jew, of the Nazis and everyone else, of power and powerlessness, of hate and love. I see in Etty a steady ability to contain these opposites and her ability to bear witness without losing her soul.

So often readers of Etty, depending on which psychological, political, or religious tradition they are conditioned by, are drawn to ask whether she was a saint or a flawed human being like the rest of us, or, at the extreme, a martyr. The answer, it seems, in keeping with this section, does not seem to fit into one or the other position, but comes, instead, from a more integral perspective where she did not reduce experience to one or the other. We have to realize that in Etty's case at the deepest level, she not only held the opposites, she had to bear the raging opposites of her time. From that perspective something entirely new was birthed: she was simultaneously a transcendent figure in her development of equanimity as well as a grounded, open, physically fragile, vulnerable woman with a strong will and huge heart.

Truth and Courage

Here we stand at another time in history in which the threat of ideology over truth is at hand, and it seems we must be diligent to discover what is truthful as news factcheckers must be on hyperdrive to constantly keep track of what is so glibly promised or threatened or fabricated. Do these threats and promises have a basis in fact, whatever that might be? Did the stories reported really happen as claimed? Well, it depends on your source. This age of information and disinformation is meant to keep us confused, to sow chaos, as some would like to keep us in a closed system—"safe" and without choice. A. H. Almaas has a quote that speaks about the love of the truth, which I believe Etty enacted:

> When you really get into seeing things about yourself, it's very painful. You don't like it, but something in you says, "I want to feel this and get to the bottom of it." Nobody's making you do it. So in that moment what is compelling you? It is somehow your desire to see the truth. Seeing the truth seems to be fulfilling in itself, it seems to bring some subtle pleasure and joy. So you want to see it regardless of how difficult it is. It is no longer a question of what is a true statement or perception or not. There is something more, and something more subtle. It is, in a sense, that the truth wants itself. And that's what is called the love of the truth for its own sake. In that situation, it is such a deep compelling desire that when it is there, nothing can stand in its way—not fear, not pain. (Almaas 2000, 96–97)

I often presented this quote from Almaas at the end of the first clinical class that I taught in a master's of counseling program at the California Institute of Integral Studies. The class was taught from an integral point of view, where spiritual, psychological, and cultural perspectives are intertwined. I consistently gave a presentation on Etty Hillesum on the last day of the semester's class, to integrate the semester's work on cultural context and liberation psychology, object relations and the relational work of intersubjectivity, and self-realization and the more boundless dimension of human experience. Some only know about the Holocaust superficially—unless they are Jewish. Although it is hugely difficult for my students, or any of us, to imagine living in such a shattering time with equanimity and purpose, they did understand "the love of the truth" as they have just moved through an intense semester of questioning all of their preconceived assumptions and fears of facing the truth—about themselves and their own conditioning through a variety of courses, including human development, their attachment style, their own repeating patterns, their parents' repeating patterns that influence them so regularly, for better or worse, and some new position that opens from this work of wanting the truth regardless of how painful or shameful it feels … it becomes freeing.

In an age of disinformation, and for large swaths of American citizens, truth, as we know it, is losing much of its value. Almaas refers here to a subjective truth that while potentially fear-inducing or painful, acts as a spark to growth. Beginning a diary unleashed in Etty an in-the-moment truth-telling; her process of "unwinding her inner ball of twine," her lived experience from 1941 to 1943, became her destiny. In regard to the question, "Was she a mystic?" Jan Geurt Gaarlandt, the editor of the first abridged publication of Etty's original diary, *Etty Hillesum: An Interrupted Life and Letters from Westerbork* (1981), provides his perspective:

> *Her mysticism led her not into solitary contemplation, but squarely back into the world of action.* Her vision had nothing to do with escape or self-deception, and everything to do with a hard-won, steady, and whole perception of reality. *Her God, in a sense resided in her own capacity to see the truth, to bear it, and find consolation in it.* (Etty 1996, xv; italics added)

Above all, in her times, Etty personifies the values of bravery and courage, which we have held as ideals since Socrates, who taught that courage is more than conquering the "other" and that an unexamined life is not worth living: "courage is the ability to conquer not others but yourself, the courage to be wise and just, the courage to cultivate your soul" (Riemen 2018, 14). Etty knew this profoundly. She lived this kind of courage; her choice to volunteer at Westerbork, to live the suffering of her people, and resist the dehumanization of the Nazis by finding beauty and meaning in life are pure articulations of the Socratic notion of courage.

Spirituality

The abridged form of Etty Hillesum's diaries and letters were first published in Dutch in 1981. The event to premiere this new book, which included significant portions of her diary, called *An Interrupted Life*, was held at the Amsterdam Concertgebouw (Concert House) in October 1981. Many of Etty's friends, still living at the time, attended, and a video of their reactions to the published diary was made during that same time. Their unanimous reaction, after seeing an English subtitled version of this video, was that they were unaware of the depth of Etty's spirituality, how serious she was about it. They knew her as committed, smart, gifted, fun, and engaged with them, but not as deeply spiritual.

Today, her writing has been embraced across the religious and spiritual spectrum; her universal messages of love of humanity and God, and acceptance of suffering, have particularly resonated with Christian and Buddhist readers. Yet, says Hila Ratzabi, Hillesum has yet to fully enter the canon of modern Jewish literature, and deserves to be counted among the great Jewish philosophers, thinkers, and mystics of the modern era. Especially during particularly difficult moments, Hillesum's writing can serve as a source of spiritual resilience for the Jewish community. In Etty's own words, she wanted to be "a balm for all wounds" (Ratzabi n.d.).

From the day I picked up the first abridged copy of *An Interrupted Life*, until now, almost twenty-five years later, I still concur with Geurt Gaarlandt, editor of that first volume, when he says in the Introduction:

> Her religiosity is totally unconventional. In Holland today Christians and Jews are claiming Etty as typically Christian or typically Jewish—an unprofitable discussion, because Etty chooses her own way. She has her own religious rhythm, not inspired by church or synagogue, or by dogmas, theology, liturgy, or tradition; all these were completely alien to her. She addresses God as she does herself. "When I pray, she writes, "I hold a silly, naive, or deadly serious dialogue with what is deepest inside me, which for the sake of convenience I call "God." (Etty 1996, xv)

In terms of mysticism, as mentioned, Etty fits with the description, if only in style and action. Mystics seem to see through a lens of opposites: darkness and light and longing that is the remedy for the longing, which is reminiscent of the poet and mystic Rumi, when he says "Longing is the core of mystery. Longing itself brings the cure. The only rule is, suffer the pain. Your desires must be disciplined and what you want to happen in time, sacrificed" (2005, 98). This seating in the opposites seems to point beyond itself to a truth that both transcends and includes logic, that is whole, embodied. And Etty was both, keenly intelligent in a left-brain way as well as a deeply embodied sensual being, with an essence of timelessness.

Etty's Jewish, Christian, and Buddhist Influences

Etty Hillesum drew from both ancient traditions of Judaism and Christianity. Alexandra Nagel, a scholar of Julius Spier, his life, relationship with Hillesum, and his work in "reading hands," which was supported by Jung, says that:

> One of the reasons that the writings of the Jewish diarist Etty Hillesum have been widely read and studied in Christian circles is the fact that she drew inspiration from the Bible and Psalms and her private notes bear witness to Biblical-mystical experiences. More than once her last surviving note has been quoted, "The Lord is my high tower," written on a postcard on September 7, 1943, and thrown out of a freight train on its way to Auschwitz. (Nagel 2022)

Hillesum was deeply influenced by her family and relatives, her first Jewish community, by Hebrew School as a child, and by a learned father who was a scholar of the Torah and considered becoming a rabbi. And she remained, as Piet Schrijvers (2018) notes, *archetypically* Jewish in her way of thinking. As Meins G. S. Coetsier and A. D. Smelik both point out "any methodology that does not take into account this 'Jewish question' or 'Jewish givenness' may lead to misinterpretation" (Coetsier 2017, 25). I explore this misinterpretation most explicitly in the Epilogue as it is a brief evolution of the responses to her diary from the beginning of its publication.

Etty also drew from Christianity through Julius Spier who was greatly influenced by their mutual friend, Henny Tideman, as well as other members of the Spier Club. Etty was also deeply moved by the passages on love in 1st Corinthians 13, a book in the New Testament written by the "Jew Paul" (ET 2002, 590–591). Rachel Brenner contests those

> critics [who] see Hillesum's references to the New Testament in the reality of the Holocaust as her Christian rather than Jewish orientation and therefore a sign of her treacherous self-exclusion from her people at a time of need. I would suggest that her reference to Paul as "the Jew Paul" is rather a sign of her stubborn, as she called it, conviction that love was an inclusive force that would erase hatred between religion and races. (Brenner 2010, 247)

Perhaps those critics would find the same complaints with her conversation with Klaas Smelik Sr. about having to do so much work on ourselves that "we shouldn't be thinking of hating our so-called enemies." "But that, that is nothing but Christianity," says Smelik Sr., an atheist. Etty responds, amused by his confusion, "Yes, Christianity, and why ever not?" (ET 2002, 212).

Etty's life and work cannot be reduced to a single or even a dual system of thought, as psychoanalysis (Freud) and archetypal and analytical systems (Jung) were also spiritual streams for Etty, as was the poetry of Rainer Maria Rilke. Spier had his group reading St. Augustine who wrote, in essence, love letters to God in a familiar, informal tone. And, per Denise de Costa (1998), the dialogical nature of her relationship with God is similar to Hasidism, which holds that direct contact with God is possible. She goes on to say:

> Hillesum arrived at her image of God in a way similar to the emergence and history of Hasidism, a Jewish mystical movement that arose amid the persecution and pogroms of eighteenth century Poland. Then, too, people felt the need for a God who was present and for a way to encounter him in daily life, in daily suffering. Hasidism was, in a sense a resistance movement. To oppose destruction, hatred, inhumanity, and murderousness, Hasidism proclaimed the sanctification of daily life, love of people, faith in God, hope and joy. ... As for the debate about how Jewish or Christian Hillesum's work is, I would prefer to transcend this distinction by focusing on her kinship with mysticism (and with Hasidism in particular). This kinship is apparent in another aspect of Hillesum's image of God, in which Jewish mysticism converge: the mother-child dynamics. My exploration of this aspect of Hillesum's spirituality once again highlights her position as a "Jewoman." (de Costa 1998, 233)

What becomes clear over time is that many people from a variety of spiritual traditions, professions, and value-based groups, in addition to Jews and Christians, have connected with Etty Hillesum. Writers, artists, feminists, and LGBTQIA+ individuals as well as Jungian and depth psychologists relate to her also. In the last year and a half or so, I have been moved by the work of a young writer, poet, and Etty Hillesum scholar, Hila Ratzabi, through an Etty Hillesum Zoom group, who has reconsidered Etty from the practice of classical Jewish mystics and Hasidic thinkers, as mentioned by de Costa. Ratzabi shares on the website *My Jewish Learning*:

> Though it is not clear that she studied traditional Jewish literature beyond the Bible, Hillesum's writing often reads like the outpourings of an iconoclastic Hasidic rebbe. For example, a statement like "If … you manage to come to grips with your inner sources, with God, in short, and if only you make certain that your path to God is unblocked … then you can keep renewing yourself at these inner sources and need never again be afraid of wasting your strength" is reminiscent of Rabbi Nachman of Breslov. And like Rabbi Menachem Mendel of Kotzk, who said, "Where is God to be found? In the place where He is given entry," Hillesum's relationship with God was existentialist, rooted in human experience: "When I pray, I never pray for myself. Always for others, or else I hold a silly, naive, or deadly serious dialogue with what is deepest inside me, which for the sake of convenience I call God." Like Martin Buber and Abraham Joshua Heschel Hillesum believed that love of God is essentially intertwined with love of humanity. (Ratzabi 2019)

As Ratzabi considers why Etty has not been accepted as a great Jewish thinker, Hila—herself schooled in the Jewish academic and religious traditions throughout her education—sees Etty in this light:

> Perhaps the reason Hillesum has yet to be canonized as a great Jewish religious thinker is that she was not an observant Jew. Her conception of God, while influenced by many different religious and literary sources, was personal and free of the strictures of religion. She rarely cites Jewish sources, except the Bible. She also preferred to be non-monogamous; she felt her love for humanity was so great that she couldn't love just one person. She also did not have a desire to have children. From a mainstream Jewish perspective this orientation would be considered radical (especially for a woman in the 1940s). (Ratzabi 2019)

As Hila Ratzabi suggests, the following quote of Etty's sounds like the outpouring of a "iconoclastic Jewish Rebbe." Here is an example of Etty's dialogue with God, written on August 18, 1943, approximately three weeks before Etty would be on the transport to Auschwitz on September 7, 1943:

> You have made me so rich, oh God, please let me share out Your beauty with open hands. My life has become an uninterrupted dialogue with You, oh God, one great dialogue. Sometimes when I stand in some corner of the camp, my feet planted on Your earth, my eyes raised toward Your heaven, tears sometimes run down my face, tears of deep emotion and gratitude. At night, too, when I lie in my bed and

rest in You, oh God, tears of gratitude run down my face, and that is my prayer. I have been terribly tired for several days, but that too will pass. Things come and go in a deeper rhythm, and people must be taught to listen; it is the most important thing we have to learn in this life. I am not challenging You, oh God, my life is one great dialogue with You. I may never become the great artist I would really like to be, but I am already secure in You, God. Sometimes I try my hand at turning out small profundities and uncertain short stories, but I always end up with just one single word: God. And that says everything, and there is no need for anything more. And all my creative powers are translated into inner dialogues with You. The beat of my heart has grown deeper, more active, and yet more peaceful, and it is as if I were all the time storing up inner riches. (ET 2002, 640)

This deep listening to God that she called "hearkening" was quite intimate: "And if I say that I hearken, it is really God who hearkens inside me. The most essential and the deepest in me is hearkening unto the most essential and deepest in the other. God to God" (ET 2002, 268–269).

Etty's Jewish friend, and member of the Spier Club, Werner Levie, Liesl's husband, read to her about Maimonides, the "foremost Jewish scholar of all time, and one of the greatest minds in the Western world," who was born circa 1138 in Cordoba Spain. He was a physician and a jurist who influenced all subsequent Jewish law codes (Kraemer 2008, 1). Maimonides said:

What is the way we should love God? We should love Him with an overwhelming and unlimited love, until our soul becomes permanently bound in the love of God like one who is love-sick ... As he commanded us, And thou shalt love the Lord thy God with all thine heart and with all thy soul. (Deuteronomy 6:5; Rich 2008)

In Melanie Rich's book, she quotes Yitzhak Buxbaum who explains this love in the following: "In Hasidism the goal of religious practice is often spoken of as *d'vekut*. Literally, this Hebrew word means 'attachment,' 'cleaving,' or 'clinging,' the full phrase usually being 'cleaving' to the *Shechinah*, the Divine Presence" (Rich 2008, 3). I feel Etty's connection to the *Shechinah* as well as something similar to a psalm, when Etty wrote:

I went to bed early last night, and from my bed I stared out through the large open window. And it was once more as if life with all its mysteries was close to me, as if I could touch it. I had the feeling that I was resting against the naked breast of life, and could feel her gentle and regular heartbeat. I felt safe and protected. And I thought, How strange. It is wartime. There are concentration camps. Small barbarity mounts upon small barbarity. I know how very nervous people are, I know about the mounting human suffering. I know the persecution and oppression and despotism and the impotent fury and the terrible sadism. I know it all and continue to confront every shred of reality that thrusts itself upon me. And yet—at unguarded moments, when left to myself, I suddenly lie against the naked breast of life, and her arms round me are so gentle and so protective, and my own heartbeat is difficult to describe: so slow and so regular and so soft, almost muffled, but so constant, as if it would never stop, and so good and merciful as well. (ET 2002, 386)

In fact, Patrick Woodhouse, long an Etty Hillesum author (*A Life Transformed*) and Hillesum Research Conference participant (also a former Canon of Wells Cathedral in Wells, Somerset, England), feels that Psalm 131 may have been on her mind when she wrote the above entry, as if a weaned child, peaceful and content in the midst of the trauma of war on May 30, 1942 (Woodhouse 2015, 83, 84, 85).

For me, it brings back the Psalm most read in my own childhood, written by David the Shepherd, ultimately, the King of Israel. Although this Psalm is often described as a metaphor for the myriad of dangers that come with sheep herding in Israel, to me, I hear Etty Hillesum in the most treacherous time in her life, still with gratefulness, who would relate as much to "I walk through the valley of the shadow of death" as to "my cup runneth over."

> The Lord is my shepherd; I shall not want.
> He maketh me to lie down in green pastures:
> He leadeth me beside the still waters. He restoreth my soul: he leadeth me in the paths of righteousness for his name's sake.
> Yea, though I walk through the valley of the shadow of death, I will fear no evil: for thou art with me; thy rod and thy staff they comfort me. Thou preparest a table before me in the presence of mine enemies: thou anointest my head with oil; my cup runneth over.
>
> (Psalm 23:4–6, KJV of the Bible)

There is another Christian author, Rowan Williams, the former Archbishop of Canterbury and today, Master of Magdalene College, in Cambridge, England, who deeply relates to Etty Hillesum. He has included her in much of his writing, in his take on Etty's relationship with God. The quote that most touches him regarding that relationship:

> But one thing is becoming increasingly clear to me: to that You cannot help us, that we must help You to help ourselves. And that that is all we can manage these days and also all that really matters: that we safeguard that little piece of You, God, in ourselves ... Alas, there doesn't seem to be much you can do about our circumstances, about our lives. Neither do I hold You responsible. You cannot help us, but we must help You and defend your dwelling place inside us to the last. (ET 2002, 488, 489)

From Williams' perspective, he does read her as not simply identifying "God with a dimension of the self, something contained in the self; yet it is clear that her sense of God is inseparable from something growing "inside." She quotes approvingly Rilke's "Even if we don't want it: God ripens." ... And above all the sense of accumulating something, growing in a way that carries a sense of responsibility. "This is a life in which a task is accepted: a task that can be defined as that of allowing God to 'ripen' in increasingly visible ways" (ET 2002, 258, 259; quoted in Williams 2012, 316)

Jung's Influence on Etty's Spiritual Perspective

Finally, I will return to Jung's significant influence on Etty's spiritual perspective and experience around the god-image. James Hillman, a famous American psychologist, often remembered as charismatic, and a Jungian "renegade," had much to do with reinvigorating Jung's ideas in the United States. "We could reappraise Jung's life-long effort to reinterpret, not so much science, philosophy, society, or even psychiatry, *but theology*" (Hillman 1975, 228). As many in depth psychology would agree, this allows us immediate access to the inner divine, or Self, or soul, or spiritual element through dreams, synchronicities, and moments of reflection, through reading spiritual, religious, historical, poetic, and psychological texts in working on ourselves, rather than through a religious institution. Etty seemed to travel such a road.

Because of the archetypal level of Etty's understanding of Jewish and Christian influences in her writing and being, I feel through her writing a timeless spiritual presence, an immediacy on the page. I also see this in the individuals from different traditions who have been influenced by her, have deepened because of her, and are having an influence on their own traditions because of Etty Hillesum.

Buddhism and Presence

Etty channeled presence. It was through integrating her flaws and vulnerability that she was able to "kneel," "sit," surrender, accept, and touch presence. Reality became radiant to itself within her, in the language of metaphysics, and she became at one with existence itself. Frits Grimmelikhuizen, along with his spouse, Manja Puch, founded the Etty Hillesum Center in Deventer, the Netherlands, in 1996, an important place that I visited it in 2006.[1] Reading Hillesum's writings, Frits was surprised by her interest in Eastern philosophy. If one is so inclined, it is difficult to miss it. Although she only casually refers to Buddhism twice, he shows the correlation between Etty and Eastern philosophy. Early in her diary, she mentions "the Buddhist quarter of an hour," which meant she was about to meditate for fifteen minutes (ET 2002, 120). Toward the end of the diary, "being left in her still corner," she uses the phrase "squatting like a Buddha" (ET 2002, 472). He notes that for a young Jewish woman to be interested in Buddhism in the 1940s was unusual. Unusual indeed, as Frits notes, because Buddhism was hardly known in the Netherlands between 1920 and 1945 (Grimmelikhuizen 2008, 429, 430). I would not doubt, however, that the practice of meditation and the notions of vastness, emptiness, emptying, and spaciousness associated with certain schools of Buddhism were practiced by the Spier group, as both Jung and Rilke were interested in Buddhism. She speaks about meditation, an important practice of Buddhism, and touching the vastness within in this way:

> So let this be the aim of meditation: to turn one's innermost being into a vast empty plain, with none of that treacherous undergrowth to impede the view. So that something of "God" can enter you, and something of "love" too. Not the kind of love-de-luxe that you revel in deliciously for half an hour, taking pride in how sublime you can feel, but the love you can apply to small, everyday things. (ET 2002, 56–57)

From a Buddhist perspective, the "present" moment contains everything, not only a person's immediate perception and emotional experience, but all experience in all times. This gives an ineffable depth to what we conventionally call the present moment, which includes life and also death. It includes joy, and it includes suffering. Etty's focus in her life, in keeping with Zen precepts, was to be present in the fuller sense of what every moment includes. "To be fully present, we have to go considerably beyond ourselves. It requires a powerful identity shift, a different way of situating oneself within experience" (Fischer 2018).

The essence of Buddhist teachings is about living in the present moment and impermanence, and Etty had similar views as she keeps bringing herself back to the present moment when she gets caught in dread, fear, and catastrophizing about the unknown but probable future. As she got closer to the final journey to Westerbork or to Auschwitz, she spoke more and more about death as the time got closer to her own death:

> By "coming to terms with life" I mean: the reality of death has become a definite part of my life; my life has, so to speak, been extended by death, by my looking death in the eye and accepting it, by accepting destruction as part of life and no longer wasting my energies on fear of death or the refusal to acknowledge its inevitability. It sounds paradoxical: by excluding death from our life we cannot live a full life, and by admitting death into our life we enlarge and enrich it. …
>
> That I should die next week, I would still be able to sit at my desk all week and study with perfect equanimity, for I know now that life and death make a meaningful whole. (Etty 1996, 155, 166)

Given our times, with so much death through the COVID-19 pandemic, the continuing horror of mass shootings, climate change, and death from fires, flooding, and earthquakes, it is wise to recognize our impermanence, whether through such trauma, or through natural aging or illness. Death is part of the natural cycle of life. Whatever is born, will die. As Jack Kornfield speaks about in his teachings on death[2]:

As we open to the nature of our mind-body, we see that it is literally—not metaphorically—being born and dying in every moment. Our breath, our heartbeats, our thoughts all arise as pulsing waves. We see that there is nothing solid, nothing static, nothing steady that goes from one year to the next, one month to the next, one moment to the next. The mind-body is a flux of constant creation and dissolution. There is no possibility of holding on, although sometimes we try very hard to do so. When we experience this process of change in a very immediate and intimate way, we realize that who we are is the ever-changing waves, and the fear of death begins to dissolve because we see that there never has been anything solid or permanent. We no longer consider death some kind of failure, apart from the natural order of things. We can be more at peace. (Kornfield 2022)

On October 9, 1942, Etty's pulsing expansiveness takes shape in this way:

Through me course wide rivers and in me rise tall mountains. And beyond the thickets of my agitation and confusion there stretch the wide plains of my peace and surrender. All landscapes are within me. And there is room for everything. The earth is in me, and the sky. And I well know that something like hell can also be in one, though I no longer experience it in myself, but I can still feel it in others with great intensity. And that is as it should be, or else I might grow too complacent. (ET 2002, 546)

Etty found a way to be more at peace. She developed equanimity.

With such little time left before her transport to Auschwitz, and her eventual death, as her own spirituality ripened, she recognized "the beat of her heart has grown deeper, more active and more peaceful." Etty wrote, it seems, to testify to the power of the human spirit, its resilience, and its resistance in facing the darkest of times. In the midst of it, she advocates for:

understanding our age, strange though that may sound. One must understand one's age, just as one understands one's contemporaries, for, after all, it is of their making, it is what it is, and must be understood as such, however perplexing it may be. (ET 2002, 499)

Her diaries and letters teach us that we all contain a deep well of strength that can help us respond to the worst suffering. Spiritual resilience is possible for Etty Hillesum and her community, she feels, when attending to her inner life, recognizing the beauty of the world, and caring for others. She knows what matters most is not about preserving one's life at any cost, but how she preserved it and how she lived it.

Etty was a human being who struggled deeply and then would soar to this joy and spiritual wisdom—from her final callup to Westerbork to her inevitable transport to Auschwitz. After realizing the truth of being ordered to leave Westerbork in the moment, not particularly knowing her destination of Auschwitz, which was then "Poland" or "the east," it was initially shocking and traumatic. Jopie Vleeschhouwer, her Westerbork and Jewish Council friend, tells us about Etty's reaction when she learned she, her parents, and Mischa, her brother, would be on the train to Auschwitz:

> Etty's departure was completely unexpected ... For her it was like a body blow which did in fact strike her down. Within the hour, however, she had recovered and adapted herself to the new situation with admirable speed ... And there she set foot onto "boulevard" the paved piece of road in front of the train tracks, which she had described just fourteen days earlier [in the letter of August 24, which I include in full in Appendix A] in her own incomparable manner. Talking gaily, smiling, a kind word for everyone she met on the way, full of sparkling good humor, perhaps just a touch of sadness, but every inch our Etty, the way you all know her. (ET 2002, 666, 667)

Was she spiritual? Jewish? Christian? Buddhist? Self-Realized? Coming face to face with the Holy, the I AM, did she have the direct experience that Zen calls Satori, or the Hindu experience of Samadhi? Twice born? Or is it because her words that speak to us today have a thread of the collective unconscious's familiarity, essentialness, and timelessness that allow so many of us to relate to Etty Hillesum? We want to continue to be touched, moved, inspired, or even transformed by her words and experiences that carry this very human and yet transcendent reality that can help us move through these times, our times, with a kind of fierce compassion and potential action that comes from our own ripening—ripening toward our own spiritual depth, radical self-acceptance, and unique contribution to a faltering world, country, state, neighborhood, religious institution, or family.

Beauty, Poetry, and Writing as Artistry and Activism

When I reflect on Etty's aesthetics, I think of the beauty of small things. Simply and tenderly described flowers on her desk or the jasmine outside in the midst of a storm and using them as an analogy to suffering and beauty, or S.'s sensual lower lip. There is the use of longing—a usual sign of beauty in writing—as she longs for less chaos and illness, the consistent attention from Spier, her longing to be a poet, her longing to protect God in these agonizing times. And the remedy is in the longing! Her writing is immediate, direct, and in the moment—on the page, filled with vulnerability and openness and self-deprecation at first and then turning into compassion for herself and others. It ranges from descriptions of joy to sorrow to tenderness in a span of sentences. She holds the opposites and seems to emerge with something new. You can feel she is living it as she is writing it. Her longing and plaintive questions turns into patience and recognition of the beauty despite the current monstrous reality:

Why did You not make me a poet, oh God? But perhaps You did, and so I shall wait patiently until the words have grown inside me, the words that proclaim how good and how beautiful it is to live in Your world, oh God, despite everything we human beings do to one another. (ET 2002, 542)

The writing transformed her. It became a practice of caring for herself, a spiritual practice, and a dedication to others. And, inevitably, it did become poetry as she bore witness:

If I have one duty in these times, it is to bear witness. I think I have learned to take it all in, to read life in one long stretch. And in my youthful arrogance I am often sure that I can remember every last thing I see and that I shall be able to relate it all one day. Still, I must try to put it down now. (Etty 1996, 219)

There is no hidden poet in me, just a little piece of God that might grow into poetry. And a camp needs a poet, one who experiences life there, even there, as a bard is able to sing about it. (ET 2002, 542)

One summer evening I sat eating red cabbage at the edge of the yellow lupin field that stretched from our dining hut to the delousing station, and with sudden inspiration I said, "One ought to write a chronicle of Westerbork." An older man to my left—also eating red cabbage—answered: "Yes, but to do that you'd have to be a great poet." He is right, it would take a great poet. Little journalistic pieces won't do. The whole of Europe is gradually being turned into one big prison camp. (ET 2002, 243)

Etty's connection to the "beauty of life" is expressed throughout her writing; her narrative "poetry" is laced with symbols reflective of nature. Her references to the sky, red cabbage, purple or yellow lupins, and fingertips, all human experiences of nature and the body, bring a sense of immediacy to the page:

The sky is full of birds, the purple lupins stand up so regally and peacefully, two little old women have sat down on the box for a chat, the sun is shining on my face—and right before our eyes, mass murder. The whole thing is simply beyond comprehension. (Etty 1996, 602)

Etty's love of beauty begins with existence itself, her developing experience of being at one with her own existence, and her commitment to "get it all down" for the sake of history and truth. She says, with clear-eyed pragmatism as well as despair and also as a record for the outside world (and to us):

The whole of Europe is gradually being turned into one great prison camp. The whole of Europe will undergo this same bitter experience. To simply record the bare facts of families torn apart, of possessions plundered and liberties forfeited, would soon become monotonous. Nor is it possible to pen picturesque accounts of barbed wire and vegetable swill to show outsiders what it's like. Besides,

I wonder how many outsiders will be left if history continues along the paths it has taken. (ET 2002, 581)

What is true is that she used her beautiful, heartbreaking, and most brilliant writing to let the outside world know, a sympathetic part of the outside world, that is, to "see" in her words, the reality of Camp Westerbork:

The letter was sent to Han Wegerif, and he had it typed out in several copies. One was given to Heleen Pimentel, and she contacted David Koning about it—they were both members of the Dutch Resistance. David Koning decided to publish it. (personal communication with Klaas A. D. Smelik)

And it has become a record for the ages (see Appendix A to read the paraphrased letter).

We must stay vigilant in the United States, as the MAGA Republican Party would like to move toward the kind of illiberal authoritarian government of Victor Orbán in Hungary. He spoke in August 2022 in Texas at the Republican CPAC (Conservative Political Action Conference) meeting for the Trump election-denying faithful "denouncing the mixing of European and non-European peoples" (Hardy 2022).

It is chilling.

Levinas and the Face of the Other

Although it is clear that Etty Hillesum was on a psychological and spiritual journey in order to "repose in" and "hearken unto herself" to a place she called God, her primary motivation was for the "other." Emmanuel Levinas, the French-Jewish philosopher who languished in a German POW camp while Etty was struggling at Westerbork, was "convinced that only our responsibility for the 'Other' will free us from our 'awful anonymity and nakedness'" (Coetsier 2014, 338). In contrast to Etty Hillesum, Levinas survived World War II and the "pre-meditated" genocide of the Jews. It is also true that he suffered the rigors and humiliation of imprisonment as a French soldier, and his family, other than his wife and daughter, was murdered. These extreme and wrenching experiences shaped his thinking. "He became convinced that what was demanded of each human person was an 'infinite' willingness to be present to and available for the other's suffering" (Putnam 2008, 68; quoted in Coetsier 2014). Finally, Levinas spoke about moral consciousness. "Ethics for Levinas was 'first philosophy,' only when ethics is the deeply human experience of infinite experience to the other person" (Coetsier 2014, 320).

As I have said throughout, Etty did feel a responsibility to her Jewish tribe. It became her destiny to bear witness as a chronicler as well as her face-to-face commitment to the ones who suffered, as the letter in Appendix A tenderly illustrates. It was also basic to her "relational" personality to serve. "I don't think I would feel happy if I were exempted from what so many others have to suffer" (ET 2002,

487–488). While friends spoke to her about her duty to go into hiding, she seemed to feel that it was her duty to share this experience. She did not feel she could write about this massive rupture in the lives of the Jews unless she had gone through it. It also seems apparent that, at some level, as much as she kept making room for death in her preparation for this next phase, that she had hope. No one could know or even imagine what was truly at Auschwitz-Birkenau at that moment, as the extermination part of the camp had been completed only months before her arrival. Levinas's work helps us to discover the ethics behind the open face-to face encounters (*le visage de l'autre*) between Etty and those she met and loved at Camp Westerbork.

We face the same urgency today, as in all times, to discover our own fear and distrust of the "other," our own biases. It is also ours to get in touch with our own responsibility to serve. This is the core of sacred teachings of all religions in all times, to love one another and to look out for the poor and traumatized. It remains the deepest work of our human condition for all time. And in this time, in particular, where trust has been extinguished through lies and hatred about the "other," whether about immigration, or racism, or banned LGBTQIA+ reading material in schools, or legal decisions that take choice away from women for their own reproductive health, or our environment, we have responsibility to act in whatever way we can.

Hope

Etty expresses hope in her final letter to the outside world and to her Jewish community scattered all over the world:

> That no words and images are adequate to describe nights like these. But still, I must try to convey something of it to you. One always has the feeling here of being the ears and eyes of a piece of Jewish history, but there is also the need sometimes to be a still, small voice. We must keep one another in touch with everything that happens in the various outposts of this world, each one contributing his own little piece of stone to the great mosaic that will take shape once this war is over. (ET 2002, 687)

Finally, there is also a prayer, sent by Judie Wexler, a friend and former provost and president of the California Institute of Integral Studies (CIIS) and currently president of the Congregation Sherith Israel in San Francisco. This is her favorite prayer and I imagine Etty would appreciate it greatly, given its archetypal images and its hope for community:

> Standing on the parted shores of history
> we still believe what we were taught
> before ever we stood at Sinai's foot;

that wherever we go, it is eternally Egypt
that there is a better place, a promised land;
that the winding way to that promise
passes through wilderness.

That there is no way to get from here to there
except by joining hands, marching
together.

Prayer during shabbat evening service (Frishman 2007, 15)

Let us in this currently democratic country on the edge, be the eyes and ears and discerning witnesses for the "other" and everything that happens in the outposts of this country and this world. And may we each contribute our own piece of stone, no matter the size, to the great mosaic that will take shape here in in this land and throughout the world. Clearly, the world is constantly crumbling and being rebuilt, and we will be the ones at any given time in history who will continue to fashion, see through, and then set the needed pieces in place.

Our hope is that in our times of societal devolution, or closed systems, we can tap into the beauty, love of the "other," truth, presence, action, and "reposing in ourselves," that Etty Hillesum knew so deeply within herself in her times. May we have the courage and guidance in our time so we, too, can live into these essential elements of the soul's journey of all time.

Notes

1 The Etty Hillesum Center is situated in the former first synagogue and Jewish school in the center of the medieval city of Deventer. It is a place open for everybody, with exhibitions, lectures, concerts, and information about Etty Hillesum, her family, and the lost Jewish life of Deventer. Special programs are developed for children about peace education and related subjects. See the website: www.ettyhillesumcentrum.nl.
2 Jack Kornfield trained as a Buddhist monk in the monasteries of Thailand, India, and Burma. He has taught Vipassana from the Theravada meditation tradition internationally since 1974 and is one of the key teachers to introduce Buddhist mindfulness practice to the West.

Epilogue
The Evolution of the Public's View of Etty Hillesum's Diary since the 1980s

Much like Etty's Hillesum's own evolution of consciousness, there has been an evolution in readers' responses to Etty's diary ever since it was first published as an abridged shorter version in 1981. Klaas Smelik Sr. had tried to get Etty's diary published in the years after World War II, but it was not possible. During that time period, there was no interest in it. His son, Klaas A. D. Smelik, took on the mantle of continuing the quest to get the diary published. Thirty years later Klaas gave the notebooks to the Dutch publisher Jan Geurt Gaarlandt to read. Gaarlandt was struck by Etty's voice:

> Klaas A. D. Smelik had delivered the material to me. And asked if I would read it. He said there was no hurry, but a certain feeling of obligation made me pick up the typed text. … I read the first sentence. Hey! And then another one. I sat down and read on, and I was fascinated. An extraordinary bundle of papers: the yellowed pages with their sentences sometimes sliding down the page in black outlined letters, old, stained, and stale. *It captivated me.* (Gaarlandt 2010, 365)

I learned what the Dutch public first thought when Etty's abridged diary was published posthumously through dialogues and presentations at my first Etty Hillesum Research Congress in 2014. One of the first articles written about the abridged diary was by a famous journalist in Holland. On December 11, 1981, the popular Dutch newspaper *NRC Handelsblad* carried several articles about the new diary publication, including one by J. H. Heldring, a popular columnist in Amsterdam at that time. His article was titled "The Saint of the Museumplein." In it, he called Etty Hillesum a saint. Klaas A. D. Smelik comments:

> Though canonization seems to be the prerogative of a pope rather than a journalist, his call struck a chord with what some readers of *An Interrupted Life* felt and still feel. Some Christians even seem to want to posthumously incorporate Etty Hillesum into the Church. (Smelik 2018, 40)

Smelik realized there should be a complete scholarly edition of the texts. The complete diary, with extensive historical notes and descriptions of people Etty mentions as well as her letters from Westerbork, was published in 1986 in Dutch and translated into English in 2002. My first trip to Amsterdam to "walk in Etty's footsteps" was in 2006, when, as I described in Chapter One, I met a Holocaust survivor, Jetteke Frijda, who lived across the street from Julius Spier's flat. I went back in 2007 to interview Frijda who, synchronistically, was Margot Frank's best friend and knew of Etty Hillesum and Julius Spier. Little did I know, I was witnessing a kind of reawakening to Etty Hillesum in Europe.

It was right around this time that I became aware of the Etty Hillesum Research Center (EHOC), which was founded by Klaas A. D. Smelik at Ghent University in Belgium. In 2015, the center moved to Middelburg, the Netherlands, Etty Hillesum's birthplace.

Klaas noticed and wrote that many Etty Hillesum authors tended to follow the Hillesum research:

> introduced by J. H. Heldring in his sanctification of Etty Hillesum as a martyr, seeing the nadir of this approach in the 1996 American book *Martyrs,* in which Etty Hillesum who wanted to share the fate of her Jewish people, is boosted as one of the Christian martyrs of the twentieth century. (Bergmann 1996; quoted in Smelik 2018, 46)

We owe gratitude to Klaas and many others, such as Meins Coetsier, for the early development of EHOC. Klaas and the EHOC staff have put on at least three major Etty Hillesum Congresses, in 2008, 2014, and 2018. I have had the privilege of presenting at two of them. At the congresses, authors from around the world, whether historians or theologians or psychologists or artists or from spiritual or religious traditions, all find a place to share their work and the inspiration they draw from Etty Hillesum's diary. Interest in her work keeps growing as the world changes and becomes more authoritarian. I see her as a guide to the raging polarities of our times. And yet this history of our responses to her writings since the 1980s helps us to see the stages along the spiral that loop back and forth depending upon the crises we face and the massive changes in our communities.

During the first forty to fifty years following the Holocaust, there was criticism of Hillesum's openness to Christianity and inferences to Buddhism as well as her hopeful and teleologically oriented thinking, warm and positive personality, and the choices she made about not going into hiding, and for some, joining the Jewish Council. Along the same vein, around 2005 when I began my own research and preparation for my journey to walk in Etty's footsteps in Holland, I came across a book called *Admitting the Holocaust: Collected Essays* by Lawrence Langer (1995). Langer was one of the first to gather information from diaries and memoirs written during or after the death camp experience at Auschwitz.

This was the era of the death of God for many Jewish religious individuals and any kind of teleological explanation or interpretation of the Holocaust was not tolerated. Understandably, nothing could be said that might convey anything other than nihilism and destruction. I remember going to an event at Boston University in my mid-twenties, around 1975 or 1976, with Elie Wiesel as the speaker. As we sat in our seats in a full, dark auditorium, only gradually did the light on the stage above Wiesel's head come on as he appeared out of the darkness and another five to eight minutes went by before he said, something like, "This is the only way to communicate about the Holocaust, by saying nothing in darkness." Eventually he spoke about his own experience and his book *Night*, which he had written fifteen years previously, as he wanted to tell the truth of his experience and did not want the media to make up stories.

Given this backdrop and my study of Etty Hillesum up to that point, I was surprised by such strong criticism of her, by Langer, in particular. Yet, I needed to consider his passionate lens. He lived in Newton Centre, in Massachusetts, the same town I had come from to California, a predominantly Jewish borough of Newton. He made it clear that the Holocaust was not a divine event; it was a secular one. He argued that Jesus was "tried" and Job was "tested" by divine permission or will, but the Jews were not (Langer 1995, 27). He felt that that "the spiritual resonance of words like 'justice,' 'injustice,' 'suffering,' 'martyrdom,' and 'heroism' depend[s] on our freedom to appeal to an external authority or established tradition for their validation" (27). And with great anguish he shared his deep conviction:

> The irreducibly terrible point of Auschwitz and other killing centers was precisely that in those places the natural completion of human life was violently, viciously, ruthlessly, and senselessly aborted. If, for example, martyrdom seeks to establish a voluntary link between how one lives and how one dies, involuntary suffocation in gas chambers rudely severs that potential connection. By the mass, anonymous manner of the executions, the killers deliberately sought to defeat martyrdom. Everything the Nazis did conspired to deprive victims of their dignity: they lied, mocked, humiliated, starved, beat, refused to differentiate by eliminating names and substituting numbers—truly, the murder of the word as well as the man and woman. They rejoiced in the sundering of the death bound from a language of appeal, as well as from each other. Afterward, however, catastrophe is what we make of it, not what it was, and if we try to restore to mute atrocity a voice of appeal in order to make it bearable to ourselves—*who can condemn this honest search for a suffering more resilient than it appears at first to have been?* (Langer 1995, 27–28; italics added)

This rings true to me. Yet, his view of Etty Hillesum does not, in that he seems to condemn her, or perhaps he doesn't see her fully because of her personality or his conviction she had converted to Christianity, or because she had not reached Auschwitz yet and her words and effort to stay conscious in the midst of this debacle seemed naive. He says about Etty, based on her diary:

> Her entries were passionately concerned with herself as a woman, an erotic being, a spiritual creature, and—what I think is the unexpressed secret of the diaries—a latent convert to Christianity. ... Although she does not repudiate her

Jewish identity, neither does she particularly acknowledge it. It lies uneasily on her shoulders like a burden she might wish to discard. Indeed, her *Diaries* are virtually unique among victim or survivor memoirs in dissociating her Jewish heritage and her fate and searching for sources of strength and consolation in a Christian vocabulary. ... Our hindsight, however, darkens her efforts, to reconcile hope with annihilation, making her buoyancy seem pathetic and exasperating rather than praiseworthy. (Langer 1995, 70)

I was struck by Langer's negative tone about Etty even though he poses this question *"who can condemn this honest search for a suffering more resilient than it appears at first to have been?"* (Langer 1995, 28; italics added). As I reflected on this quote by Langer, I focused on two things: first, his comment about Etty, "while not repudiating her Jewish identity, she did not acknowledge it"—in fact, he felt that she disassociated her identity from her fate. On the first matter of not acknowledging her Jewish identity, it seems important to remember that Etty was an assimilated and secular Jew and that it was the Nazis who forced her and entire family back to their Jewish origins in such a time of absolute destruction of a People. By not going into hiding, however, she was actually acting on a strong feeling, of a sense of responsibility to her fellow Jews and took such a step to actually help others in a tangible way. If she was going to be a chronicler, she felt she had to be there to share this fate, to bear witness, come what may.

Next, I was referred to books on Holocaust diaries in my search to understand. One of those that gave me insight was *The Diary: The Epic of Everyday Life* (Ben-Amos and Ben-Amos 2020) generally, and a chapter on Holocaust diaries specifically. It was helpful to understand that Langer did not know about diaries and the "sacred voice" of the author and what makes a Holocaust dairy, from a comparative literature and life-writing point of view:

> People often start to write diaries when an imbalance occurs in their lives, between a previously coherent social situation with their clear social norms and a new, normless situation. Holocaust diaries certainly fit into that category, but their writers had additional goals: to bear witness, to sound an alarm to the world, to seek future revenge, or to leave traces of their existence. ...
>
> ... The representation and ethics of Holocaust narratives and scholarship were discussed by historians, philosophers, and literary critics into the 1990s and the 2000s. One example is Lawrence Langer's refusal to find collective redemption or individual resolution or adventure-type narrative in any of the memoirs (and, by extension, diaries) of the Holocaust. Langer insists that readers or listeners cannot draw any meaning from them and that historians will never fully explain the Holocaust. (Ben-Amos and Ben-Amos 2020, 365, 367)

Today, another historical event is happening in the Etty Hillesum literary world. Jan Geurt Gaarlandt's publishing company, Balans, is publishing a brand-new biography of Etty, the only one ever written. Entitled *Etty Hillesum: The Story of Her*

Life, written by Judith Koelemeijer, it was published on September 20, 2022, in the Netherlands. This premiere was also held at Amsterdam Concertgebouw (Concert House) on September 20, 2022, forty-one years after the first launch of her diary! This long-awaited biography, which fills in needed research, will be translated into English, hopefully, in the near future.

After offering online programs for the last year, the Etty Hillesum House, at Molenwater 77 in Middelburg, Etty's birthplace, opened the weekend of September 17–18, 2022. Lotte Bergen, long involved as an Etty author and with Klaas A. D. Smelik and EHOC, is the director. The mission and purpose of the house is as follows:

> Etty Hillesum's ideas remain topical and socially relevant. The question of how to relate as an individual to themes such as enemy thinking, polarization, anti-Semitism, but also solidarity and freedom is a permanent challenge and a necessary and pressing question. All the more reason to want to safeguard the history and ideas of Etty Hillesum for future generations.

It is important that her legacy is preserved, as the last witnesses of World War II are dying, and future generations are moving further and further away from this history. The Etty Hillesum House wants to keep the memory of this special diarist and her fellow sufferers alive and contribute to knowledge and insight about a period of persecution and oppression, a time when people were confronted with war, dictatorship, and the serious dilemmas that this entailed. In addition, the house assumes the very important social role of contributing to awareness (and combating) of contemporary antisemitism by anticipating this worrying trend in an educational and pedagogical way.

The Etty Hillesum House will serve as an institute for education, science, art, and culture. Various activities will be developed from these four pillars, including exhibitions, children's lectures, poetry workshops, symposia, educational activities, and lectures. In addition, the Etty Hillesum Research Center will move to the birthplace as well to continue this important work.

It is also an interesting time in United States, as we are seeing an Etty Hillesum renaissance here as well, in this dire period in our history that mirrors the 1930s and 1940s in multiple ways. The most frightening is the actual possibility of the demise of democracy and its potential consequences of more violence, chaos, and lack of personal freedoms.

Someone on the front line of writing opinion pieces in the *New York Times* about this political period as well as a commentator for NPR, National Public Radio, is journalist and author David Brooks, a prominent American writer and commentator known for his work on morality, values, integrity, and ethics. Recently, Etty has emerged in a book by David Brooks, *Second Mountain: The Quest for a Moral Life* (2019, 75–82). Values and morality, character and integrity are squarely in Brook's wheelhouse. He is Jewish by birth and was married to a woman who converted to Judaism early in their relationship. After being married for twenty-seven years with grown children, he went through a painful divorce and a time of deconstruction and suffering. David began to trace his spiritual journey via his own Second Mountain experience and subsequent relationship with a second spouse, a Christian, his former assistant, who attended Wheaton College, an elite evangelical school in Illinois (Bailey 2019).

The Second Mountain is the transformation that can arise after some initiation, usually causing suffering, that radically alters one's life toward the "Second Mountain" of life—or the "twice born," as William James would say, who are apt to feel a strong sense of renewal or even a deeper sense of conscious "being" after facing into challenges or tragedies, in fact, much like Etty herself. Brooks's *Second Mountain* writing project was inspired by his own experience. He began interviewing people with Second Mountain experiences and groups with the motivation to give back to society in fresh ways. With amazement I turned to his last example and there was Etty Hillesum. He chose her as an example of a Second Mountain person and gives a brief summary of her story that shows, as we have seen thus far, that after Spier's death Etty was on a Second Mountain journey, the fast track to the Divine, so to speak:

> Few of us are going to experience a personal transformation as complete as the one Hillesum experienced. … But their lives serve as models. They are models [she is a model] for many reasons, but in part because they illustrate a core point: One task in life is synthesis. It is to collect all the fragmented pieces of a self and bring them to a state of unity, so that you move coherently toward a single vision. (Brooks 2019, 81–82)

I get a sense of Brooks himself, who was interviewed about his book and his life, when he says: "I really do feel more Jewish than ever before. It felt like more deepening of faith, instead of switching from one thing to another." He has no plans to leave Judaism. He calls himself "a wandering Jew and a very confused Christian. If Jews don't want me as a Jew, they're going to have to kick me out. On the other hand, I can't unread Matthew" (Bailey 2019).

Although books also had quite the impact on Etty, she often had the actual, sometimes mystical, experiences of inner freedom through energy, images, or sensations like vastness within, as if the world was within her that she spoke about in her writing. As human beings we can be somewhat certain that at times she acted "as if," as we all are apt to do. I can imagine Etty's response to David Brooks, who also grew up as a secular Jew, how natural it would seem to her, given her own modernity, almost eighty years ago, refusing to choose between one and another religious path and, instead, drawing from many. It is also interesting that Etty Hillesum and David Brooks both began their spiritual inquiries as atheists.

It surely seems Etty's time has come, for introducing her more fully to the United States, where she is mostly unknown in spite of all that has been written about her. It seems our times are calling forth her spirit, her presence. *"We must act as if we are free and life is meaningful even though we can't be sure of either"* (James 1902, 157, 169; italics added).

Etty Hillesum found a way out of no way. She not only unfolded toward the realization of her being, her transformed Self as Jung would call it, acted through love and empathy and through writing to warn the world of what was coming to fruition in those East European "killing fields." She modeled how to live fully while we are alive, even in the worst of times. In all of the EHOC conferences hundreds of individuals from all over the world have participated in writing articles published after the conferences about any number of topics that Etty Hillesum inspired. She became the chronicler that she wished to be for all time. May we, in our times of a fragile democracy and closed systems, tap into the courage, beauty, love of the "other," truth, presence, action, and "reposing in ourselves," that Etty Hillesum knew so deeply within herself in her times. May it give us the courage that we, too, can live into these essential elements of the soul's journey of all times, and change our world from the inside out.

Acknowledgments

It is amazing to contemplate that opening a small book called *An Interrupted Life*, about an unknown young Dutch woman named Etty Hillesum, would make such a lasting impact on my life. The book, which I discovered in the late 1990s, is about her rich life of spiritual exploration, about love and beauty, a life that would be so radically and cruelly ended in Auschwitz in 1943. Even more amazing is that this book about her would be born in 2023. As an English-speaking American, I could not have written this book without a Dutch village of Etty's diary holders, publishers, translators, and other authors.

Etty told her friend and housemate, Maria Tuinzing, to give her spiral notebook diaries to Klaas Smelik Sr., her friend and former lover who was also a publisher. It took the passion and commitment of his son, Klaas A. D. Smelik, for this diary to be published, first as an abridged copy by the publisher Jan Geurt Gaarlandt in 1981 and then, in 2002, was responsible for editing the unabridged copy with extensive footnotes of the people and historical events of Etty's lifetime.

I could not have written this book without the support of Klaas A. D. Smelik. His writing and scholarship continue to enlarge the context of Etty's world. He began the Etty Hillesum Research Center (EHOC) from Ghent University in Belgium, and my first contact with the Etty world was through Klaas and Meins Coetsier, who also played a significant role in the development of EHOC and has written many significant books about Etty Hillesum in relationship to a variety of philosophical schools of thought. I joined this organization in 2008 after my own journey to Amsterdam to "walk in Etty's footsteps" in 2006. Speaking at my first EHOC conference in 2014 was my initiation into the Etty Hillesum world, which includes Alexandra Nagel, a Julius Spier scholar with whom I developed a lasting connection. Alexandra, a generous and gifted researcher and author herself, continues to offer her invaluable guidance in monthly Zoom meetings.

That first conference set the stage along with my connections with Alexandra Nagel, Denise de Costa, Anna van der Wel, Meins, and Klaas. My visit with Denise de Costa and her family in Den Bosch was foundational—and from her home base I visited the former transit Camp Westerbork and prepared to go onto Auschwitz. We discovered on that trip that as she was working on one of her children's books on Anne Frank that Margot's childhood friend, Jetteke Frijda, who was the same person I met, quite synchronistically, in South Amsterdam twelve years earlier. It was on that trip in 2017 that I also discovered that Nico Frijda and his sister Jetteke had died, Nico in 2015 and Jetteke in 2017. These deaths not only personally impacted me; they also signaled the ending of a generation of survivors and all the potential for more Holocaust denial. These experiences in my Etty journey have nurtured this book.

The most recent conference in 2018 reconnected me with all these friends. There I presented on Etty Hillesum on "The Contours of Her Time, Our Time and All Time," the article that formed the basis of this book. Klaas included my article in his edited book *The Lasting Significance of Etty Hillesum's Writings*. I am honored that he agreed to write the Foreword for this book. No one is closer to the source of Etty Hillesum's work and vision than he has been, and we would not have the gift of her unique and poignant voice without him. That visit also connected me further to Lotte Bergen, who was very involved with Klaas in putting on this congress in 2018. Lotte is now the director of the Etty Hillesum House in Middelburg. Her presentation on Gemmeker, based on her book, haunted me at that conference and I am grateful to have drawn upon it for this book.

Closer to home, Michael Strange, an Oakland resident who has connections to Middelburg, Holland, was at the 2018 Middelburg conference and has edited many of Klaas's books for an English audience. After discovering how close we lived to each other, we have developed a friendship based on our Etty experience. She advocated for me to make the connection between Etty's writings and current US politics.

Next, I want to thank my Etty Hillesum online group. Hila Ratzabi, Rabbi Dorothy Richman, Kristin Kane, Rabbi Emma Sham-ba Ayalon (Etty Hillesum Cards, see Appendix B), Shoshana Lavan, Rabbi Havia Ner-David, Jenny Golub, Judith Koelemeijer, Alexandra Nagel, Susan Stein (Etty Project, see Appendix B), Nancy Anderson, John Smith, Laura Petracek, and additional rotating members. We have been meeting for almost three years and we have members from Holland, Israel, and the United States—Jewish, Buddhist and Christian. From this group, I have gotten to know Judith Koelemeijer, the author of the first biography of Etty Hillesum, which was published on September 20, 2022 in Dutch with fanfare and very high ratings. Her commitment to accurate research on Etty was inspiring and she was generous with her sharing of it.

Next is Rabbi George Gittelman of Shomrei Torah Synagogue and Alissa Hirshfeld of the same community who asked me to present a talk about Etty and a year later I interviewed Rabbi Gittelman for this book. It was a special connection and I am so grateful to explore Etty Hillesum, and her choices and the Holocaust itself with him and discuss the story of Job.

Given that this is a "life book" my family of friends is next. Their love has given me a conscious "family" of support as I've traveled along my Etty journey. In order of years known—my longest and sister-like friend of fifty years plus is Cathy Kuhn. She was my college roommate (oh the joy and laughter) and to this day a kind of "ground" for me. She is truly engaged with the story of Etty and always wants to know everything going on with this book. Next are my East Coast, Newton Centre friends, JoAnn and Michael Feldstein. They are lifelong friends and I have been involved with their daughters' welcoming to the world with showers and Naming ceremonies and one of their Bat Mitzvahs. They have inspired me around Judaism and have been supportive since the day I "met" Etty Hillesum and walked in her footsteps. These days JoAnn's first words to me are "How's the book?" My close friend Alzak Amlani, who came to this country as a refugee from Uganda and is of Indian descent, has been a colleague and friend on the spiritual journey for the past thirty-five years. We've been together through graduate school, our journey with the Diamond Approach, and as faculty at the California Institute of Integral Studies. He knows Etty through osmosis. Julia Voinche started as an assistant to my ex-husband and myself for over a decade and then became my billing and tax person and, of course, along the way a lifelong friend. She has gone through some very intense struggles and reminds me of Etty in her faith and creativity. Helen Marlo, another close soul friend and the mother of my godchild, Renee, as well as her siblings, Andre and Audrey, and their Dad Larry are my California family. Helen is also a psychologist, faculty member, and Dean of Notre Dame's master's psychology program. She is a Jungian analyst who makes a difference in this world. She inherited this impulse from her Italian father who cared deeply about protecting Jewish people in Italy and did so during WWII. She has supported my work from the beginning.

Theresa Silow, a deep soul friend, somatic therapist, faculty member at CIIS, and German by birth, visited Auschwitz with me where we did a ritual for Etty Hillesum. We have been on this spiritual and writing journey together. Marilyn Fowler, another soul friend who was a chair of the Consciousness department at John F. Kennedy University, has done her own roots journey to the Indigenous Sami people in Scandinavia and written a book about their contributions to leadership. She read the first half of my manuscript and gave me critical feedback and encouragement to go forward. And she couldn't wait for the next part of Etty's story! That was the best encouragement I could have received.

And last but not least—the "newest" is my very close friend, Judie Wexler. Judie was the provost at CIIS when I was hired. She did that job impeccably and with vision for fourteen years and then became president for another four years. Judie is a gifted leader and it is no surprise that she is now the president of one of the largest synagogues in San Francisco, Sherith Israel. At dinner every other week, she is the one who opens our conversations with "How is the book going?" A conversation of discovery always follows. I am grateful for her wisdom and leadership at CIIS through all these years; after almost fifteen years, we are family.

Heather Cox Richardson needs recognition for her *Letters from an American*, a daily newsletter with a historical lens, and being a guide for so many of us who have relied on her to see the radical changes in our political landscape and frankly the loss of civility and bipartisan politics in our US government … clearly and without rancor.

Other important sources of inspiration for this book through the years include, from the C. G. Jung Institute of San Francisco, the late Joseph Wheelwright and Tom Singer, author and analyst whose writing and support of this book has been instrumental in the writing and publishing of it. Other Jungians: Christine Hejinian, Fanny Brewster, and Sam Kimbles; from the California Institute of Integral Studies, my academic home for fourteen years Robert McDermott, who I taught "Karma and Biography" with and knows Etty Hillesum well through that class – a true friend and supporter, Rick Tarnas, Arisika Razak, Shirley Strong, and Brant Cortright have been inspiration to me. I also want to thank those who inspired me in the Diamond Approach, including A. H. Almass (Hameed Ali), Karen Johnson, and Doriena and Rueben Wolff; and from Spirit Rock Meditation Center's teacher training program, Jack Kornfield and Tara Brach.

And finally, closest to home on the family side, my brother, "father," "friend," and family is Richard Morrill, the Spier figure, particularly in the area of education and spirituality, in my life. Rich has supported and encouraged his "little sister" all these years. He has a brilliant career because of his passion for values, the truth, and the deep "Sources of the Self," as Charles Taylor the philosopher has written about extensively. Further back than that, Richard Niebuhr's notion of "responsibility" has shaped his personal and leadership philosophy. We share Kierkegaard's notion that "Purity of Heart is to will one thing" as we both have "evangelical" zeal (the only thing we could not shed) in our pursuit of justice, democracy, and the Mystery that underlies all things. I can always count on his support and he mine.

I have such gratitude toward my "pre-editor" Leeann Pickrell, managing editor of *Jung Journal: Culture & Psyche*. She is gifted at her work, knows the ethos of this Jungian oriented book, is touched by Etty, and makes magic out of my run-on sentences! I have confidence in this manuscript because of her. I am grateful, Leeann, and feel you so strongly on team Etty and your support of Etty Hillesum's voice in this volatile time in the United States on so many levels.

I am going to add another person who has contributed to this Etty Village. Jennifer Hill, a skilled and thoughtful developmental editor has helped me to integrate Chapter Five, "Our Times," in a more thematic fashion. I am grateful to her for her depth, skill, and immediate understanding of the importance of Etty's story, encouraging me near the end of a very long journey.

To you, Jill Mellick, my former doctoral chairperson, a courageous warrior, and beauty lover. The moment with you two years ago after so many years, was so deeply touching and inspirational. You signed your amazing new book *The Red Book Hours: Discovering C. G. Jung's Art Mediums and Creative Process* and then asked, "What about writing a book about Etty?" Thank you for your deep creative inspiration … Jill Mellick passed away from cancer in December of 2022. She is greatly missed.

And finally, gratitude to my Routledge editor, Katie Randall, who believed in and championed this book about Etty Hillesum for our times.

Appendix A

Etty Hillesum's Letter to Friends That Was Sent to the Dutch Resistance Two Weeks before Her Own Departure for Auschwitz

The author has both quoted and paraphrased this letter.

To Han Wegerif and others
Westerbork, Tuesday, 24 August 1943

24 /8 / 43

There was a moment when I felt in all seriousness that after this night, it would be a sin ever to laugh again …

Although Etty believes her words and images can't possibly convey the horror of the camp, this letter grips the reader as we walk with her through those hours she spends watching the guards with their empty faces, the men standing with their packs waiting to be deported, listening to the babies' "piercing screams." A young, terrified boy in blue pajamas runs off and hides so he won't be taken away. They find him, of course, yet still, fifty more victims are placed on the transport as punishment. She worries how he will be treated on the train.

The evening before, as Etty walks through the camp, she notices people are grouped together between the barracks under a menacing sky. "Look, that's just how people behave after a disaster, standing about on street corners discussing what's happened," her companion, Philip Mechanicus, says to her. Etty reminds him that this is what makes it difficult to understand because it is "*before* the disaster!" She notes that whenever there is a crisis, people naturally lean toward helping each other and that she would be assisting with the babies and trying to calm the mothers before escorting them to the cattle cars.

In the afternoon Etty does a round of the hospital barracks for the last time, going from bed to bed. She wonders which beds will be vacant the next day. She knows that the transport lists are not published until the absolute last second, but some of the staff know well in advance that their names will be on it. She continues to speak about the tragic encounter with the paralyzed girl mentioned earlier in the story of Westerbork.

Etty shares that she really could not tell who was going and who was not this time. She notices that almost everyone is up and dressed as the sick help each other to get ready. Some have no clothes at all. Young mothers are preparing milk bottles to take on the train to feed their babies. She describes the young mother who almost apologizes for her crying child.

Etty faces agonizing moments, the pressure of being asked to take or hide the children designated to go with their parents. The woman with her wet laundry and sick child who begs her to help because "they take the sick children away, and you never get them back." A woman comes to comfort her: "There now, you're just an ordinary Jew, aren't you? So you'll just have to go, won't you …?"

She comes to the moment a few beds farther along when "I suddenly catch sight of the ash-gray, freckled face of a colleague. She is squatting beside the bed of a dying woman who has swallowed some poison and who happens to be her mother …"

"God Almighty, what are You doing to us?" The words just escape me. Over there is that affectionate little woman from Rotterdam. She is in her ninth month. Two nurses try to get her dressed. She just stands there, her swollen body leaning against her child's cot. Drops of sweat run down her face. She stares into the distance, a distance into which I cannot follow her, and says in a toneless, worn-out voice, "Two months ago I volunteered to go with my husband to Poland. And then I wasn't allowed to, because I always have such difficult pregnancies. And now I do have to go … just because someone tried to run away tonight." The wailing of the babies grows louder still, filling every nook and cranny of the barracks, now bathed in ghostly light. It is almost too much to bear. A name occurs to me: Herod.

Etty and other staff are able to take a woman who begins labor on the stretcher on the way to the train back to the hospital instead—which, for Etty seems like "a rare act of humanity …" She then takes some time to sit and squeeze tomato juice for the babies and describes another kind of story told with passion and a degree of defiance.

A young woman sits down beside her who Etty remembers admitting. This woman seems ready and actually eager to leave "and is beautifully turned out." She has been there only a short time and came from the punishment block and has been ready and impatient to leave since the afternoon. She has with her a heavy rucksack and a blanket roll. This woman is eating moldy sandwiches to prepare for the trip. She had been thrown in prison when she was pregnant. When she told the guards she couldn't stand, they wouldn't let her sit. Her baby died but she still has milk and says she can help feed the babies on the train.

Then Etty spots a woman she recognizes and has even admired for the "aristocratic way in which she reclines on her shabby bunk." She recognizes this woman is unsteady on her feet yet finely dressed and proud. This woman's husband died at Westerbork a few weeks prior. "She answers in a hoarse voice, 'Yes, I'm here as well. They wouldn't let me share my husband's grave.'"

And then there is the story of "the tough little ghetto woman." This woman always seemed to be starving because she never received any packages of food. She has seven children there at Westerbork and is bustling about packing, kind and almost cheerful, on her way to the transport with all her children.

Next comes the young woman who is used to luxury and Etty thinks that she must have been very beautiful. She is a recent arrival and had gone into hiding to save her baby. Betrayed, she is now here wearing several layers of clothes, looking close to collapse. Etty wonders how she'll survive the three-day transport.

> What will this young woman, already in a state of collapse, look like after three days in an overcrowded freight car with men, women, children, and babies all thrown together, bags and baggage, a bucket in the middle their only convenience?

She keeps wandering "in a daze" through other barracks. She walks past scenes "that loom up before my eyes in crystal-clear detail and at the same time seem like blurred age-old visions." She sees a dying old man being carried away, "reciting the Shema to himself."

The train is due to depart at eleven, and they start loading it with people and luggage. Paths to the train are staked out by men of the Ordedienst, the Camp Service Corps. Anyone not involved with the transport has to stay in the barracks. Etty slips into one just across from the siding. "There's always been a splendid view from here," a cynical voice says.

> a depressing series of bare, unpainted freight cars in the front, and a proper coach for the guards at the back. Some of the cars have paper mattresses on the floor. These are for the sick. ... Men from the "Flying Column" in brown overalls are bringing the luggage up on wheelbarrows.

She sees "two of the commandant's court jesters." One of them, a songwriter named Willy Rosen, had been selected for transport but sang to save himself, delighting the commandant. He was spared and even given a house.

The men in green uniforms swarm the walkway. Etty reflects on some of the earlier transports, when she thought that some of the guards were simple, possibly kindly types "with puzzled expressions who walked about the camp smoking their pipes and speaking in some incomprehensible dialect. ... Now I am transfixed with terror. Oafish, jeering faces, in which one seeks in vain for even the slightest trace of human warmth."

Etty's companion, Philip Mechanicus, who is at the window, shudders at these guards as well. Months ago Philip was brought to Westerbork from Amersfoort, "in bits and pieces." More and more people are filling up the spaces in the freight cars. The head of the Antragstelle, the camp Appeals Department, tries to save people off the transport, yet because of the young boy who tried to run away it won't be possible to save many.

One can't really call it a serious attempt to escape—he absconded from the hospital in a moment of panic, a thin jacket over his blue pajamas, and in a clumsy, childish way took refuge in a tent, where he was picked up quickly enough after a search of the camp. But if you are a Jew you may not run away, may not allow yourself to be stricken with panic. The commandant is remorseless. As a reprisal, and without warning, scores of others are being sent on the transport with the boy, including quite a few who had thought they were firmly at anchor here. This system happens to believe in collective punishment.

In Etty's opinion the cars are full, and yet another large group shows up:

"God Almighty, does all this lot have to get in as well?" The children are still standing with their noses glued to the windowpane; they don't miss a thing. "Look over there, a lot of people are getting off; it must be too hot in the train." Suddenly one of them calls out, "Look, the commandant!"

Etty is on to this psychopathic commandant. Her writing captures, in the most withering and ironic way, the utter disgust of this cartoonish figure who perhaps sees himself as a royal dispensing favors to his subjects. His artistic palate has been described in the Westerbork chapter as he was the biggest consumer of the performances and jokes told on cabaret nights. Perhaps this is how he denied the truth of what he was actually doing at Westerbork. He only served ten years in prison after the war. He said at his trial, with his known charisma, that he did his job, and really never knew what happened in Poland.

"They also say that he especially loved children." In the Westerbork section, that piece of information could be highly debated as the story of an infant, Machieltje, tells the truth of his motives. "Children must be looked after" he asserts:

In the hospital they even get a tomato each day. And yet many of them seem to die all the same ... So far not a single great mind has been able to fathom why that should be. I could go on quite a bit longer about "our" commandant.

He walked with a military bearing, "inspecting his troops: the sick, infants in arms, young mothers, and shaven-headed men. A few more ailing people are being brought up on stretchers. He makes an impatient gesture; they're taking too long about it." His Jewish secretary accompanies him, "with the sporty demeanor yet vacuous expression of the English whisky drinker."

Etty feels the outside world sees the Jews as a "gray uniform mass," never recognizing them as individual people. "Could one ever hope to convey to the outside world what has happened here today?"

She goes on to tell us that the commandant was joined by the *Oberdienstleiter,* the head of the Camp Service Corps. The *Oberdienstleiter* was a German Jew of massive build, and Commandant Gemmeker "looked slight and insignificant by his side. Black top boots, black cap, black army coat with yellow star. He has a cruel mouth and a powerful neck. Several years before he was a digger in the outworkers' corps …"

The doors to the train shut:

Shut on the herded, densely packed mass of people inside. Through small openings at the top we can see heads and hands, hands that will wave to us later when the train leaves. The commandant takes a bicycle and rides once again along the entire length of the train. Then he makes a brief gesture, like royalty in an operetta. … The train gives a piercing whistle. And 1,020 Jews leave Holland. This time the quota was really quite small, all considered: a mere thousand Jews, the extra twenty being reserves. For it is always possible—indeed, quite certain this time—that a few will die or be crushed to death on the way. So many sick people and not a single nurse …

Etty watches as the crowd recedes, the tide of helpers gradually go back to their sleeping quarters. Next week there will be another transport, as there has been each week for a year, week in, week out. There are now only a few thousand left in Westerbork. Hillesum believes:

that a hundred thousand Dutch members of our race are toiling away under an unknown sky or lie rotting in some unknown soil. We know nothing of their fate. It is only a short while, perhaps, before we find out, each one of us in his own time. For we are all marked down to share that fate, of that I have not a moment's doubt. But I must go now and lie down and sleep for a little while. I am a bit tired and dizzy. Then later I have to go to the laundry to track down the facecloth that got lost. But first I must sleep. As for the future, I am firmly resolved to return to you after my wanderings. In the meantime, my love once again, you dear people.

Etty
(ET 2002, 644–654)

Appendix B

Examples of Action Based upon Etty Hillesum's Writings Today

The Etty Hillesum Cards

Peace Activism

"Etty Hillesum Cards" come in a box in which you can find a booklet and 100 cards with her quotes in three languages; English, Hebrew, and Arabic. We are two women peace activists, Dina Awwad-Srour and Emma Sham-Ba Ayalon, a Palestinian and an Israeli. We believe that Etty Hillesum's words carry the wisdom of deep humanism that the world needs now so urgently.

Emma and Dina are currently working with Israelis and Palestinians with their cards, courses, and film, as they try to contribute to the spreading of Etty's words and spirit. The film shows how Etty's words inspire peace workers in the Middle East and help overcoming hatred, dehumanization, victimhood, and despair. To open dialogue and understanding about the animosity and hatred between these two alienated groups of people sharing the same land. They have created these cards with Etty Hillesum quotes that they use to facilitate new growth in the middle of a renewed hostility and violence between the two groups given Netanyahu's recent return to power with a far-right coalition.

Emma Sham-Ba Ayalon

As a Jewish woman who grew up in Israel, I know that we carry a trauma that influences us as individuals and as a nation. The trauma that we carry from the Holocaust plays a big role in our behaviour as a nation and especially in the way we treat Palestinians. As a peace worker I know that we cannot go forward toward a vision of peace if we don't heal the wounds from the past. As a Jewish woman who grew up in Israel, I know that we carry a trauma that influences us as individuals and as a nation. The trauma that we carry from the Holocaust plays a big role in our behavior as a nation and especially in the way we treat Palestinians. As a peace worker I know that we cannot go forward toward a vision of peace if we don't heal the wounds from the past. Etty wanted to be a remedy of healing. I believe that her spiritual path that allowed her to never hate and to find inner peace, even in the very dark times of the Holocaust, can serve as a healing force and as a role model for what is possible for us as Jews and as humans. Her writings deeply healed my heart and helped me step out of a victim's perspective and to find the power from within myself to contribute to the creation of a better world.

Dina Awwad-Srour

My name is **Dina Awwad-Srour**. I am a Palestinian, originally from the town of Beit Sahour, a small town in east Bethlehem—Palestine. I now live in Eilaboun, a small Arab village in the north of Israel. I am a lecturer and a writer and my main passion is to empower women and mothers. I encountered Etty's diaries eight years ago when I was 27 years old, exactly the same age as Etty was when she started writing her diaries. I immediately felt connected to her and her challenges as a young woman. I learned a lot from her about love and freedom; for example, how to stay independent and free even when you love someone. For my spiritual path I learned a lot from her about prayer and connecting to God. As a Palestinian, I find Etty very inspiring as she helped me learn to look at the Palestinian/Israeli conflict from a wider angel beyond a black & white or a good & evil perspective. I learned to ask questions and look for the answers within myself. I learned from her to see the human inside every Israeli soldier. I gained a deeper understanding of how war is a system that misuses young men.

The Etty Project—Susan Stein

The roots of the Etty Project lie in the diaries of Etty Hillesum, a young Jewish Dutch student living and writing in occupied Amsterdam in 1942. Etty committed herself to rooting out her own hatred as the next step in building a better world, a choice that inspired Susan Stein to write the one-woman play, *Etty*. With help from director Austin Pendleton, Susan began performing *Etty*, first in living rooms and museums then in theaters, universities, schools, prisons, and houses of worship throughout the United States and Europe.

Etty Project expanded to include educational programming that connects today's youth with other young people in history. Etty Project helps recover lost voices from the diaries, narratives, and songs from the Holocaust, American slavery and civil rights, Japanese concentration camps, the Rwandan genocide, and the Sudanese civil war, with the aim of building bridges between people from diverse histories, sensibilities, and circumstances. Participants bear witness to those who have come before, faced injustice, and resisted racism. Etty Project stretches boundaries, bringing live theater to underserved communities, creating theater in non-traditional spaces with those who have never imagined performing, and treating primary source documents as living texts.

Over 65,000 people have attended an *Etty* performance; more than 5000 students have participated in Etty Project classes, and over 200 teachers have attended professional development workshops run by Etty Project teaching artists. Susan Stein has presented at universities, and more than a dozen conferences, including the International Conference on Holocaust Education at Yad Vashem, the International Teachers Conference.

Bibliography

Alexander, Elizabeth. 2022. *The Trayvon Generation.* New York: Grand Central Publishing.
Almaas, A. H. 2000. *Diamond Heart, Book 1: Elements of the Real in the Man.* Boston: Shambhala.
Assagioli, Roberto. 1991. *Transpersonal Development: The Dimension beyond Psychosynthesis.* Crucible.
Bailey, S. 2019. "Is David Brooks a Christian or a Jew?" *The Washington Post*, April 29.
Ben-Amos, Batsheva, and Dan Ben-Amos. 2020. *The Diary: The Epic of Everyday Life.* Bloomington, IN: Indiana University Press.
Bergen, Lotte. 2019. "Etty Hillesum & Albert Konrad Gemmeker: A Twofold Analysis of the Perpetration of the Westerbork Commander." In *The Lasting Significance of Etty Hillesum's Writings,* edited by Klaas A. D. Smelik. Amsterdam: University of Amsterdam Press.
Bergmann, Susan, ed. 1996. *Martyrs: Contemporary Writers Lives of Faith.* San Francisco: Harper Collins.
Borradori, Giovanna. 2003. *Philosophy in a time of Terror; Dialogues with Jurgen Habermas and Jacques Derrida.* Chicago: The University of Chicago Press.
Bolen, Jean Shinoda. 1993. *Gods in Everyman: Archetypes that Shape Men's Lives.* New York: HarperCollins.
Braxton, Joanne. 1989. *Black Women Writing Biography.* Philadelphia: Temple University Press.
Brenner, Rachel F. 1997. *Writing as Resistance: Four Women Confronting the Holocaust.* State College, PA: Penn State University Press.
———. 2010. "Etty Hillesum: A Portrait of a Holocaust Author." In *Spirituality in the Writings of Etty Hillesum,* edited by Klaas Smelik, Ria van den Brandt, and Meins G. S. Coetsier. Leiden: Brill.
Brewster, Fanny. 2017. *African Americans and Jungian Psychology: Leaving the Shadows.* London: Routledge.
Brooks, David. 2019. *Second Mountain; The Quest for a Moral Life.* New York: Random House.
Carroll, John. 2002. *Constantine's Sword: The Church and the Jews.* New York: Houghton Mifflin.
Christ, Carol. 1980. *Diving Deep & Surfacing: Women Writers on Spiritual Quest.* Boston: Beacon Press.
Church of England. 2000. *Common Worship: Services and Prayers for the Church of England.* London: Church House Publishing.

Claremont de Castillejo, Irene. 1973/1979. *Knowing Woman: A Feminine Psychology.* Boston: Shambhala.
Coetsier, Meins. 2014. *The Existential Philosophy of Etty Hillesum.* Leiden: Brill Publishing.
———. 2017. "Etty Hillesum's Ethical Consciousness and the History of Jewish Philosophy." In *The Ethics and Religious Philosophy of Etty Hillesum,* edited by Klaus A. D. Smelik, Meins G. S. Coetsier, and Jurjen Wiermus, 21–48. Leiden, The Netherlands: Brill.
Collins, P. 1991. "Learning from the outsider within: The sociological significance of Black Feminist Thought." In *Beyond Methodology: Feminist Scholarship as Lived Research,* edited by M. M. Fonow and A. Cook. Indianapolis, IN: Indiana University Press.
de Beauvoir, Simone. 1970. *The Coming of Age.* New York: W. W. Norton & Co.
de Costa, Denise. 1998. *Ann Frank and Etty Hillesum: Inscribing Spirituality and Sexuality.* New Brunswick, NJ: Rutgers University Press.
de Jong, Louis. 1990. *The Netherlands and Nazi Germany.* Cambridge, MA: Harvard University Press.
Fandos, Nicolas, and Michael D. Shear. 2019. "Trump Impeached for Abuse of Power and Obstructions of Congress." *New York Times,* December 19. https://www.nytimes.com/2019/12/18/us/politics/trump-impeached.html.
Fischer, Norman. 2018. "Our Grand Delusion: Norman Fischer on the Tyranny of the Self." *The Sun,* August.
Flinders, Carol Lee. 2006. *Enduring Lives: Portraits of Women and Faith in Action.* New York: Penguin.
Frank, Anne. 1952. *The Diary of a Young Girl.* New York: Doubleday.
Frankel, Viktor. 1970. *Man's Search for Meaning.* New York: Washington Square Press.
Frenk, Hannon. n.d. "Etty Hillesum Jan 15 1914–1943." *Shalvi/Hyman Encyclopedia of Jewish Women.* https://jwa.org/encyclopedia.
Frishman, Elyse D. 2007. *MISHKAN T'FILAH: A Reform Siddur.* New York: Central Conference of American Rabbis.
Gaarlandt, Jan Geurt, ed. 1981. *An Interrupted Life and Letters From Westerbork.* New York: Henry Holt and Company.
———. 2010. "Context, Dilemmas, and Misunderstandings During the Composition and Publication of An Interrupted Life: Etty Hillesum's Diary, 1941–1943." In *Spirituality in the Writings of Etty Hillesum,* edited by Klaus Smelik, Ria van den Brandt, and Meins G. S. Coetsier, 377–398. Leiden, The Netherlands: Brill.
Garman, Emma. 2019. "Feminize Your Canon: Etty Hillesum." *The Paris Review,* April 4. https://www.theparisreview.org/blog/2019/04/04/feminize-your-canon-etty-hillesum/.
Greenblatt, Jonathan. *It Could Happen Here: Why America is Tipping from Hate to the Unthinkable and How We Can Stop It.* Boston: Mariner Books.
Greene, Daniel. 2008. In dialogue with James Carroll. *Voices on Antisemitism,* January 31. https://www.ushmm.org/antisemitism/podcast/voices-on-antisemitism/james-carroll.
Goldenberg, Naomi. 1979. *Changing of the Guards: Feminism and the End of Traditional Religions.* Boston: Beacon Press.
Grimmelikhuizen, Frits. 2008. "The Road of Etty Hillesum to Nothingness." In *Spirituality in the Writings of Etty Hillesum,* edited by Klaus Smelik, Ria van den Brandt, and Meins G. S. Coestier, 429–445. Leiden, The Netherlands: Brill.
Haberman, Maggie. 2022. "Before Jan. 6. Aide Warned Secret Service of Security Risk to Pence." *New York Times,* June 3. https://www.nytimes.com/2022/06/03/us/politics/trump-pence-safety-jan-6.html.

Bibliography

Hardy, Michael. 2022. "Hungarian Prime Minister Viktor Orbán Got a Standing Ovation from the Trump Faithful." *The Texas Monthly*, August. https://www.texasmonthly.com/news-politics/viktor-orban-cpac-dallas/.

Hett, Benjamin Carter. 2018. *The Death of Democracy: Hitler's Rise to Power and the Downfall of the Weimar Republic*. London: Penguin Random House.

Hillesum, Etty. 1996. *An Interrupted Life: The Diaries of Etty Hillesum, 1941–1943* (*Het Vestoorde Leven: Dagboek Van Etty Hillisum* [1981]). Notes and introduction by Jan G. Gaarlandt. New York: Henry Holt and Company.

Hillman, James. 1975. *Re-Visioning Psychology*. New York: Harper Perennial.

Hodge, Nathan. 2022. "Restoration of Empire Is the Endgame for Russia's Vladimir Putin." *CNN World*, June 10.

Horn, Dara. 2021. *People Love Dead Jews: Reports from a Haunted Present*. New York: W. W. Norton and Co.

Hull, G., P. B. Scott, and B. Smith, eds. 1982. *All the Women are White, All the Blacks are Men, But Some of Us Are Brave*. New York: The Feminist Press.

Iannacci, Nicandro. 2016. "'Nothing Less Than a Miracle': The Constitution and the Peaceful Transition of Power." *Constitution Daily*, October 21. https://constitutioncenter.org/blog/nothing-less-than-a-miracle-the-constitution-and-the-peaceful-transition-of.

Jacobi, Jolande. 1967. *The Way of Individuation*, 2nd Ed. New York: Meridian Press.

Jaffé, A. (1971). *From the life and work of C.G. Jung* (R. F. C. Hull, Trans.). Harper & Row. (Original work published 1968)

James, William. 1902. *The Varieties of Religious Experiences*. London: Longman's Green and Co.

Jung, C. G. 1928/1969. "On Psychic Energy." In *The Collected Works of C. G. Jung*. Vol. 8, *The Structure and Dynamics of the Psyche*. Princeton: Princeton University Press.

———. 1928/1969. "The Relations between the Ego and the Unconscious." In *The Collected Works of C. G. Jung*. Vol. 7, *Two Essays in Analytical Psychology*. Princeton: Princeton University Press.

———. 1929/1968. "Commentary on the 'Secret of the Golden Flower.'" In *The Collected Works of C. G. Jung*. Vol 13, *Alchemical Studies*. Princeton: Princeton University Press.

———. 1930–31/1969. "The Stages of Life." In *The Collected Works of C. G. Jung*. Vol. 8, *The Structure and Dynamics of the Psyche*. Princeton: Princeton University Press.

———. 1933. *Modern Man in Search of a Soul*. New York: Harcourt, Brace & World.

———. 1934/1969. "The Soul and Death." In *The Collected Works of C. G. Jung*. Vol. 8, *The Structure and Dynamics of the Psyche*. Princeton: Princeton University Press.

———. 1934/1954. The Development of Personality. In *The Collected Works of C. G. Jung*. Vol. 17, *The Development of Personality*. Princeton: Princeton University Press.

———. 1946/1989. *Essays on Contemporary Events: The Psychology of Nazism, with a New Forward by Andrew Samuels*. (Bollingen Series XX—Original work published in Vols. 10, 16) Princeton: Princeton University Press.

———. 1957. *The Undiscovered Self: The Dilemma of the Individual in Modern Society*. New York: Little, Brown and Company.

———. 1964. The Meaning of Psychology for Modern Man. In *The Collected Works of C. G. Jung*. Vol. 10, *Civilization in Transition*. Princeton: Princeton University Press.

———. 2009. The Red Book: Liber Novus. Edited by Sonu Shamdasani. New York: W. W. Norton & Co.

Knoop, Hans. 1983. *De Joodsche Raad: hat drama van Abraham Asscher en David Cohen.* Amsterdam: Elsevier.

Koelemeijer, Judith. 2022. *Etty Hillesum: Het verhaal van haar leven* (The Story of Her Life). The Netherlands: Balans.

Kornfield, Jack. 2022. "Fearing Death." Internet lecture.

Kristof, Nicholas. 2023. "What We Get Wrong About Israel and Gaza." *New York Times*, November 15.

Kraemer, Joel L. 2008. *Maimonides: The Life and World of One of Civilization's Greatest Minds.* New York: Doubleday Religion.

Kushner, Harold. 1981. *When Bad Things Happen to Good People.* New York: Schocken Books.

Langer, Lawrence: 1995. *Admitting the Holocaust: Collected Essays.* New York: Oxford University Press.

Last, Jonathan V. 2022. "Mike Pence Is an American Hero: Democrats Should Honor the Republican Who's Trying to End Trumpism." *The Atlantic*, June 9. https://www.theatlantic.com/ideas/archive/2022/06/january-6-hearings-mike-pence-service-democracy/661224/.

Lauter, Estella, and Carol Rupprecht. 1985. *Feminist Archetypal Theory.* Knoxville: University of Tennessee Press.

Lifton, Robert J. 1986. *The Nazi Doctors.* New York: Basic Books.

———. 2017. "Our Witness to Malignant Normality." In *The Dangerous Case of Donald Trump: 27 Psychiatrists and Mental Health Experts Assess a President*, edited by Bandy X. Lee. New York: Thomas Dunne Books

Maritz, Dominique. 2012. "What Are the Main Causes of Genocide." *E-International Relations*, July 12. https://www.e-ir.info/2012/07/12/what-are-the-main-causes-of-genocide/.

Matza, Max. 2021. "Who's Behind Recent Rise in U.S. Anti-Semitic Attacks?" *BBC News*, May 28. https://www.bbc.com/news/world-us-canada-57286341.

Mechanicus, Philip. 1968. *Waiting for Death.* London: Calder and Boyars.

Miller, Jean Baker. 1986. *Toward a New Psychology of Women.* Boston: Beacon Press.

Nagel, Alexandra. 2022. "Julius Spier read the Bible for Guidance—Etty Hillesum Followed Him." *Psychology & the Cross*, June 17. https://centerofthecross.substack.com/p/julius-spier.

Nawaz, Amna, and Dorothy Hastings. 2022. "Jewish Americans Are Terrified Amid Rising Anti-Semitic Attacks. How Can They Feel Safe?" *PBS News Hour*, January 17.

Neiman, Susan. 2019. *Learning from the Germans; Race and the Memory of Evil.* New York: Picador.

Neri, Nadia. 2010. "Etty Hillesum's Psychological and Spiritual Path." In *Spirituality in the Writings of Etty Hillesum*, edited by Klaus Smelik, Ria van den Brandt, and Meins G. S. Coestier, 419–427. Leiden, The Netherlands: Brill.

O'Brian, Phillips Payson. "Tanks for Ukraine Have Shifted the Balance of Power in Europe." *The Atlantic*, January 27. https://www.theatlantic.com/ideas/archive/2023/01/us-germany-ukraine-tanks-russia-nato/672859/.

Orenstein, Anna. 2020. "The Relativity of Morality in the Contemporary World." *Psychoanalytic Inquiry* 40, no. 4: 223–233.

Peck, M. Scott. 1983. *People of the Lie: The Hope for Healing Human Evil.* New York: Simon & Schuster.

Perera, Sylvia Brinton. 1981. *Descent to the Goddess. A Way of Initiation for Women*. Toronto: Inner City Books.

Pfeffer, Dan. 2022. *Battling the Big Lie; How Fox, Facebook, and the MAGA Media Are Destroying America*. New York: Hatchette Book Group.

Presser, Jacob. 1968. "Introduction." In *Waiting for Death* by Philip Mechanicus. London: Calder and Boyers.

———. 2010. *Ashes in the Wind: The Destruction of Dutch Jews*. London: Souvenir Press.

Pulliam Bailey, Sarah. 2019. "Is David Brooks a Christian or a Jew? His latest book Traces His Faith—and His Second Marriage." *The Washington Post*, May 3.

Putnam, Hilary. 2008. *Jewish Philosophy as a Guide to Life: Rosenzweig, Buber, Levinas, Wittgenstein*. Bloomington, IN: Indiana University Press.

Ratzabi, Hila. n.d. "The Wisdom of Etty Hillesum." *My Jewish Learning*. https://www.myjewishlearning.com/article/the-wisdom-of-etty-hillesum/.

Reuther, Rosemary Radford. 1997. *Faith and Fratricide*. Eugene, OR: WIPF – Stock Publishers.

Rich, Melanie. 2008. *Jews in Psychology and the Psychology of Judaism*. Piscataway, NJ: Tigris.

Richardson, Heather Cox. 2020. *How the South Won the Civil War*. New York: Oxford University Press.

Riemen, Rob. 2018. *To Fight Against This Age: On Fascism and Humanism*. New York: W. W. Norton & Company, Inc.

Rilke, Rainer Maria. 2005. *The Book of Hours*. Translated by Joanna Macy and Anita Barrows. New York: Penguin.

Robertson, Campbell, Christopher Mele, and Sabrina Tavernise. 2018. "11 Killed in Synagogue Massacre; Suspect Charged with 29 Counts." *New York Times*, October 27. https://www.nytimes.com/2018/10/27/us/active-shooter-pittsburgh-synagogue-shooting.html.

Ruane, Michael E. 2022. "Putin's Attack on Ukraine Echos Hitler's Takeover of Czechoslovakia." *Washington Post*, February 24.

Rumi, 2005. *The Book of Love; Poems of Ecstasy and Longing*. San Francisco: Harper

Schrijvers, Piet. 2000. "Truth is the Daughter of Time: Prof. David Cohen as Seen by Himself and Others." In *Dutch Jews as Perceived by Themselves and Others: Proceedings of the Eighth International Symposium on the History of the Jews in the Netherlands*, edited by Chaya Brasz and Yosef Kaplan, 355–370. Leiden: Brill.

———. 2018. "Etty Hillesum in Jewish Contexts." In *Reading Etty Hillesum in Context: Writings, Life, and Influences of a Visionary Author*, edited by Klaas A. D. Smelik, Gerrit van Ord, and Jurjen Wiersma. Amsterdam: Amsterdam University Press.

Shorto, Russell. 2013. *Amsterdam: A History of the World's Most Liberal City*. New York: Doubleday.

Siertsema, Bettine. 2019. "New Light on Etty Hillesum's Actions in Camp Westerbork." In *The Lasting Significance of Etty Hillesum's Writings*, edited by Klaas A. D. Smelik, 341–352. Amsterdam: University of Amsterdam Press.

Singer, Thomas. 2017. "Trump and the American Collective Psyche." *The Dangerous Case of Donald Trump: 27 Psychiatrists and Mental Health Experts Assess a President*, edited by Bandy X. Lee. New York: Thomas Dunne Books.

———, ed. 2020. *Cultural Complexes and the Soul of America*. London: Routledge.

Singer, Thomas, and Samuel L. Kimbles, eds. 2004. *The Cultural Complex: Contemporary Jungian Perspectives on Psyche and Society.* London: Routledge.

Smelik, Klass A. D., ed. 2002. *Etty: The Letters and Diaries of Etty Hillesum, 1941–1943.* Grand Rapids, MA, and Cambridge, UK: William Eerdmans Publishing.

———. 2018. "Etty Hillesum's Choice not to go into Hiding." In *Reading Etty Hillesum in Context: Writings, Life, and Influences of a Visionary Author,* edited by Klaas A. D. Smelik, Gerrit van Ord, and Jurjen Wiersma. Amsterdam: Amsterdam University Press.

———, ed. 2019. *The Lasting Significance of Etty Hillesum's Writings.* Amsterdam: University of Amsterdam Press.

Smelik, Klaas A. D., Gerrit van Ord, and Jurjen Wiersma, eds. 2018. *Reading Etty Hillesum in Context: Writings, Life, and Influences of a Visionary Author.* Amsterdam: Amsterdam University Press.

Smelik, Klaas A. D., Ria van den Brandt, and Meins G. S. Coetsier, eds. 2010. *Spirituality in the Writings of Etty Hillesum.* Leiden, The Netherlands: Brill.

Smith, Ben. 2020. Heather Cox Richardson Offers a Break from the Media Maelstrom. It's Working." *The New York Times,* December 27. https://www.nytimes.com/2020/12/27/business/media/heather-cox-richardson-substack-boston-college.

Smith, Curtis D. 1990. *Jung's Quest for Wholeness: A Religious and Historical Perspective.* Albany: State University of New York Press.

Snyder, Timothy. 2017. *On Tyranny: Twenty Lessons from the Twentieth Century.* New York: Random House.

———. 2018. "How Did the Nazis Gain Power in Germany?" Review of the *Death of Democracy* by Benjamin Carter Hett. *The New York Times,* June 14.

Spetter, Ies. 2018."Buna." In *Erste Nederlandse getuigenissen van de Holocaust 1945–1946,* edited by Bettine Siertsema, 395–453. Laren: Verbum.

Spier, Julius. 1944/2014. *The Hands of Children: An Introduction to Psycho-Chirology.* London: Routledge.

Stelter, Brian. 2021. "This Infamous Steve Bannon Quote Is Key to Understanding America's Crazy Politics." *CNN Business,* November 16. https://www.cnn.com/2021/11/16/media/steve-bannon-reliable-sources/index.html.

Sullivan, Barbara S. 1989. *Psychotherapy Grounded in the Feminine Principle.* Ashville, NC: Chiron Publications.

Tarnas, Richard. 1993. *Passion of the Western Mind.* New York: Ballantine Books.

Tillich, Paul. 1952. *The Courage to Be.* New Haven, CT: Yale University Press.

Trump, Mary. 2020. Too Much and Never Enough; How my Family Created the World's Most Dangerous Man. New York: Simon & Schuster.

van Ord, Gerrit. 2010. "Two Voices from Westerbork: Etty Hillesum and Philip Mechanicus on the Transport from Camp Westerbork on 24 August 1943." In *Spirituality in the Writings of Etty Hillesum,* edited by Klaas Smelik, Ria van den Brandt, and Meins G. S. Coetsier, 313–334. Leiden, The Netherlands: Brill.

Washington, M. H. 1982. "Teaching Black-eyed Susans: An Approach to the Study of Black women writers." In *All the Women are White, All the Blacks are Men, but Some of Us are Brave,* edited by G. Hull, P. B. Scott, and B. Smith. New York: The Feminist Press.

Wehr, Demaris S. 1987. *Jung and Feminism: Liberating Archetypes.* Boston: Beacon Press.

Weinreb, Friedrich. 1969. *Collaboration and Resistance 1940–1945, Part II.* Amsterdam: Meulenhoff.

Wilkerson, Isabelle. 2020. *Caste: The Origin of Our Discontents*. New York: Penguin Random House.
Williams, Rowan. 2012. *Faith in the Public Sphere*. London: Bloomsbury.
Woodhouse, Patrick. 2015. *Life in the Psalms; Contemporary Meaning in Ancient Texts*. London: Bloomsbury Continuum.
Woodward, Bob. 2018. *Fear: Trump in the Whitehouse.* New York: Simon & Schuster.
———. 2020. *Rage.* New York: Simon & Schuster.
Woodward, Bob, and Robert Costa. 2020. *Peril.* New York: Simon & Schuster.
Yahil, Leni. 1987. *The Holocaust: The Fate of European Jewry.* New York: Oxford University Press.
Young-Eisendrath, Polly. 1986. "New Contexts and Conversations for Female Authority." Paper presented at the Colloquium for Social Philosophy, Pennsylvania State University, April 19.

Index

Note: Page numbers in *italics* refer to photographs.

ableism 98
abortion 87–88, 121
Admitting the Holocaust: Collected Essays (Langer) 124
African Americans *see* Black people
African Americans and Jungian Psychology: Leaving the Shadows (Brewster) 28
albedo 27
Alexander, Elizabeth 98
Alito, Samuel 87
Almaas, A. H. 8, 108
Amsterdam: A History of the World's Most Liberal City (Shorto) 21
androcentrism 29
Anne Frank and Etty Hillesum: Inscribing Spirituality and Sexuality (de Costa) 41
Anne Frank House 8
Anti-Defamation league 81, 92
antisemitism 6, 7, 10, 15, 17–18, 22, 24, 90–94, 127
Apprentice, The (television show) 86
Arbury, Ahmaud 98
archetypal psychology 6, 7, 28–29
archetypes 29, 115
Armenia 103
Ashes in the Wind: The Destruction of Dutch Jewry (Presser) 22–23
Assagioli, Roberto 31
Asscher, Abraham 22–23, 61
atheism 111
Augustine (saint) 37, 111
Auschwitz/Auschwitz-Birkenau concentration camp 3–4, 10, 11, 19, 57, 58, 68, 72, 89, 105, 117–118, 121, 124, 125; cross controversy 90–92;
Etty's deportation to 73–74; medical experimentation on women at 88–89
Austria 78
Austrian Freedom Party 78
authoritarian regimes 15, 18, 77–78, 83–86, 94, 120, 124
awakening stage, 31–32, 42–50, 65
Awwad-Srour, Dina 139–140
Ayalon, Emma Sham-Ba 139–140

Baeck, Leo 96
Baker Miller, Jean 29
Bannon, Steve 81
Battling the Big Lie: How Fox, Facebook, and the MAGA Media Are Destroying America (Pfeffer) 80–81
beauty 54, 118–120
Beauvoir, Simone de 32, 40
Ben-Amos, Batsheva 126
Ben-Amos, Dan 126
Bergen, Lotte 59, 73, 127
Bergen Belsen concentration camp 10, 23, 63
Bible: book of Corinthians 102, 111; book of Job 51–52; Psalms 114
Biden, Hunter 84
Biden, Joseph 82, 84, 85, 97, 99
Biden administration 93
Big Short (Lewis) 81
Black Lives Matter movement 103
Black people 15, 18, 79, 97–98; as analysts/psychologists 94; women 65; *see also* slavery
Black Women Writing Biography (Braxton) 65
Blinken, Antony 93

Bolsonaro, Jair 18, 77
Book of Hours, The (Rilke) 50
boundless dimension stage 33, 58, 65
Brandt, Willy 24
Braxton, Joanne 65
Brenner, Rachel 64–65, 105, 106, 111
Brewster, Fanny 28
Brexit vote 78
Brooks, David 127
Buber, Martin 112
Buddhism 115–118, 124
Burns, Ken 54
Bush, George W. 83
Buxbaum, Yitzhak 113

California Institute of Integral Studies (CIIS) 10, 108, 121
Cambodia 103
cancel culture 95–96
Capitol insurrection 82–83, 99
Carroll, James 91
Caste (Wilkerson) 17
Chauvin, Derek 98
Cheney, Liz 83
Cheney, Richard 83
China 83
Christ, Carol 14, 28, 29, 30, 33, 42, 50, 54; stages of spiritual quest 30–33
Christianity 5–6, 102, 110–111, 123, 124, 125–126
Christian Nationalism 78
civil rights movement 6, 103
Cixous, Helene 41
Clark, Stephon 98
classism 7
Clauberg, Carl 88–89
Clinton, Hillary 84, 103
Coetsier, Meins G. S. 50, 110, 124
Cohen, David 22–23, 61
collective conditioning 13
Collins, Patricia 7
colonialism 98
color blindness 7
complexes: collective 96; individual vs. cultural 13–14, 94, 107
concentration camps: Bergen Belsen 10, 23, 63; Ohrdruf 4; Sobibor 72; Theresienstadt 63; *see also* Auschwitz/Auschwitz-Birkenau concentration camp
Confederacy 86
Confederate flag 86

Connecticut Works 7
conspiracy theories 80, 81, 103
Constantine's Sword: The Church and the Jews (Carroll) 91
Costa, Robert 82
Courage to Be, The (Tillich) 54
COVID-19 pandemic 97, 116
creativity 28
Croatia 103
cultural complexes 13–14, 94, 107
Czechoslovakia 78

Darfur 103
dark night of the soul 31
David the Shepherd (biblical) 114
death 116–117
Death of Democracy, The: Hitler's Rise to Power and the Downfall of the Weimar Republic (Hett) 17
de Costa, Denise 11, 12, 41, 111
de Jong, Louis 21
democracy 81, 97, 98–99, 101, 122, 127
Denmark 85
depression 11, 88
depth psychology 6, 8, 28, 111, 115
DeSantis, Ronald 106
Descent of Inanna 31
Diamond Approach 8
Diary, The: The Epic of Everyday Life (Ben-Amos and Ben-Amos) 126
disinformation 80, 109
Dostoevsky, Fyodor 37
Douglas, Claire 28
drama therapy 89
dualisms 32

Eastern philosophy/spiritualism 6, 8, 115–118
Eichmann, Albert 72
Electoral College 82
Enduring Lives: Portraits of Women and Faith in Action (Flinders) 37
Erdogan, Recep Tayyip 77
Essays On Contemporary Events: The Psychology of Nazism (Jung) 96
essentialism 7
Etty (play) 140–141
Etty Hillesum: An Interrupted Life and Letters from Westerbork 109, 124
Etty Hillesum Center 115, 122n1
Etty Hillesum Congresses 123, 124
Etty Hillesum House 127

Etty Hillesum Research Center (EHOC) 124, 127
Etty Hillesum: The Story of Her Life (Koelemeijer) 126–127
Etty Project, The 140–141
Etty: The Letters and Diaries of Etty Hillesum 60
eugenics 88, 97–98
Existential Philosophy of Etty Hillesum, The (Coetsier) 50

fascism 97
Fear (Woodward) 97
feminism 6–7, 14, 32, 41; first-wave 40; and individuation 28–30; Jungian 14
feminist psychology 29
Finland 85
Flinders, Carol Lee 36–37
Floyd, George 98
Ford, Christine Blasey 88
Fox News 87
France 78, 93
Frank, Anne 8, 9–10, 63, 90; diary writing 10–13
Frank, Margot 8, 9–10, 11, 63, 124
Frank, Otto 9–10
Frankl, Viktor 8
Frazier, Darnella 98
Freud, Sigmund 48, 102, 104, 111
Frijda, Jetteke 9, 10, 11, 124
Frijda, Nico 9, 10

Gaarlandt, Jan Geurt 109, 110, 123, 126
Garman, Emma 88
Garner, Eric 98
Garrison, Lloyd 6
Gemmeker, Albert Konrad 59–60, 71–73, 74, 95
General Medical Society 96
genocide 60, 84, 103, 120, 140
Genocide Convention (1948) 103
Germans 17, 21–24, 54, 59, 73, 78, 80, 89, 94–95, 96
Germany 78–79, 93
Gesammelte Werke (Jung) 102
Ghent University 124
Gies, Miep 10
Gittelman, George 51, 58n1
globalization 17
God: death of 124–125; Etty's notion of 12, 50–53, 102, 109–115, 119; and Job 51–52; Jung's idea of 50–51

Goebbels, Joseph 17
Goldenberg, Naomi 28
Goldwater, Barry 86
Greenblatt, Jonathan 81
Greene, Marjorie Taylor 92
Grimmelikhuizen, Frits 115

Haberman, Maggie 82
Hageman, Harriet 83
Haley, Nikki 106
Hamas 93
Hands of Children, The: An Introduction to Psycho-Chirology (Spier) 26
Hasidism 111, 112
Heldring, J. H. 123, 124
Herzburg, Abel 23
Heschel, Abraham Joshua 112
Hett, Benjamin Carter 17–18
Hill, Anita 88
Hillesum, Etty: as activist 103–106, 118–120; attempts to persuade her to go into hiding 60–64, 121; on beauty 54, 118–120; as chronicler 11, 14, 15, 23, 34, 43, 54–55, 67, 73, 100, 105, 120, 126, 129; death at Auschwitz 89, 116–117; deportation to Auschwitz 3–4, 73–74, 117–118; diary writing 3–4, 8, 10–13, 14, 15, 20–21, 34, 37, 47, 49, 60, 68, 71, 94, 95, 100, 102, 104, 117, 124, 140–141; education 1; family 1–2, *2*, 37–39, 50, 66, 89, 110, 118; Holocaust experience of 9–10, 15; on hope 121–122; and Ies Spetter 68–70; influence of Jung on 55, 100, 101–102, 104, 115; influence of Rilke on 37, 50, 55, 101, 111, 115, 116; as Jew 22, 30, 62–65, 102, 110–111, 120, 126; and the Jewish Council 22–23, 55, 56, 59, 60, 61–63, 72, 124; Kaddish for 75–76; last postcard 74, 110; letters to friends 66, 67, 117, 120, 121–122, 134–138; as martyr 107, 124–125; memories of Bonger 20–21; notion of God 12, 50–53, 56, 75–76, 102, 109–115, 119; and Philip Mechanicus 70–73; photos *19*, *57*, *61*, *75*; pregnancy experience 88; process of self-discovery 42–50; relationship with Spier 2–3, 8, 9, 21–22, 34, 35, 37, 39–50, 55–57, 110, 111; relationship with Wegerif 1; Second Mountain journey 128; self-awareness struggle 37–42; sexuality of 12, 39–40, 43; and

spirituality 33, 109–115; teaching about 108; therapy with Spier 11, 33, 34, 35–37, 41, 96; "thinking heart" of 63, 65, 67, 104; and truth 108–109; and the union of opposites 106–108; work at Westerbork 3, 11, 14–15, 23, 37, 55–60, 65–74, 91, 103, 105–106, 109, 121, 134–135
Hillesum, Jaap 1, 12, 38, 39, 88
Hillesum, Mischa 1, 3, 12, 38, 39, 59, 66, 88, 118
Hillesum Research Conference 114
Hillman, James 115
Himmler, Heinrich 18, 89
Hindenburg, Paul von 17, 18
Hitler, Adolf 11, 14, 17–19, 54, 71, 78, 79, 96, 97, 106
Hodge, Nathan 85
Holocaust 8, 9, 53–54, 108, 124–125; education about 24, 141; in the Netherlands 22–23
Holocaust Liberation Day 4
homophobia 94, 97
hope 121–122
Horn, Dara 90
humanism 139
human rights 6
Hungary 83, 120

identity, ethnic 14
Ies Spetter, Matthew *see* Spetter, Ies
Importance of Psychology for the Present (Jung) 102
individual complexes 13–14
individuation 14, 26, 42, 100; alchemical stages of 27–28, 32; feminist perspectives on 28–30; Jung's stages of 26–27; and women 28–29
insight stage 32, 42–50, 65
Institute for War, Holocaust and Genocidal Studies (NIOD) 68
Institute of Transpersonal Psychology 7
integral psychology 6, 10, 13
integration stage 33, 58, 65
intergenerational trauma 7
International Conference on Holocaust Education 141
Interrupted Life, An (Hillesum) 8, 60, 109–110, 123
Irigaray, Luce 41
Israel 62, 63, 139–140; attacks on 93–94
Italy 93

Jackson, Andrew 86
Jacobi, Jolande 27
James, William 128
Jesus Christ 17, 91, 101, 107
Jewish Council 3, 22–23, 55, 56, 58, 59, 60, 61–63, 68, 72, 74, 118, 124; Spetter and 68–69
Jews: assimilated 12, 63, 102, 126; clashing opposites, 107; converting to Christianity 90, 91; Dutch 14, 19–24, 59, 65, 66, 137–138; in France 24; German 137–138; and the Holocaust 53–54; and Jewish identity, 127–128; Jung's views on 96; *Massenschicksal* of 63–65; as refugees 54; as scapegoats 17, 97; wearing the yellow star 21–22, 47, 91, 137; *see also* antisemitism
Job (biblical) 51–52
John Paul II (pope) 90, 91
Johnson, Karen 8
Johnson, Lyndon B. 86
Joodse Raad see Jewish Council
Judaism 12, 17, 87, 110; Hasidic 111, 112; intellectual 50
Jung, C. G.: break with Freud 102; and Buddhism 116; on God 12, 50–51, 102; on individuation 14; influence on Etty 55, 101–102, 115; influence on Spier 2, 26, 34–35, 100, 104; philosophy of 47, 50, 65, 96, 100–101; psychotherapeutic system of 26, 107; on the Self, 129; views on women 28–29; writings of 96, 100, 102, 106
Jung and Feminism (Wehr) 28
Jungian psychology 6, 7, 8, 13, 28, 94, 102, 111
Jung Institute 6

Kavanaugh, Brett 88
Kennedy v. Bremerton School District 87
Kimbles, Samuel 94
Kim Jong Un 84
Kinzinger, Adam 83
Knoop, Hans 22
Koelemeijer, Judith 63, 89, 127
Koning, David 120
Kormann, Osias 68
Kornfield, Jack 116–117, 122n2
Kristeva, Julia 41
Kristof, Nicholas 93–94
Kushner, Harold 51–52

Land Grant Acts 4
Langer, Lawrence 124, 125–126
Latin Americans 98
Lauter, Estella 31
Learning from the Germans: Race and the Memory of Evil (Nieman) 24
Lee, Robert E. 92
Lentz, Jacob 21
Leonard, Linda 28
Le Pen, Marine 78
Levi, Herta 3, 34, 44, 47, 49
Levi, Primo 8
Levie, Liesl 61–62, *62*, 63, 113
Levie, Werner 61–62, *62*, 63, 113
Levinas, Emmanuel 120–121
Lewis, Michael 81
LGBTQ community 87, 111, 121
liberation psychology 108
Life Transformed, A (Woodhouse) 114
Lifton, Robert J. 97
Lincoln, Abraham 4

MacDonald, Laquan 98
Maimonides 113
malignant normality 97–98
Martin, Trayvon 98
martyrdom 107, 124–125
Martyrs (Heldring) 124
Mechanicus, Philip 68, 70–73, 134, 136
meditation 115–116
Mendel, Menachem 112
mental illness 1, 38, 39, 88
Merkel, Angela 24
#MToo movement 36, 88
misogyny 97
Modern Man in Search of a Soul (Jung) 100
moral consciousness 120
Morrill, Justin Smith 4
Morrill, Richard 9
Morrill Land Grant Act 4
Movement Conservatives 86
Muslims 93
My Jewish Learning (Ratzabi) 112
mystical experience 32
mysticism 109, 110, 128
myths: German 96–97; of the hero's journey 58; importance of 28; Sumerian 31

Nagel, Alexandra 110
National Front 78
National Peace and Justice Memorial 24–25
National Socialist Party 8, 11, 18, 46, 48, 52, 105, 109
Native Americans 18, 80
nativism 78
NATO 85–86
Nazis *see* National Socialist Party
Neri, Nadia 102
Netanyahu, Benjamin 18, 77, 139
Netherlands: Geert Wilders in 78; German occupation of 21–22; and the Nazis 19–20, 98
Newman, Naomi 1
New Naming stage 32, 33, 50–58, 65
Nichols, Tom 97
Nieman, Susan 24
Night (Wiesel) 125
nigredo 27
nihilism 124
NIOD (Institute for War, Holocaust and Genocidal Studies) 68
Norway 85
nothingness stage 30, 31, 37–42, 65
NPR (National Public Radio) 127

Obama, Barack 98
object relations 44
Ohrdruf concentration camp 4
Orbán, Victor 18, 77, 84, 120
Orenstein, Anna 78–79, 81, 83
"Other" 11, 120–121

Palestine/Palestinians 62, 63, 94, 139–140
palm-reading 26
Passion of the Western Mind, The (Tarnas) 104
patriarchy 12, 29–30, 40, 87, 97
Paul the apostle 102, 111
peace activism 139–140
Peck, M. Scott 94
Pence, Mike 82
Penney, Bernard 63
Penney, Walter 63
People Love Dead Jews: Reports from a Haunted Present (Horn) 90
Perera, Sylvia Brinton 28, 31
Peril (Woodward) 97
Peter the Great 85
Pfeffer, Dan 80–81
Philippines 83
pillarization 21
Pimentel, Heleen 120
Playback theater 89

Poland 78, 83, 89, 90, 103, 111; deportation to 22, 59, 63, 65, 71, 72, 118, 135, 137
polarization 80, 87
populism 78
presence 115–118
Presser, Jacob 22–23, 72
propaganda 80
psyche 14
psychochirology 2, 26
psychology: analytical 96; archetypal 28–29; depth 6, 8, 28, 111, 115; feminist 29; integral 6, 10, 13; Jungian 6, 7, 8, 13, 28, 94, 102; liberation 108; mass 96; transpersonal 6, 7, 9, 32
Puch, Manja 115
Putin, Vladimir 18, 78, 84–86

QAnon 103

racism 6, 7, 24, 28, 29, 41, 86, 94, 97, 98, 121, 140
Rage (Woodward) 97
rationalism 101
Ratzabi, Hila 75–76, 109, 112
Reagan, Ronald 81–82
rebirth 27, 29, 32
Red Book, The (Jung) 102
repetition compulsion 48
Rice, Tamir 98
Rich, Melanie 113
Richardson, Heather Cox 80, 84, 86, 93
Richman, Dorothy 51–52, 58n2
Rilke, Rainer Maria 37, 50, 55, 101, 111, 115, 116
rituals 28
Robers, Betty 61
Roe v. Wade 87–88
Rohingya people 103
Roosevelt, Eleanor 5
Roosevelt, Franklin 54
Rosen, Willy 136
rubedo 27–28
Rupprecht, Carol 31
Russia 78, 83, 85, 103
Rwanda 103, 140

Samuels, Andrew 96
schizophrenia 12, 88; *see also* mental illness
Scholz, Olaf 85
Schrijvers, Piet 23, 110
Second Mountain 127–128

Second Mountain: The Quest for a Moral Life (Brooks) 127–128
Second Sex, The (Beauvoir) 40
Segal, Oren 92
Select Committee to Investigate the January 6th Attack on the US Capitol 82–83
self-realization 11, 26, 33, 49, 58, 59, 70, 73, 100, 105, 108
sexism 7, 29
shadow work 94–97
Shechinah 113
Sherith Israel 121
Shinoda Bolen, Jean 28, 29–30
Shomrei Torah 51, 58n1
Short, Marc 82
Shorto, Russell 21, 23
Siertsma, Bettine 68, 69
Silow, Theresa 89
Singer, Thomas 13–14, 94
slavery 4, 65, 77, 78, 80, 86
Smelik, Johanna 60
Smelik, Klaas A. D. Sr. 4, 50, 60, 63, 110, 111, 120, 123, 124, 127
Smith, Curtis 27
Snatager, Leonie 60–61, *61*, 63
Sobibor concentration camp 72
socialism 95
social media 81, 97
Society Organized Against Racism (SOAR) 7
Spetter, Ies 68–70, 73
Spier, Julius: approach to women patients 2, 35–37; *The Hands of Children: An Introduction to Psycho-Chirology* 26; and Herta Levi 3, 34–35, 49; illness and death 11, 13, 55–56; Jung's influence on 2, 26, 34–35, 100, 104; photos *3, 35, 36*; relationship with Etty 2–3, 8, 9, 21–22, 33, 34, 35, 37, 39–50, 55–56, 110; spirituality of 111; work with Etty 34–37, 41, 96
Spier Club 3, 35, 60, 111, 113
spiritual awakening 28
spirituality 109–115
spiritual quests 30–33, 128; awakening/insight stage 31–32, 42–50, 65; integration/boundless dimension stage 33, 58, 65; New Naming stage 32, 33, 50–58, 65; nothingness stage 31, 37–42, 65
Stalinism 78, 85
Stein, Edith 90, 91

Stein, Susan 140–141
stereotypes 29
Sudan 140
suffering 104, 120
Sullivan, Barbara 63
Supreme Court (US) 87–88
Sweden 85
symbols 28

Tarnas, Rick 104
Teresa Benedicta of the Cross (saint) 91
terrorism 93
theology, feminist 28
Theresienstadt concentration camp 63
Thomas, Clarence 87–88
Tideman, Henny 111
Tillich, Paul 54
Too Much and Never Enough: How My Family Created the World's Most Dangerous Man (Mary Trump) 95
totalitarian regimes 79
transcendence 32
transpersonal psychology 6, 7, 9, 32
Traveling Jewish Theatre 1
Trayvon Generation, The (Alexander) 98
triple jeopardy 7
Trump, Donald: agenda of, 79–80; anger and paranoia of 86–87; and the "big lie" 81–84; and the Capitol insurrection 82–83, 99; on Charlottesville rally 92–93; compassion for 95; as dictator, 18, 77; Muslim travel ban 93; as presidential candidate 79, 99, 103, 106, 120; as reflection of modern culture 94; on Twitter 97; Veteran's Day speech 97; worldview of, 78
Trump, Fred 95
Trump, Mary 95
truth 108–109
Tuinzing, Maria 2, 4, 60
Turkey 83
Turksma, Suze 68

Ukraine 84–86
Undiscovered Self, The (Jung) 100
United Kingdom 78, 93
United States 78, 93, 97, 101, 103, 105, 120; *see also* Trump, Donald
United States Holocaust Museum 91
"Unite the Right" rally 92
U.S. and the Holocaust, The (docuseries) 54
Uyghur people 103

Van Creveld 73
van Ord, Gerrit 68, 70
Venezuela 83
Vleeschhouwer, Jopie 68, 70, 73–74, 118
Volkas, Armand 89

Wannsee Conference 19
Way of Individuation, The (Jacobi) 27
Wegerif, Han 1–2, 3, 8, 46, 56, 57, 60, 73, 134
Wehr, Demaris 28, 29, 31
Weimar Republic 17; *see also* Germany
Weinreb, Friedrich 66
Westerbork transit camp: daily life at 65–68; Etty and Mechanicus at 70–73; Etty and Spetter at 68–70; Etty's work at 3, 11, 14–15, 23, 37, 55–60, 65–74, 103, 105–106, 109, 121, 134–135; Jewish Catholics at, 91
Westerweel group 68
Wexler, Judie 121–122
Wheaton College 6–7, 128
Wheelwright, Joseph 6
When Bad Things Happen to Good People (Kushner) 51
white supremacy 15, 92–93
wholeness 14, 32
Wiesel, Elie 8, 125
Wilders, Geert 78
Wilhelmina (queen of Netherlands) 21
Wilkerson, Isabel 18–19
Williams, Rowan 114
women: Black 65; as housewives and mothers 5–6, 11, 38; Jewish 65; Jung's views on 28–29; medical experimentation on 88–89; and the patriarchy 29–30, 40; at Westerbork transit camp 135–136
Woodhouse, Patrick 114
Woodman, Marion 28
Woodward, Bob 82, 97

Xi Jinping 84

Yad Vashem 140
Yahil, Leni 23
Yaron, Mikey 63
Yazidi people 103
Young-Eisendrath, Polly 28, 31
Yudnik, Hagar 63

Zelensky, Volodymyr 84, 85
Zionism 62, 73